The Best Places To Kiss™ In Northern California

A Romantic Travel Guide

Third Edition

by

Stephanie C. Bell & Elizabeth Janda

Beginning Press

Other Books in THE BEST PLACES TO KISS... Series

The Best Places To Kiss In Southern California, 3rd Edition $12.95

The Best Places To Kiss In Hawaii $10.95

The Best Places To Kiss In The Northwest, 4th Edition $12.95

The Best Places To Kiss In New England $13.95

The Best Places To Kiss In And Around New York City, 3rd Edition $13.95

Any of these books can be ordered directly from the publisher.

Please send a check or money order for the total amount of the
books, plus $2 for shipping and handling per book ordered, to:
Beginning Press
5418 South Brandon
Seattle, Washington 98118
To place an order using Visa or MasterCard,
call (800) 831-4088.

Art Direction and Production: Design Source
Cover Design: Design Source
Typography: Design Source
Editor: Miriam Bulmer
Printing: Gilliland Printing
Contributors: Kristin Folsom, Pamela P. Hegarty, and Avis Begoun

Copyright 1990, 1992, 1994 by Paula Begoun

First Edition: June 1990
Second Edition: June 1992
Third Edition: June 1994
1 2 3 4 5 6 7 8 9 10

The Best Places To Kiss™
is a registered trademark of Beginning Press
ISBN 1-877988-12-X

This book is distributed to the U.S. book trade by:
Publisher's Group West
4065 Hollis Street
Emeryville, CA 94608
(800) 788-3123

This book is distributed to the Canadian book trade by:
Raincoast Books
112 East Third Avenue
Vancouver, BC V5T 1C8
Canada
(604) 873-6581

Special Acknowledgment
To Avis Begoun, for her extremely creative and romantic
original idea for this book.

Dedication
Kissing is a fine art. To our partners, who helped us hone our craft.

Publisher's Note

Travel books have many different formats and criteria for the places they include. We would like the reader to know that this book is not an advertising vehicle. As is true in all **The Best Places To Kiss** books, none of the businesses included were charged fees, nor did they pay us for their review. This book is a sincere effort to highlight those special parts of the region that are filled with romance and splendor. Some of those places were created by people, such as restaurants, inns, lounges, lodges, hotels, and bed and breakfasts. Some of those places are untouched by people and simply created by G-d for us to enjoy. Wherever you go, be gentle with each other and gentle with the earth.

The recommendations in this collection were the final decision of the publisher, but we would love to hear what you think of our suggestions. It is our desire to be a reliable guide for your amorous outings, and in this quest for blissful sojourns your romantic feedback assists greatly in increasing our accuracy and resources for information. If you have any additional comments, criticisms, or cherished memories of your own from a place we directed you to or a place you discovered on your own, feel free to write:

Beginning Press
5418 South Brandon Street
Seattle, WA 98118

We would love to hear from you!

"As usual with most lovers in the city,
they were troubled by the lack of that
essential need of love — a meeting place."

Thomas Wolfe

TABLE OF CONTENTS

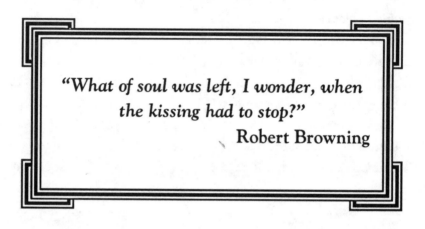

"What of soul was left, I wonder, when
the kissing had to stop?"
                                    Robert Browning

THE FINE ART OF KISSING

Why It's Still Best To Kiss In Northern California

It is no secret that Northern California is a splendid part of the world. For those of us who kiss and tell for a living, it is simply our favorite place to visit again and again. Every region is filled with all the things you might require for a romantic experience. From the brilliant lights of San Francisco, it is only a short drive to mountains, forests, vineyards, rugged shorelines, and sandy beaches. Regardless of the season or the area, misty mornings, sultry afternoons, and cool evenings are standard. The seasons themselves are all exhilarating and temperate: mild, warmish winters, lush autumns, vivid springs, perfect summers. In short, there probably is not a more diverse, yet compact, place in the world in which to pucker up.

From the North Coast and the wine country to San Francisco, the Bay Area, and the fascinating terrain of the South Coast—all will ignite your imagination and passions. If you've ever longed for a special place where you can share closeness, you can find it here. Wine tastings, bed and breakfasts, hot-air balloon rides, vibrant nightlife, alluring restaurants, country hikes, lofty woods, city streets filled with extravagant shopping, expansive parks, not to mention the ocean and the bridges and the valleys and the entertainment and . . . in short, Northern California is an adult carnival. From shore to valley, the vitality and romance here are contagious, and when you're accompanied by the right someone the only challenge will be to find the lovable niche that serves your hearts best.

You Call This Research?

This book was undertaken primarily as a journalistic effort. It is the product of earnest interviews, travel, and careful investigation and observation. Although it would have been nice, even preferable, kissing was not the major research method used to select the locations listed in this book. If smooching had been the determining factor, several inescapable problems would have developed. First, we would still be researching, and this book would be just a good idea, some breathless moments, random notes, and nothing more. Second, depending on the mood of the moment, many kisses might have occurred in places that do not meet the requirements of this travel guide. Therefore, for both practical and physical reasons, more objective criteria had to be established.

You may be wondering how, if we did not kiss at every location during our research, we could be certain that a particular place was good for such an activity? The answer is that we employed our reporters' instincts to evaluate the heartfelt, magnetic pull of each place visited. If, upon examining a place, we felt a longing inside for our special someone to share what we had discovered, we considered this to be as reliable as a kissing analysis. In the final evaluation, we can guarantee that once you choose where to go from among any of the places listed, you will be assured of some degree of privacy, a beautiful setting, heart-stirring ambience, and first-rate accommodations. When you get there, what you do romantically is up to you and your partner.

What Isn't Romantic

You may be skeptical about the idea that one location is more romantic than another. You may think, "Well, it isn't the setting, it's who you're with that makes a place special." And you'd be right. But aside from the chemistry that exists between the two of you without any help from us, there are some locations that can facilitate and enhance that chemistry, just as there are some that discourage and frustrate the magic in the moment.

For example, holding hands over a hamburger and fries at McDonald's might be, for some, a blissful interlude. But the french-fry fight in full swing near your heads and the preoccupied employee who took a year and a day to get your order would put a damper on heartthrob stuff for most of us, even the most adoring. No, location isn't everything; but when you're at a certain type of place with all the right atmospheric details, including the right person, the odds are better for achieving unhindered and uninterrupted romance.

With that in mind, here is a list of things that we consider to be not even remotely romantic: olive green or orange carpeting (especially if it is mildewed or dirty); anything overly plastic or overly veneered; an abundance of neon (even if it is very art deco or very neo-modern); most tourist traps; restaurants with no-smoking sections that ignore their own policy; overpriced hotels with impressive names and motel-style accommodations; discos; the latest need-to-be-seen-in nightspots; restaurants with officious, sneering waiters; and, last but not least, a roomful of people discussing the stock market or the hottest and latest business acquisition in town.

Above and beyond these unromantic location details, unromantic *behavior* can negate the affection potential of even the most majestic surroundings. These are mood killers every time: any amount of moaning over the weather; creating a scene over the quality of the food or service, no matter how justified; worrying about work; getting angry about traffic; incessant backseat driving, no matter how warranted; groaning about heartburn and other related symptoms, no matter how painful or justified.

Rating Romance

The three major factors that determined whether or not we included a place were:

1. Surrounding splendor
2. Privacy
3. Tug-at-your-heartstrings ambience

Of the three determining factors, "surrounding splendor" and "privacy" are fairly self-explanatory; "heart-tugging ambience" can probably use some clarification. Wonderful, loving environments are not just four-poster beds covered with down quilts and lace pillows, or tables decorated with white tablecloths and nicely folded linen napkins. Instead, there must be more plush or other engaging features that encourage intimacy and allow for uninterrupted affectionate discussions. For the most part, ambience was rated according to degree of comfort and number of gracious appointments, as opposed to image and frills.

If a place had all three factors going for it, inclusion was automatic. But if one or two of the criteria were weak or nonexistent, the other feature(s) had to be superior before the location would be included. For example, if a breathtakingly beautiful panoramic vista was in a spot that was inundated with tourists and children on field trips, the place was not included. If a fabulous bed and breakfast was set in a less than desirable location, it would be included if, and only if, its interior was so wonderfully inviting and cozy that the outside world no longer mattered.

Kiss Ratings

If you've flipped through this book you're probably curious about the miniature lips that follow each entry. The rating system notwithstanding, *all* of the places listed in this book are wonderfully special places to be, and all of them have heart-pleasing details and are worthwhile, enticing places to visit. The tiny lips indicate only our personal preferences and nothing more. They are a way of indicating just how delightfully romantic a place is and how pleased we were with our experience during our visit. The number of lips awarded each location indicates:

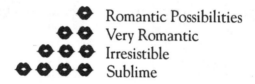

❖	Romantic Possibilities
❖ ❖	Very Romantic
❖ ❖ ❖	Irresistible
❖ ❖ ❖ ❖	Sublime

Cost Ratings

We have included additional ratings to help you determine whether your lips can afford to kiss in a particular restaurant, hotel, or bed and breakfast. (Almost all of the outdoor places are free; some charge a small fee.) The price for overnight accommodations is always based on double occupancy; otherwise there wouldn't be anyone to kiss. Eating establishment prices are based on a full dinner for two, excluding liquor, unless otherwise indicated. Because prices and business hours change, it is always advisable to call each place you consider visiting, so your lips will not end up disappointed.

Restaurants

Inexpensive	Under $25
Moderate	$25 to $50
Expensive	$50 to $80
Very Expensive	$80 to $110
Unbelievably Expensive	$110 and up

Lodgings

Very Inexpensive	Under $75
Inexpensive	$75 to $90
Moderate	$90 to $125
Expensive	$130 to $175
Very Expensive	$185 to $240
Unbelievably Expensive	$250 and up

Wedding Bells

One of the more auspicious times to kiss is the moment after wedding vows have been exchanged. The setting for that moment can vary from your own cozy living room to a lush garden perched at the ocean's edge to a grand ballroom at a downtown hotel. As an added service to those of you in the midst of prenuptial arrangements, we have indicated which places have wedding facilities and how many people they can serve. For more specific information about which facilities and services are offered, please call the establishment directly. They should be able to provide you with menus, prices, and all the details needed to make your wedding day as spectacular as you have ever imagined.

◆ **Romantic Note:** If wedding bells aren't in your near future and you are going to an establishment that specializes in weddings and private parties, call ahead to ensure that a function isn't scheduled during your stay. Unless you're hoping that seeing a wedding will magically inspire your partner to "pop the question," you might feel like uninvited guests.

What If You Don't Want To Kiss?

Some people we interviewed resisted the idea of best kissing locales. Their resistance stemmed from potential expectations regarding intimate interaction. They were apprehensive that once they arrived at the place of their dreams, they'd never get the feeling they thought they were supposed to have. Many imagined spending time setting up itineraries, taking extra time to get ready, making the journey to the promised land, and, once they were there, not being swept away in a flourish of romance. Their understandable fear was, what happens if nothing happens? Because in spite of the best intentions, even with this book in hand, romance is not always easy.

Those of us involved in writing this book have experienced situations like this more than once; we empathize and are prepared with solutions. To prevent this anticlimactic scenario from becoming a reality and to help you survive a romantic outing, consider the following suggestions.

When you make decisions about where and when to go, pay close attention to details; talk over your preferences and discuss your feelings about them. For some people there is no passion associated with fast pre-theater dinners that are all but inhaled, or with walking farther than expected in overly high, high heels, or with finding a place closed because its hours have changed. Keep in mind the difficulty of second-guessing traffic patterns in San Francisco, along the coast, or through the wine country. Our strong recommendation, although we know this is problematic, is not to schedule a romantic outing too tightly or you will be more assured of a headache than an affectionate interlude.

Do not discuss money, family, or the kids. If you have a headache, take some aspirin now and not later. Regardless of how good-looking the person at the next table is, remember that distractions are never considered to be in romantic good taste. How different factors might affect your lips, not to mention your mood, is something to agree on before you head out the door, not after—or during.

Remember that part of the whole experience of an intimate time together is to allow whatever happens to be an opportunity to let affection reign. Regardless of what takes place, that is what is romantic. For example, remember the scene between Kevin Costner and Susan Sarandon in *Bull Durham* where he throws his full cereal bowl against the wall, clears the kitchen table with a sweep of his arm, then picks Susan up and throws her passionately on the table? How romantic would that have been if Kevin had started complaining about the broken china in his hair and the spilled milk running down his arms? Get the idea?

So, if the car breaks down, the waiter is rude to you, your reservations get screwed up, or if both of you tire out and want to call it a day, you can still be endearing and charming. Really, it only takes an attitude change to turn any dilemma into a delight.

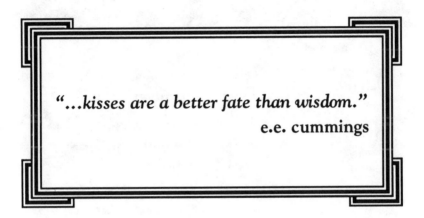

"...kisses are a better fate than wisdom."

e.e. cummings

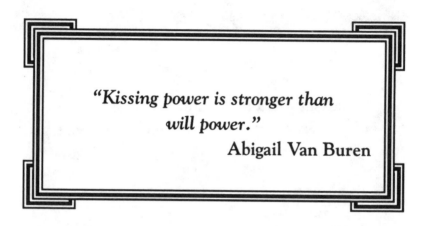

"*Kissing power is stronger than will power.*"

Abigail Van Buren

NORTH COAST

If you've never witnessed the North Coast's indescribably dramatic and arresting scenery, be prepared for the visual experience of a lifetime. Unlike the developed coastline south of San Francisco, this rugged, breathtaking shoreline remains relatively pristine and unblemished. Interestingly, much of the surrounding region consists of sprawling farmland, enhancing the rural setting. In some areas the turbulent, white-capped surf thunders against the coast's tall, rocky cliffs; in other areas, waves lap gently at beaches or sand dunes overgrown with grass and wildflowers. Not surprisingly, there are many superlative places to stay, eat, and hike along this coastline, though not in such abundance that the region's natural beauty has been obstructed in any way. I can't think of a better setting for romance—kissing here just seems inevitable.

HIGHWAY 1

Take the Golden Gate Bridge out of San Francisco and follow the signs for Highway 1.

Northern California Coast Highway 1 is an exhilarating roller-coaster ride of a lifetime. The road writhes its way along terrain that would otherwise seem impassable. Following the ocean from atop towering cliffs, each turn capriciously switches back on itself, hugging the edge so closely that you may feel more like you're hang-gliding than motoring along. At other times, feeling the ocean mist on your face and hearing the roar of the surf, you can imagine you're boating instead of just driving.

Be sure to allow enough time to travel this highway at a leisurely, touring pace. There are scads of turnoffs that will demand your attention, so the slower your speed, the easier it will be to stop at any given point and enjoy. The picture-perfect panorama of the pounding surf splashing against dramatic palisades continues on forever. Each corner, each turn, has a view so like Eden that a warning seems in order: driving and kissing don't mix! Before you indulge, be sure you are parked and not negotiating the narrow turns on Highway 1.

♦ **Romantic Warning:** If you are in a hurry to get to points north at a faster clip, do yourselves and the rest of the traffic on Highway 1 a favor and take Highway 101.

Stinson Beach

Although technically part of Marin County, this area is the threshold to the North Coast. Until recently, the only way to stay in Stinson Beach (without moving there) was to spend the night with friends who live there, or rent a vacation home. A few bed and breakfasts have since opened, but this seaside town, located within the Golden Gate National Recreation Area, is far from overdeveloped. **STINSON BEACH STATE PARK** is three miles of sandy white beach. It is crowd-crazed in the summer, but you can still take off your shoes, close your eyes, and bask in the sun and sand. The Golden Gate Bridge is in clear sight, but you'll feel far away from the city.

Hotel/Bed and Breakfast Kissing

CASA DEL MAR, Stinson Beach
37 Belvedere Avenue
(415) 868-2124
Moderate to Very Expensive

As you enter Stinson Beach, heading north on Highway 1, a firehouse is the first building on the right. Turn right there onto Belvedere Avenue; Casa del Mar is about one block up, on the left.

A fresh approach to innkeeping is alive and well in this towering Mediterranean-style villa. Tropical foliage and flowering cactus fill the terraced, landscaped front yard, and a path leads to bright and sunny accommodations. All six rooms are colorfully decorated and enhanced by contemporary local art. Each room has a queen-size bed with a down comforter, plus a private patio facing either the ocean or the forested hillside of Mount Tamalpais. The penthouse on the top floor has the best of both worlds, with two patios, one on each side of the building, a large soaking tub for two, and skylights. The Garden Room, on the lowest level, has a view of the ocean from a garden patio, and breakfast is delivered to this room. For everyone else, the delightfully creative full breakfast, which might feature apple-ricotta pancakes flavored with cinnamon, or homemade blueberry-poppyseed coffee cake, is served fireside on the airy main floor.

◆ **Romantic Suggestion:** If you don't stay the night at Casa del Mar, you won't be able to sample the luscious breakfast in the morning, but fear not: Casa del Mar is open for dinner November through April, on Friday and Sunday nights. The menu is fixed and reservations are required, but you are encouraged to bring your own bottle of your favorite wine and dinner is only $20 per person. The varying Mediterranean menu might include an unusual main dish like chicken breasts baked with walnuts, yogurt, ginger, curry, and mango chutney, or fresh asparagus lasagne with goat cheese. Of course, your meal wouldn't be complete without a delectable dessert such as lemon soufflé served with berries and whipped cream, or rum-orange bread pudding. You'll wish you were spending the night just to sample more of the same scrumptious cooking the following morning.

Olema

Hotel/Bed and Breakfast Kissing

POINT REYES SEASHORE LODGE, Olema
10021 Coastal Highway 1
(415) 663-9000
Inexpensive to Expensive
Wedding facilities are available; call for details.

At the intersection of Highway 1 and Sir Francis Drake Boulevard.

Despite a slight hotel-like feel, the ambience inside this cedar lodge is at once polished and provincial, commodious and congenial. All 22 rooms have views of the inn's pleasantly landscaped backyard and the forested hills of Point Reyes beyond. If you can afford to splurge, the spacious Sir Francis Drake Suite, where breakfast is delivered right to your room, has a separate sleeping loft with a curtained, four-poster feather bed, tiled fireplace, and a sitting area with a two-story atrium window. Several other rooms feature ceramic tile fireplaces, whirlpool tubs, down comforters, and bay window seats. Afternoons can be spent lounging on Nantucket-style lawn furniture in the grassy courtyard. You probably have your own ideas of how to spend the evening, but just in case, the game room downstairs is equipped with an antique billiards table and plenty of puzzles and games. Continental breakfasts are served in a sunny room that opens to the backyard and is warmed by an immense stone hearth beautified with dried flowers.

◆ **Romantic Warning:** This lodge is located right on Highway 1. Request a room in the northern wing, where road noise shouldn't be a problem.

ROUNDSTONE FARM, Olema
9940 Sir Francis Drake Boulevard
(415) 663-1020
Moderate

Heading north on Highway 1, turn right onto Sir Francis Drake Boulevard. Roundstone Farm is a couple of blocks up, on the left.

Step into the spacious living room with its wood stove and soaring skylighted ceiling and you are at once drawn to the provincial landscape framed by a wall of picture windows. Roundstone Farm is set on ten verdant acres, so the view out of almost every window is serene and captivating. Rolling meadows, a tranquil pond, and the innkeeper's extraordinary Connemara and Arabian horses create a purely pastoral scene. Four of the five rooms here have a fireplace, and all are spacious, bright, and cozy with down comforters, private baths, simple lacquered furnishings, and soft floral linens. The upper-level rooms have high ceilings and the same uncluttered feel. Beyond the rolling hills, you can watch the sun set in the distance over Tomales Bay. A full breakfast including fresh baked goods is served family-style in the airy dining room or on the garden patio, depending on the weather.

Inverness and Point Reyes

The towns of Inverness and Point Reyes, which border the Point Reyes National Seashore and Marin County, are the entry point into this gorgeous coastal area. These two small, quaint villages, spread along the shores of Tomales Bay, harbor numerous waterside and hillside romantic retreats. Even though this area is sparsely populated and quiet in the winter months, it is almost too well traveled in the spring and summer. Nevertheless, if you can ignore the crowds, a stay at one of the special bed and breakfasts in the area can be utterly romantic and memorable any time of year. For more information regarding accommodations, write or call **INNS OF POINT REYES,** P.O. Box 145, Inverness, CA 94937; (415) 485-2649.

Hotel/Bed and Breakfast Kissing

BLACKTHORNE INN, Inverness Park
266 Vallejo Avenue
(415) 663-8621
Moderate to Expensive

Heading north on Highway 1, look for the sign for a left turn to Inverness (near Point Reyes Station). Turn left onto Vallejo Avenue (the Knave of Hearts Bakery is on the corner). When you think an inn can't possibly be this far down this narrow country lane, look for the small sign with "266" on the right.

Nesting high in the trees, this popular four-story wooden castle with twin turrets, high peaked gables, and multipaned windows is crowned with an octagonal tower and surrounded by an expansive redwood deck, complete with a fireman's pole to the drive below. Inside, classical music casts a cultivated spell in the spacious living room with its immense stone hearth. Spiral staircases lead upstairs and down to the guest rooms. The Overlook has a Juliet-style balcony overlooking the living room, a private outdoor terrace, and stained glass windows. The Eagle's Nest occupies the octagonal tower, with windows on all sides looking out to the treetops and a steep ladder to its own sun deck. (The bath for this room, however, lies across a 40-foot-high outdoor walkway leading to the uppermost deck.) A jetted hot tub is available for the use of the guests, and, in true California spirit, clothing is optional after dark.

◆ **Romantic Note:** For the most part this is a unique bed and breakfast, but it can feel cramped and crowded when full, which is most of the year.

DANCING COYOTE BEACH
GUEST COTTAGES, Inverness
12794 Sir Francis Drake Boulevard
(415) 669-7200
Moderate

From the town of Inverness, follow Sir Francis Drake Boulevard south. The cottages are on the left.

This getaway is made to order when you're in need of quiet time together. Nestled on the shore of Tomales Bay, these four connecting beachfront cottages are sheltered in the shade of sturdy pine and cypress trees. Fireplaces, skylights, floor-to-ceiling windows, loft bedrooms, and pastel shades of green and peach adorn each bungalow. Breakfast provisions are provided for guests to eat at their leisure in the privacy of their own small galley kitchen, and each cottage has access to private beachfront a few feet from its front door.

◆ **Romantic Note:** When making your reservation, request the cottage nearest the water—it has the most privacy and the best views.

JASMINE COTTAGE, Point Reyes Station
(415) 663-1166
Moderate

Call ahead for reservations and directions.

Get back to the basics at Jasmine Cottage, a genuine country escape settled on a residential hillside and surrounded by herb, flower, and vegetable gardens, fruit trees, and a flock of clucking chickens that provide fresh morning eggs for guests. The tiny, self-contained cottage is charmingly cozy, with a floral-cushioned window seat overlooking the garden, lace curtains, a wood-burning stove, a full kitchen stocked with tasty breakfast items, and Oriental rugs strewn over a rock floor. Another romantic perk is the hot tub situated just outside, secluded behind a lattice fence. Though it feels like the country, don't forget that the innkeeper's home is just on the other side of the garden.

MARSH COTTAGE, Point Reyes Station
(415) 669-7168
Moderate

Call ahead for reservations and directions.

As you might deduce from the name, this small, weathered cottage is sequestered on the shores of a marsh in Tomales Bay. Cattails, wildflowers, and long, honey-colored grasses grow up around the cabin, framing a nature lover's paradise. Country prints and fabrics, a woodburning fireplace, and French doors that open onto a sun deck overlooking the marsh enhance the cabin's natural mood. A more than ample breakfast of fresh orange juice, homebaked bread or muffins, seasonal fruits, milk and granola, a basket of eggs, cheeses, tea, and coffee awaits guests in the semi-modern, fully equipped kitchen. Your only complaint here will be the fact that you can't stay longer.

THE NEON ROSE, Point Reyes
76½ Overlook Road
(415) 663-9143
Moderate

Call ahead for reservations and directions.

The only neon to be found at this supremely private country retreat is one red rose, set above the arched door frame of the bedroom. Perched on a hillside overlooking Tomales Bay, the Neon Rose caters to those who really want to escape the city—neon lights included. Pass through a delightful small garden into the modern, self-contained stucco-and-wood cottage that surveys sweeping views of Point Reyes and the bay below. The cottage is sparsely attractive, with hardwood floors and Santa Fe-style appointments, and has a fully equipped kitchen, a chic bedroom, and a cozy living area with a Jacuzzi tub, wood stove, and complete stereo system. An abundant supply of breakfast foods and hors d'oeuvres is provided for you to prepare at your convenience.

SANDY COVE INN, Inverness
12990 Sir Francis Drake Boulevard
(415) 669-COVE, (800) 759-COVE
Moderate

One mile south of the village of Inverness, just before the intersection of Camino Del Mar and Sir Francis Drake Boulevard; look for signs on the right.

Sandy Cove Inn is aptly named, due to its location on a stretch of sandy shore along Tomales Bay. Four acres of country landscape envelop the weathered gray Cape Cod-style house imbued with a sleepy country charm. Guest rooms have private entrances, refrigerators, sun decks, queen beds, and private baths; several even have wood-burning fireplaces. Each room is appointed with Turkish rugs, antique pine furniture, and colorful artwork. An abundant country breakfast, complete with farm-fresh eggs and garden herbs, is served in the lovely solarium that overlooks the countryside.

◆ **Romantic Note:** Surprise your loved one with a pre-arranged appointment with a certified massage therapist, available to guests for an extra charge.

SEA STAR COTTAGE, Inverness
(415) 663-1554
Moderate

Call ahead for reservations and directions.

The utmost in seclusion is yours for the taking at the Sea Star Cottage, harbored along placid Tomales Bay. A 75-foot-long wooden walkway stretches over the tidal waters and leads to the door of this petite, weathered cottage. The cozy living room overlooking the water has a wood-burning fireplace and comfortable, albeit timeworn, furnishings. The bedroom features a queen-size four-poster bed and an adjacent blue-and-white-tiled bathroom. Watch the ducks swim beneath you at high tide from the vantage point of a hot tub set in a solarium on the outside deck. A breakfast of fresh juice, fresh fruit salad, quiche, and almond croissants can be enjoyed in the sun-filled breakfast room that overlooks the yacht club next door or, better yet, in the privacy of the solarium.

TEN INVERNESS WAY, Inverness
10 Inverness Way
(415) 669-1648
Moderate to Expensive

Follow Sir Francis Drake Avenue south to Inverness Way. The inn is on your right.

Set just off Inverness' surprisingly quiet main thoroughfare, this weathered gray clapboard house is tucked among overgrown gardens and foliage. The inn's rustic though comfortable parlor has a large stone fireplace, dark wood-paneled walls and ceiling, and antique accents (including a player piano). The parlor's rusticity contrasts sharply with the two bright, airy, countrified guest rooms, decorated with white lace curtains and patchwork quilts, that overlook the inn's cheerful English gardens. Generous country repasts of buttermilk spice coffee cake, cheese and basil scrambled eggs, or Blitz soufflés are served in the sun-soaked breakfast room. Best of all, a hot tub sheltered in its own petite cabin and enveloped by trees can be reserved for private candlelight soaks for two.

Restaurant Kissing

MANKA'S RESTAURANT, Inverness
Argyle Drive and Callendar Way
(415) 669-1034
Expensive
Wedding facilities are available for a maximum of 100 people.

Heading north on Highway 1, look for a sign for a left turn to Inverness (near Point Reyes Station). Once in Inverness, turn left onto Argyle Drive at Manka's sign.

Dinner at Manka's is a once-in-a-lifetime romantic experience, though it might turn out to be more than just once (we returned here several times while staying in the area). The turn-of-the century hunting lodge, a magnet for locals and visitors alike, is set alongside a steep residential street that leads into the deep forest. A fire blazes in the first of three intimate, dark, wood-paneled rustic dining rooms, while tapers flicker on linen-cloaked tables. Serene melodies from the grand piano waft through the room, along with the mouthwatering aromas of seasonal specials. Appetizers of clam and mussel soup with fennel and cilantro puree or grilled polenta with local wild mushrooms are just the beginning. Entrées like the house-cured grilled pork chops with lodge mashed potatoes, Italian black cabbage, and pear-kumquat chutney or the grilled buffalo with a wild mushroom-tarragon sauce are excellent and satisfying, though not so satisfying that you're willing to forgo the pumpkin pie with maple mascarpone cream or a chocolate sour cream cake with vanilla whipped cream.

◆ **Romantic Note:** Manka's serves dinner Thursday through Monday only.

Outdoor Kissing

POINT REYES NATIONAL SEASHORE
(415) 663-1092

Just off Highway 1, about 35 miles north of San Francisco.

Point Reyes National Seashore is noted for acre after exquisite acre of wild land, colored by winter grass and patterned with chiseled rock, cascading waterfalls, calm sandy beaches, precarious primitive coastline, and turbulent breakers crashing against haystack rocks and spewing streams of water into the fresh air above. Follow one of the many trails that interlace this prime hiking kingdom; some end near the edge of the land, where the ocean reveals itself nestled between interwoven hills. (Now is the time to kiss.) There are too many spectacular treks in this area to list in this book. Realistically, not everyone who wants to find romance owns hiking boots or, for that matter, sturdy thighs and a disposition that can survive the walk. For a beautifully written examination of the hikes available, we strongly recommend the book *Point Reyes Secret Places and Magic Moments,* by Phil Arnot. His descriptions and instructions are accurate and fairly easy to follow.

◆ **Romantic Suggestion:** Three of our favorite places in Point Reyes National Seashore are **ALAMERE FALLS, TOMALES POINT,** and **WILDCAT BEACH.** Each is dramatically different from the others, and the natural glory that exists here is worth discovering for yourselves.

Check at the ranger station for hiking information about these areas, or use the book by Phil Arnot mentioned above.

◆ **Second Romantic Suggestion:** Rent a pair of ponies at **FIVE BROOKS STABLES,** 8001 Highway 1, three and a half miles south of Olema, (415) 663-1570. This is a fabulous horse ranch with hourly rentals at Point Reyes National Seashore.

◆ **Third Romantic Suggestion:** Along the western edge of Tomales Bay, in Tomales Bay State Park, is **HEART'S DESIRE BEACH.** Do the views of this tranquil, sparkling bay live up to the beach's name? You'll have to see for yourselves.

WHALE WATCHING

From numerous viewpoints along the Coast Trail in the Point Reyes National Seashore, and especially from Point Reyes Lighthouse, (415) 669-1534, at the end of Sir Francis Drake Boulevard due west of Inverness.

If you have always secretly longed to witness firsthand the passage of whales on their yearly migration to warmer waters, then the Northern California coast is a great place to live out your cetacean fantasy. December to April is the best time to witness this odyssey, particularly when the weather conditions are clear and sunny. Be sure to go early in the morning, about the time when the sun is warming the cool morning air. As you stand at the edge of a cliff towering over the depths below, you will have a tremendous view of this tortuous coastline. Find a comfortable position, snuggle close together, and be patient. This performance is intermittent at best and requires careful study and diligence. Be prepared for an amazing encounter.

Take in the open, endless ocean, lined with staggered cliffs haloed with green and gold chaparral for as far as the eye can see. Allow your vision to slowly scan the calm, azure waters. Then suddenly, in the distance, breaking the still of a silent, sun-drenched spring morning, a spout of bursting water explodes from the surface. A giant, arched black profile appears boldly against the blue sea, followed by an abrupt tail slap and then stillness once more. It's hard to explain the romance of that moment, but romantic it is. Perhaps it's the excitement of observing such an immense creature gliding effortlessly through the water with playful agility and ease. Or perhaps it's the chance to celebrate a part of nature's mysterious aquatic underworld together.

Marshall

Hotel/Bed and Breakfast Kissing

POET'S LOFT, Marshall   ❖ ❖ ❰
19695 Highway 1
(415) 453-8080
Moderate

Call ahead for reservations and directions.

If you aren't a poet, a weekend here might just inspire you to become one. Though the loft is set just off the highway, the otherwise spectacular setting speaks for itself. Perched on stilts, this multi-angled wood cabin juts out over the placid waters of Tomales Bay. A wood-burning fireplace warms the cozy interior, appointed with contemporary furnishings, a full kitchen, outdoor hot tub, and sweeping views of the bay and Point Reyes peninsula. If this doesn't fuel your poetic inclinations, what will?

◆ **Romantic Warning:** This is considered a vacation rental, not a bed and breakfast. Guests are required to provide their own food and linens. (Yes, linens. In other words, if you didn't bring your sleeping bags, you're out of luck.)

Bodega Bay

Perched above the rocky coast, Bodega Bay and the other small towns dotting this shoreline boast spectacular views, wonderfully romantic accommodations, and several marvelous beaches accessible from Highway 1. Keep watch for the "COASTAL ACCESS" signs, which pop up inconsistently and direct you to many secluded, windswept beaches—enticing to beachcombers and romantics alike.

Hotel/Bed and Breakfast Kissing

BAY HILL MANSION, Bodega Bay   ◆ ◆ ❮
3919 Bay Hill Road
(707) 875-3577, (800) 526-5927
Inexpensive to Expensive
Wedding facilities and services are available for a maximum of 150
people; call for details.

*Highway 1 leads directly into Bodega Bay. Look for Bay Hill Road and follow
it east to Bay Hill Mansion.*

Set on a hillside above the village, this gleaming white mansion with
a Queen Anne motif is Bodega Bay's most romantic retreat. In the
evening, wine, appetizers, and glorious sunsets draw guests into the spacious parlor with its immense wood stove and expansive bay window. Soft
pastels and dainty florals adorn the six comfortable guest rooms. The
unique Whale Watch Room is built into one of the turrets, so it has
octagonal walls that soar to a high oak ceiling and windows that face the
village and sea. The dining room, where a full gourmet breakfast is served
family-style, has more wonderful windows that overlook the ocean and
Bodega Bay.

Jenner

Hotel/Bed and Breakfast Kissing

FORT ROSS LODGE, Jenner
20705 Highway 1
(707) 847-3333
Inexpensive to Expensive

*On the west side of Highway 1, two miles north of Historic Fort Ross State Park,
about 14 miles north of the town of Jenner.*

Fort Ross Lodge rests on a rocky pinnacle above the rugged azure sea,
encircled by rolling meadows dotted with wildflowers and dried golden

brush. A mowed path leads to the edge of a cliff and a trail you can climb down to explore interesting tide pools or catch a stupendous sunset. The 16 units in the Lodge section have simple floral or paisley linens; hotel-like amenities such as a small refrigerator, coffee maker, and television; and sliding glass doors that open to a private, enclosed deck with a barbecue for your use. Many rooms overlook the unobstructed beauty of the Pacific, and some have a fireplace or a little hot tub for two on their private patio. A glass-enclosed hot tub with the same view is available for all guests.

There are six more units in the Hill section, located across the street on a forested hillside. Even though you are farther from the ocean in these units, a tree-framed view of the sea is still visible in all but one of the rooms, and every room has a small sauna and whirlpool tub for two. These rooms are simply decorated with dark tones and feel like studio apartments where you can host your own private party for two.

◆ **Romantic Note:** To make things easier when you make your reservations, you should know that Rooms 5 through 8 and 14 through 17 are closest to the ocean and have the best views. Rooms 9 through 12 and 19 have no view.

◆ **Romantic Alternative: MURPHY'S JENNER INN**, 10400 Highway 1, Jenner, (707) 865-2377, (800) 732-2377, (Very Inexpensive to Expensive), offers a variety of bed-and-breakfast accommodations, from houses to individual units within homes. Even the most expensive vacation rentals are too rustic with outdated, mismatched furnishings to award them lips, but many of them are set right on the sparkling shore of the Russian River estuary and have incredible views of the beach and ocean. Call and ask for a brochure that describes what is available, because saving money and/or being this close to the glistening water might be more important to you than glistening chandeliers and sumptuous linens.

Restaurant Kissing

RIVER'S END, Jenner   ❧ ❧
11048 Highway 1
(707) 865-2484
Moderate to Expensive
Wedding facilities for a maximum of 70 people are available only in the
off-season or weekdays.

On the west side of Highway 1, a quarter mile north of the town of Jenner.

The view of swirling white water and turbulent eddies that explode
over and around the rock outcroppings of the Pacific Ocean can change at
night into a placid, almost surreal, composition. As sunset nears, a single
path of sunlight glosses the surface, illuminating only the water and the
horizon, with the hills veiled in darkness. Evening announces its finale
with a crescendo of colors that fade slowly to black. From the deck, dining
room, or solarium lounge area of the River's End restaurant, perched at the
edge of the Russian River estuary, this daily, sparkling performance is yours
to behold. The menu offers traditional seafood items; our meal was just
average, but with the glistening ocean outside we hardly noticed.

◆ **Romantic Note:** The days and hours that the restaurant is open vary
depending on the season, but it is usually closed December and January.

◆ **Romantic Warning:** River's End is also a lodge with guest rooms
that have the same view as the restaurant, only closer to the water. Why
the warning? Because the decor can only be described as tacky and old,
which hardly makes the rooms romantic. The price and scenery are certainly desirable, so if proximity to the ocean and bargain accommodations
are paramount concerns, this place is a gem.

◆ **Romantic Alternative:** In any other setting **JENNER BY THE
SEA**, 10400 Highway 1, Jenner, (707) 865-1192, (Moderate), might be
considered a little too rustic or too casual, and too near the highway for a
romantic dinner. Here on the Sonoma coast, however, almost any restaurant with a large fireplace and hearth, windows that survey the meandering Russian River emptying into the Pacific, and a kitchen staff that
prepares very fresh seafood dishes is indeed a special spot.

Outdoor Kissing

GOAT ROCK STATE PARK, Jenner

From Highway 1, watch for signs to Goat Rock State Park.

This dramatic location would have been awarded four lips except that, like so many state parks, it is so packed with people during the summer and on weekends that privacy is impossible. Still, this place is so alluring that you shouldn't let the crowds deter you. Here the milky green and blue waters of the Pacific crash into the surf and meet the mouth of the Russian River estuary. Water laps on both sides of this small strip of beach, and the massive rocks protruding from the sea are covered with colonies of sea lions and seals basking in the sun.

♦ **Romantic Suggestion:** There might be fewer people at **SHELL BEACH**, just south of Goat Rock State Park. A beat-up trail leads down to this little section of sand, which is best at low tide when there are diverse tide pools to study. Also, you should be able to find some shells to take home as mementos of a day of fun in the sun. Just make sure that a little crustacean isn't living in the shell you choose.

Cazadero

Hotel/Bed and Breakfast Kissing

TIMBERHILL COUNTRY INN
AND TENNIS RANCH, Cazadero
35755 Hauser Bridge Road
(707) 847-3258
Unbelievably Expensive
Wedding facilities are available for a maximum of 30 people.

Drive north on Highway 1. Five miles north of Jenner, turn right onto Meyers Grade Road (the first right after Seaview Plantation Road) and climb to the ridge. Follow this country road for 13.7 miles from Highway 1. Six miles down, the Meyers Grade Road turns into Seaview and then Seaview turns into Hauser Bridge Road, which ends at the ranch.

You don't have to cuddle a racquet or chase tennis balls in the hot sun to consider this tennis ranch a perfect place for romance. Be open-minded. Even if you can't tell a tennis racquet from a baseball bat, you can still enjoy this retreat, enveloped by 80 wooded acres of nature's finest greenery, far removed from the pressures of the real world. The ranch is home to ten handsome cedar-log cabins, all with the appropriate romantic accoutrements: knotty pine walls, Southwestern themes, wicker furniture, tiled wood-burning fireplaces, views of the sunset from your private deck, and (most important) seclusion. Acres of woodland that ramble on endlessly next to the ranch will tempt you to take long hikes. Or stay on the grounds and swim, or relax in the Jacuzzi till dinnertime nears. Even the dining room has a serene elegance that enhances the enticing meals, all prepared by a skilled chef. And you don't even have to play tennis.

◆ **Romantic Note:** The daily room rate here includes all meals.

Gualala

Hotel/Bed and Breakfast Kissing

ST. ORRES INN, Gualala
36601 Highway 1 South
(707) 884-3303
Inexpensive to Expensive
Wedding facilities are available for a maximum of 150 people.

As you head north out of Gualala on Highway 1, the spires of St. Orres will appear on the right. If you reach Anchor Bay, you have gone too far.

Finding words that succinctly express the richness and architectural intrigue of this bed and breakfast is a challenge. Across the street from a cloistered sandy cove, this structure appears suddenly out of nowhere, a fascinating hand-carved, wood-and-glass Russian-style chalet. The stained glass windows of this inn's two intricately crafted towers twinkle in the daylight. This same prismatic light bathes the interior in a velvety amber glow. The guest accommodations here are varied, from simple, sparse, unromantic rooms in the main house to splendid, intimate cottages scattered about the grounds. Each cottage has its own spirit and tone, with modern furnishings and varying color schemes; some have unobstructed ocean views, others have sun decks, fireplaces, and sunken tubs.

Breakfast is served in the main house in the small, sunlit arboretum and dinner is served nightly (except for Tuesdays and Wednesdays in the winter months) in the spires of the fabulous St. Orres Restaurant (see "Restaurant Kissing").

WHALE WATCH INN, Gualala   ❖ ❖ ❖ ❢
35100 Highway 1
(707) 884-3667
Expensive to Very Expensive
Wedding facilities are available for a maximum of 36 people.

On Highway 1, just north of Gualala, on the west side of the road.

Most modern hotels or resorts remind me of suburban condominium developments: functional, but not necessarily romantic. The refreshingly artistic Whale Watch Inn gives new meaning to contemporary architecture. Just reading through previous guests' comments in the journals found in each of the rooms is enough to assure anybody that they've come to the right place for a romantic encounter. The sound of the careening surf resounds through the five compact buildings that make up this complex set above the rugged shoreline and sandy beach inlet of Anchor Bay. The buildings' wood exteriors are stained a weathered seaside gray that harmonizes with the landscape. The inn has only 18 suites, each endowed with a unique style. Skylights, sun decks, whirlpools, and wood-burning fireplaces enhance the comfortable furnishings and pastel fabrics in several of the nicest suites, though some of the remaining rooms have a slightly more dated feeling and decor.

A delicious gourmet breakfast is served in the privacy of your room, where you can savor ocean views and sometimes even sight a pod of whales.

◆ **Romantic Alternative:** Across the street and up from the Whale Watch Inn is the **NORTH COAST COUNTRY INN**, 34591 South Highway 1, Gualala, (707) 884-4537, (Moderate), residing on a forested hillside with a view of the Pacific in the distance. All four suites at this terraced redwood home have private entrances with French doors that open onto decks, large bay windows (two with distant ocean views), fireplaces, skylights, kitchenettes, and comfortable (though outdated) American furnishings. There is also a steamy outdoor hot tub for soaking tired spirits back to life. Breakfast is delivered to your room for the most intimate dining possible.

◆ **Romantic Warning:** Having said all that, I must also inform you that this attractive inn is located right next to Highway 1, which is hardly what you would call secluded or serene.

Restaurant Kissing

THE OLD MILANO RESTAURANT, Gualala
38300 Highway 1
(707) 884-3256
Moderate to Expensive
Wedding facilities are available for a maximum of 40 people.

The hotel is one mile north of the town of Gualala, on Highway 1. Watch for a small, easily missed sign for the hotel on the west side of the road.

As you veer off the highway and start down the sandy driveway toward the ocean, you will readily appreciate the enveloping seclusion of this modest turn-of-the-century restaurant. Besides its wondrous location (a stone's throw from the ocean), this restaurant's most irresistible quality is its unsurpassed enthusiasm for antique country finery. Every corner of the dining area boasts a memento from the past; the cozy tables are draped in white linens and garnished with candles. The creative menu is consistently delicious, though it changes daily; we enjoyed garlic-eggplant pita with hummus, skewered Portuguese scallops, braised monkfish with nicoise olives, and roasted salmon. After dinner, take a stroll along the shore and admire the heavenly scenery.

◆ **Romantic Note:** Though this restaurant is delightfully romantic, the accommodations here leave much to be desired. Stick to dinner.

ST. ORRES RESTAURANT, Gualala
36601 Highway 1 South
(707) 884-3303
Inexpensive to Expensive
Wedding facilities are available for a maximum of 50 people.

As you head north out of Gualala on Highway 1, the spires of St. Orres will appear on the left. If you reach Anchor Bay, you have gone too far.

St. Orres' Russian-inspired architecture is anything but ordinary, and the restaurant here exemplifies this property's flair for the unusual. A three-story-high wooden tower, patterned with stained glass windows and stenciled woodwork, creates a dramatic dining climate, ideal for romancing the night away. Distant views of the ocean are visible from some of the candlelit two-person tables clustered at the base of the tower. Dinner here is a prix fixe three-course delight and, as you might expect, features unusual entrées like wild boar stuffed with dates and walnuts, served with Rosemary's apple-ginger chutney from St. Orres' orchards; grilled vegetable tart in a flaky pastry shell with fresh corn beignets and a smoked tomato sauce; or grilled Sonoma County quail marinated in tequila, served with yam and green onion pancakes, quail won tons, and a blood orange-jalapeno pepper glaze. Don't worry—the food is as delicious as it is interesting!

Outdoor Kissing

ROTH RANCH, Gualala
37100 Old Stage Road
(707) 884-3124

Head north on Highway 1 for one mile past the town of Gualala. Turn left onto Pacific Woods Road, which dead-ends at Old Stage Road, where you turn left. The ranch is two miles down the road.

Roth Ranch provides healthy, energetic horses for gallops along logging trails lined with redwoods, rhododendrons, and flowering wild azaleas. Prices are reasonable and horse rentals are by the hour; if this isn't long enough for you and yours, request a three-hour excursion that includes a picnic lunch (optional) along the rushing Gualala River.

♦ **Romantic Suggestion:** Those interested in exploring Gualala's spectacularly private beaches might want to consider packing their own lunch and making a day of it. **THE FOOD COMPANY,** 38411 Robinson Reach, Gualala, (707) 884-1800, (Inexpensive to Moderate), located off Highway 1 in Gualala, is an excellent place to pick up a carry-out gourmet lunch. Whether it's wild mushroom lasagne, deep-dish pizza, or a tempting chocolate soufflé roll with mocha cream, you're sure to find something appetizing. So appetizing, in fact, that it might be gone by the time you reach the beach.

Elk

Hotel/Bed and Breakfast Kissing

ELK COVE INN, Elk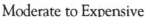
6300 South Highway 1
(707) 877-3321
Moderate to Expensive
Wedding facilities are available for a maximum of 50 people.

On the west side of Highway 1, in the town of Elk.

The views from the Elk Cove Inn are stunning, and sunset will leave you speechless (which makes kissing that much easier). The eight sparsely decorated rooms are spacious, with standard bedspreads and wood-paneled walls. The upstairs rooms in the main house have arched ceilings and dormer windows with window seats that face windblown cypresses and the shimmering sea. Four small guest cabins are perched on the edge of a bluff so the view is even more up-close and personal; two have bay windows, high beamed ceilings, skylights, and wood stoves. There is a roof deck atop the main house if you want a bird's-eye view, or you can wander outside for a kiss in the newly built gazebo. Did I forget to mention the driftwood-scattered beach below the inn? There are so many potential kissing spots that this is one place you really should check out for yourselves. A gourmet European breakfast, served at separate tables in the wood-paneled, ocean-view dining room, will leave you satisfied until dinner.

GREENWOOD PIER INN, Elk
5928 South Highway 1
(707) 877-9997
Moderate to Very Expensive
Wedding facilities and services are available for a maximum of 50 people.

On the west side of Highway 1.

Copious flower gardens cover the grounds of the Greenwood Pier Inn, a peaceful and earthy oasis that could easily be mistaken for a Zen Buddhist retreat. Several uniquely crafted redwood cottages house 11 different rooms. Each has artsy decor, a fireplace or wood-burning stove, and knotty pine paneling; some have private decks, stained glass windows, a canopied bed, or a spiral staircase leading up to a loft with a whirlpool tub for two. Sound great? Well, even though it is a little funky, it is wonderful and a refreshing change of pace.

A continental breakfast is delivered to your room for a leisurely morning. Although breakfast in bed is an affectionate option, it isn't every morning that a glorious garden perched at the edge of the Pacific awaits right outside the door (at least not at our house). We forced ourselves to get dressed so we could enjoy freshly baked breads and muffins in this serene setting, overlooking massive ocean-carved rocks and the brilliant blue sea.

GRIFFIN HOUSE COTTAGES, Elk
5910 South Highway 1
(707) 877-3422
Inexpensive to Expensive

On the west side of Highway 1.

Behind a pub, where you might expect a parking lot, are seven small white cottages with green trim. Each one is modestly decorated and has a wood-burning stove and private bath; a few have brass beds, claw-foot tubs, and private decks with views overlooking the endless Pacific. Note that some of the cottages have a double bed, so you might have to cuddle a little closer than usual. A creative full breakfast is brought to your cottage in the morning.

HARBOR HOUSE INN BY THE SEA, Elk
5600 South Highway 1
(707) 877-3203
Moderate to Expensive

Just outside the town of Elk, on the west side of Highway 1.

The word "rustic" usually makes me nervous. It's hard to know exactly what is meant by the term. Rustic can conjure up images of knotty wood paneling, alcove sitting areas next to bay windows, crackling fireplaces, and down quilts three inches thick. It can also suggest paneling that is falling off the walls, drafty fireplaces that provide no warmth, and torn quilts that have seen better days. This inn by the sea is best described as a rustic sanctuary—of the first type and not anything like the second type. It is a place where the hours drift by and your mood is enhanced by the tranquillity around you.

The inn is constructed of redwood and resides on a bluff with awesome views of the water and the private beach below. The sweeping bay window in the dining room looks out onto haystack boulders and sea-worn rock arches that dot the ocean's surface. In this imposing setting, exceptional gourmet breakfasts (for guests only) and dinners are served with flair. The food is as fresh as the location, with preference given to homegrown vegetables and herbs. You will find everything about Harbor House amorous and relaxing.

The moderate price for staying here includes a full breakfast and dinner for two. There are ten rooms at Harbor House, and almost all are decidedly romantic. The Lookout Room is the only one without a fireplace or wood stove, but it has a private deck with an amazing view. The Seaview and Oceansong cottages have semiprivate decks, fireplaces, and full ocean views. The Cypress and Harbor rooms are more spacious and also have fireplaces and incredible ocean views.

◆ **Romantic Suggestion:** Even if you don't spend the night here, you can still make a reservation for a magnificent meal at the **HARBOR HOUSE RESTAURANT** (Moderate). The gorgeous scenery outside the expansive windows is absolutely breathtaking, and dinner is equally satisfying. The fixed menu might begin with tomato basil soup, pepper cheese bread, and mixed garden greens with lemon-chive vinaigrette, followed by salmon fillets in phyllo pastry with Parmesan mornay sauce, polenta, and fresh asparagus spears, and finally dessert, a light peach crisp that is the perfect finale to your perfectly prepared meal.

SANDPIPER HOUSE, Elk
5520 South Highway 1
(707) 877-3587
Moderate to Expensive

Just outside the town of Elk, on the west side of Highway 1.

Even if the Sandpiper House didn't have outstanding amorous touches such as whirlpool tubs for two, fireplaces, bay windows, down comforters, canopied beds, and a complimentary bottle of wine the first night of your stay, the awesome view would still command attention. All of the comfortable, homey rooms are decorated with soft floral fabrics, antiques, and fresh flowers. Strange as it seems, the original master bedroom is the only one of the five rooms that doesn't have a water view and instead looks out onto Highway 1. Greenwood Cove was once so busy that when the original owners built this home in 1916, a peaceful meadow view was preferred. Oh, how the times have changed.

A colorful garden and sitting area look out over the ocean; the inn shares beach access with its neighbor, the Harbor House. A two-course gourmet breakfast is served in the sunny dining room. Afternoon tea and evening sherry are also included with your stay.

Albion

Hotel/Bed and Breakfast Kissing

ALBION RIVER INN, Albion
3790 North Highway 1
(707) 937-1919, (800) 479-7944
Inexpensive to Expensive
Wedding facilities are available for a maximum of 125 people.

On the west side of Highway 1, near the town of Albion, six miles south of Mendocino.

We suggest you book your reservations two months ahead of time at the celebrated Albion River Inn—everybody wants to stay here. Fortunately, the inn's popularity in no way hampers its romance potential. If, after a long day of touring, you want a secluded, beautiful place to watch the golden sunset turn the sky to fiery red as the ocean thunders against the shore below, this is the place to be. The inn sits on a precipice directly on the coast, towering above Albion Cove and the Pacific. All of the 24 rooms have private decks with superlative views, attractive antique and white wicker furnishings, floral linens, and Oriental throw rugs; four of the luxury rooms even have Jacuzzis. A generous breakfast of home-baked breads, homemade granola, eggs to order, fresh fruit, and juices, served in the inn's waterfront restaurant, is included with your stay. The food is truly delicious and the view is mesmerizing.

◆ **Romantic Note:** If you want to take a walk during your stay here, there is a private headland pathway that leads to great vistas of the expansive water and sky.

FENSALDEN INN, Albion   ◆ ◆
33810 Navarro Ridge Road
(707) 937-4042
Moderate
Wedding facilities are available for a maximum of 40 people.

From Highway 101 south, turn left onto Navarro Ridge Road. Follow this for a quarter mile; the inn will be on your left.

Don't be upset with Fensalden Inn for making you turn your back on the coastline. Look at it this way: you're also leaving the highway behind you. Besides, you can still appreciate distant ocean views from your room in the lovely, wood-shingled provincial home, the water tower, or the bungalow, set among 20 acres of quiet country. Five of the eight guest rooms are located in the main house, and although they have king- and queen-size beds, private porches, and ocean views, they lack the affection required to set the stage for a romantic encounter.

Our favorite spot at Fenselden is the self-contained wooden bungalow found just down the street, also overlooking the ocean in the distance. The cozy wood interior exudes a country charm and provides ample privacy for a weekend getaway, with a loft bedroom, full kitchen, and private bath. Breakfast and hors d'oeuvres are included in your stay.

Restaurant Kissing

ALBION RIVER INN RESTAURANT, Albion
3790 North Highway 1
(707) 937-1919, (800) 479-7944
Inexpensive to Expensive
Wedding facilities are available for a maximum of 125 people.

On the west side of Highway 1, near the town of Albion, six miles south of Mendocino.

Albion River Inn shares its glorious clifftop setting with this highly acclaimed restaurant, also perched above the ocean. The views alone make this small dining room a worthwhile romantic venture. Though the tables are crowded together, the amorous mood is enhanced by candles at every table and soft piano music on Friday and Saturday nights. At dusk on weekends you might also catch glimpses of a bagpipe player in a kilt on the bluff. Though the menu features fairly typical seafood fare, it's delicious, from spicy rock shrimp and angel-hair pasta tossed with roasted red peppers to the breast of Muscovy duck served crisp with an apricot glaze.

THE LEDFORD HOUSE, Albion
3000 North Highway 1
(707) 937-0282
Moderate to Expensive
Wedding facilities are available for a maximum of 35 people.

Off Highway 1, four miles south of Little River, on the east side of the road.

Sited on a bluff with a spectacular view of the ocean, the Ledford House is one of the most elegant places to dine along the coast. Candlelight casts flickering shadows on whitewashed walls, infusing the dining room with warmth. When the area is shrouded in fog (which occurs more often than some would like to admit), the Ledford House becomes still more cozy and inviting. The food here is equally enticing: steamed green mussels with white wine, drizzled with garlic butter, or fresh Maine lobster in citrus and saffron broth with fermented black beans and a cilantro-red pepper pasta are two of the wonderful choices.

◆ **Romantic Note:** Be sure to call for reservations. This restaurant, like many others in this part of the world, is closed during the winter.

Little River

Hotel/Bed and Breakfast Kissing

GLENDEVEN INN AND GALLERY, Little River   ❖ ❖ ❖
8221 North Highway 1
(707) 937-0083, (800) 822-GLEN
Moderate
Wedding facilities are available for a maximum of 25 people.

On Highway 1, just one and a half miles south of Mendocino, look for the Glendeven sign on the east side of the road.

This is country living at its best (though the nearby highway is still distantly audible). The charming New Englandesque farmhouse, annex, and rustic barn house are poised on verdant meadowland brushed by fresh ocean air. Glendeven has ten unique guest suites in all, and each is more engaging and provocative than the last. All of the rooms are replete with lovely bay or garden views, affectionate details, and cozy furnishings. Of special interest are the spacious, airy rooms in the annex with water views, fireplaces, balconies, high vaulted ceilings, redwood paneling, French doors leading to sunny decks, and large tiled bathrooms. If these rooms don't help set the mood, nothing will.

HERITAGE HOUSE, Little River   ❖ ❖ ❖ ❖
5200 North Highway 1
(707) 937-5885, (800) 235-5885
Expensive to Unbelievably Expensive
Wedding facilities are available for a maximum of 20 people.

About five miles south of Mendocino, on the ocean side of Highway 1.

It's not surprising that the movie *Same Time, Next Year* was filmed at the Heritage House—this spellbinding hostelry boasts one of the most spectacular panoramas on California's northern coast. But if you're thinking of kissing in the room where Alan Alda and Ellen Burstyn romanced, you'll have to reserve months in advance. In fact, reserve as far in advance as possible for any room here. The estate embraces no fewer than 72 guest rooms in a series of small buildings terraced above the Pacific. Almost all of the uniquely decorated rooms have private entrances and share a dazzling view of a pristine cove where waves crash majestically against rugged cliffs. Views from a Sunset room are pure inspiration; unbelievably, the view from the Carousel Suite is even more sensational. Throw open the windows to welcome the Pacific's music and sink into the double whirlpool set beneath the starry skylight. A two-sided fireplace warms both the living room and bedroom.

Don't be taken aback by the Unbelievably Expensive cost rating here—room rates include breakfast and dinner for two served in the elegant dining room perched above the Pacific (see "Restaurant Kissing").

◆ **Romantic Warning:** Heritage House is closed in December and January.

◆ **Romantic Alternative:** STEVENSWOOD LODGE, 8211 Highway 1, Little River, (707) 937-2810, (Inexpensive to Very Expensive), is set back from the road on nicely landscaped grounds and offers ten surprisingly contemporary, crisp rooms in a small, rustic lodge setting. Though the rooms are sparsely decorated and seem to be designed more for traveling executives (there are remote-control televisions and phones in every room), the wood-burning fireplaces, decks, and partial water views in some of the rooms suggest romantic possibilities. The inn's nicest feature is the colorful local art featured in the gallery-like hallways. Generous evening appetizers, wine, and gourmet breakfasts are served in the cheerful, firelit common room.

Restaurant Kissing

HERITAGE HOUSE RESTAURANT, Little River   ◆ ◆ ◆ ◆
5200 North Highway 1
(707) 937-5885, (800) 235-5885
Expensive to Very Expensive
Wedding facilities are available for a maximum of 20 people.

About five miles south of Mendocino, on the ocean side of Highway 1.

If you want to reserve a table at this elegant oceanside restaurant, your best bet is to spend the night at the Heritage House Inn. Dinner and breakfast are included in the price of your stay, and dinner reservations are guaranteed to guests only. (Once guests have been accommodated, the restaurant opens to envious nonguests.) Set above the sparkling Pacific, nearly every linen-cloaked table in the restaurant's three dining rooms has a glimpse of the ocean. In one room, chandeliers softly illuminate a painted dome ceiling that endows the restaurant with a feeling of spaciousness. The menu changes daily, but can include saffron mussel bisque or crab and smoked almond salad to start; entrées like grilled salmon with artichokes, leeks, and pistachios, or African pheasant with spicy vegetable pot-stickers; and, of course, luscious desserts.

LITTLE RIVER RESTAURANT, Little River   ❖
7750 North Highway 1
(707) 937-4945
Inexpensive to Moderate

Heading south on Highway 1, look for Little River's one and only post office and gas station on the right-hand side of the road; the restaurant is connected to the gas station.

I can't think of a more unlikely location for a restaurant. This obscure, thoroughly pleasing place to dine is attached to the back of the town's gas station and post office. Antiques and framed turn-of-the-century photos adorn the tiny restaurant's walls, which embrace a cozy group of seven tables covered with pink tablecloths. (Now this is intimate!) A remarkably adept kitchen staff serves creatively prepared fresh fish and seafood to its small clientele. Dinner is served Friday through Monday only; the reasonably priced entrées include soup and salad.

Outdoor Kissing

VAN DAMME STATE PARK, Little River   ❖ ❖ ❖ ❖
Two miles south of Mendocino on Highway 1; look for signs on the right.

Footpaths from the highway lead through meadows, weaving past small groves of gnarled trees, while the sound of the Pacific grows ever nearer. Suddenly, the trail climaxes at a stunning seascape of rugged cliffs, mighty surf, and an azure ocean that stretches as far as the imagination. Below, waves send miniature waterfalls rippling over sculptured rocks, and if you're lucky you might even catch a glimpse of seals playing in the breakers or a whale spouting in the distance.

Sea Ranch

SEA RANCH LODGE, Sea Ranch
60 Sea Walk Drive
(707) 785-2371, (800) SEA-RANCH
Moderate to Expensive

Heading south on Highway 101 in the small town of Sea Ranch, look for signs to the lodge. It will be on your right.

The boundless drama of the Pacific Ocean is romantic in and of itself, and the closer your accommodations are to this magnificent shoreline, the better. It doesn't get much closer than the Sea Ranch Lodge, perched on a bluff directly above the sand dunes and ocean. Though the lodge's common areas are modestly appointed with dated Southwestern-style decor, the large stone fireplace in the Piano Bar and gorgeous, unhindered views from the Solarium are all the inspiration you need. Guest rooms are even more subdued, with simple artwork and country patchwork quilts, but the extraordinary views, occasional fireplace or Jacuzzi, and lack of television and telephones give the otherwise standard hotel rooms some romantic potential.

If a lodge isn't your idea of romantic (it can get fairly crowded when the inn is operating at full occupancy), you're still not without options at Sea Ranch. Private oceanfront rental homes are available through the lodge for an extra price (sometimes outrageously extra). Truly escape and relish breathtaking ocean views from the privacy of your own home. (Linens, breakfast basics, and snack items are provided.)

Mendocino

If there is one place that is representative of coastal life in Northern California, it is Mendocino. Words that appropriately fit this seaside town are "quaint" and "serene." Well, at least during the winter that's true. Other times of the year, "crowded" best characterizes this Cape Cod-style village. Its quiet streets are lined with whitewashed storefronts that house small art galleries and specialty shops ripe for browsing. There are also enviable bed and breakfasts that are frequently fully booked on week-ends—months in advance. Of course, the main attraction is the view of the tranquil bay and rocky shoreline that surround Mendocino. In essence, this town offers the yin and yang of getaway spots. The very elements that make it so wonderful are also why everyone and their cousins know about it. Still, there is the off-season, when the crowds and sun are less prevalent and fog shrouds the area in a veil of misty white. And that's what down comforters, fireplaces, and snuggling close are for.

Hotel/Bed and Breakfast Kissing

AGATE COVE INN, Mendocino
11201 North Lansing Street
(707) 937-0551, (800) 527-3111 (in California)
Inexpensive to Expensive
Wedding facilities are available for a maximum of 20 people.

From northbound Highway 1: Take the Lansing Street exit after the traffic light. From southbound Highway 1: Take the first Lansing Street exit. The inn is a half mile north of the village of Mendocino.

The wonderful thing about oceanfront accommodations is that the surf is close enough to serenade you all night long. The Agate Cove Inn is right across the street from the ocean, and luckily the crashing waves drown out any road noise that might otherwise be a problem. Nine of these ten cozy English country-style cottages have mesmerizing views of the ocean beyond a well-cared-for garden courtyard. Every room has comfortable country furnishings, and some have canopied beds, handmade quilts, and a Franklin fireplace. The premier Emerald and Obsidian rooms each have a "companion" tub for two, double-headed shower, king-size bed, fireplace, and a spectacular water view.

The full country breakfasts served here are cooked on an antique wood-burning stove; you may be greeted by omelets with five fillings of your choice, eggs Benedict, or French toast. This generous meal is served in the inn's extremely pleasant, window-outfitted dining room, with a ringside view of the potent, rugged shoreline.

BREWERY GULCH INN, Mendocino
9350 North Highway 1
(707) 937-4752
Inexpensive to Moderate
Wedding facilities are available for a maximum of 10 people.

Just south of Mendocino, on the inland side of Highway 1.

Even though the Brewery Gulch Inn is located just outside lively little Mendocino, it feels like a down-home country retreat. From the moment you enter the weathered gate, you'll find serenity and generous hospitality. Two of the five homey rooms here share a bath, and all have queen-size beds. The spacious Garden Room has a comfy sitting area next to a brick fireplace and French doors that open to a private deck and secluded garden area. Nature paths along the hillside allow you to explore the lovely grounds before devouring a hearty breakfast, served in the lush garden when the weather permits.

THE HEADLANDS INN, Mendocino
Howard and Albion streets
(707) 937-4431
Moderate to Expensive

Follow Highway 1 north to Mendocino. Turn left to the business district, drive two blocks to Howard Street, and turn right. The inn is a block and a half up, on the left, at the corner of Howard and Albion streets.

The new owners of the Headlands Inn have tastefully blended charm and comfort to create a light, airy atmosphere in this Cape Cod-style Victorian. Each of the five distinctive rooms has a feather bed, down comforter, or handmade quilt; overstuffed European reading pillows; and a fireplace or parlor stove. The views of the Pacific's churning white water are outstanding in the spacious Bessie Strauss Room, which features a huge bay window, and in the cozy top-floor George Switzer Room, with its arched ceiling and window seat. The other rooms view the village. A cottage on the property offers a four-poster bed and a large sunken soaking tub: the ultimate in privacy.

In the morning, an exceptional gourmet breakfast is brought directly to your room. Do not be surprised to find Florentine ham rolls with cheddar-sherry sauce, peach or blackberry crêpes in an amaretto sauce, and fresh pastries and fruits on your personalized tray.

REED MANOR, Mendocino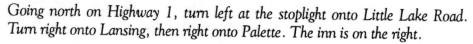
Palette Drive
(707) 937-5446
Expensive to Unbelievably Expensive

Going north on Highway 1, turn left at the stoplight onto Little Lake Road. Turn right onto Lansing, then right onto Palette. The inn is on the right.

For opulently voluptuous kissing in earthy Mendocino, check into this stately new manor. All five of the palatially sized guest rooms feature gas fireplaces, ample whirlpool tubs, sumptuous decor, high wood-beamed ceilings, mini-fridges, coffee makers, teapots, stereos, televisions tucked away in cabinets, and VCRs hidden in bedside drawers. High-power telescopes are set up on some of the private decks for viewing the village below and the ocean beyond; complimentary wine encourages you to toast it all. In the Napoleon Room, a double-sided fireplace warms both the bathroom, with its whirlpool and dual-headed shower, and the silvery French Provincial bedroom, with its romantic four-poster bed. Josephine's Garden Room opens to a delightful redwood patio laced with colorful blooms. Even the smallest, least expensive Imperial Room is elegant and cozy, adorned with Oriental flair and peach florals.

A continental breakfast of nut breads, fruit, and locally made apple juice is wrapped and delivered to your room in the evening, so you can enjoy it at your leisure in the morning.

STANFORD INN BY THE SEA, Mendocino
Comptche-Ukiah Road
(707) 937-5615, (800) 331-8884
Expensive to Unbelievably Expensive

Just south of Mendocino, turn inland from Highway 1 onto Comptche-Ukiah Road.

This expansive lodge is the perfect marriage of quintessential luxury and a woodsy naturalness true to its ruggedly beautiful setting. Step onto your private deck (all 24 rooms have one) to absorb the remarkable scene of the sun setting on the far horizon and casting its golden glow across the Pacific, over the inn's herd of graceful llamas grazing in the meadow, and past terraced flower and vegetable gardens. If the evening chills, cuddle by the firelight in your knotty pine-paneled room, pop open the complimentary bottle of wine, and slide a mood-setting CD into your stereo. Each room, even the smallest, has a fireplace, private balcony, stereo, television, VCR, and a sleigh or four-poster bed. In the morning, take a dip in the alluring greenhouse-enclosed pool or luxuriate in the spa and sauna. The warmth of this bright and humid solarium might make you think you're actually in the South Pacific.

A champagne breakfast of cereals, yogurt, pastries, fruits, and more is served in the cozy firelit parlor.

◆ **Romantic Note:** See the coast in style on one of the inn's state-of-the-art mountain bikes, available at no cost to guests. Or rent a canoe for a romantic paddle along the Big River, following it inland to secluded picnicking and kissing spots.

WHITEGATE INN, Mendocino
499 Howard Street
(707) 937-4892, (800) 531-7282
Moderate to Expensive
Wedding facilities are available for a maximum of 25 people.

Take Highway 1 into Mendocino and turn west onto Little Lake Road (the only stoplight). Go two blocks, turn left onto Howard Street, and go south one block. The inn is on the corner of Howard and Ukiah streets.

In some towns, Victorian-style bed and breakfasts are so abundant that they start to look alike. In Mendocino this is not the case. The Whitegate Inn stands out as one of the few traditionally Victorian bed and breakfasts in town, with its elegant crystal chandeliers, antique furniture, claw-foot tubs, and floral and textured wall coverings. The six guest rooms all have ocean or village views, cozy down comforters, and five have a fireplace. Unwind on the expansive redwood deck or in the gazebo, where you can gaze at the clear blue sea, then roam to the parlor for afternoon wine and cheese.

A full breakfast is served family-style at one large table in the morning; it isn't very intimate, but you might overhear some good ideas on how to spend your day (just in case you've already done everything we've suggested).

Restaurant Kissing

CAFE BOUGELAIS, Mendocino
961 Ukiah Street
(707) 937-5614
Moderate to Expensive

On Ukiah Street, between Howard and Evergreen.

Some say this is the most romantic restaurant in Mendocino. Others say that the tables are a little too close together for comfort. Everyone agrees that the wood-burning stove and the candles at every table warm the oak-paneled interior and create a cozy atmosphere. Additional tables in a casual atrium look out over the green garden; they attract lots of couples on a sunny day, but the room gets too hot to be comfortable when the sun beats down.

Let your dining experience be an unhurried one at Cafe Bougelais; the menu boasts "Good food takes time to prepare—we do not have a microwave oven (and never will)." You'll appreciate this philosophy once you taste the fresh bread, baked in a brick oven outside, or a lamb shank marinated and braised with brandy, red wine, carrots, and onions, or farfalle with prawns, calamari, garlic, and leeks braised in red wine, with toasted breadcrumbs, lemon, and fresh herbs. For dessert, we couldn't decide between the French chocolate mousse cake with warm chocolate sauce and vanilla ice cream or the ginger-pumpkin crème brûlée, so we had to order both. Ah, if only all choices in life could be so easy, and so satisfying!

◆ **Romantic Alternative:** Right next door, **955 UKIAH STREET**, 955 Ukiah Street, Mendocino, (707) 937-1955, (Moderate to Expensive), serves dinner Thursday through Sunday only. Because of their limited hours, we didn't actually get to see this popular new restaurant, but, boy, did we hear about it! Everyone in town was talking about the exquisite, inventive cuisine and the dramatic split-level dining room with vaulted ceilings. We didn't eat there, so we can't award it any lips, but we hear that the most romantic tables are downstairs, where the 20-foot ceiling helps to create a sense of space even when the room is packed with diners.

CHOCOLATE MOOSSE CAFE, Mendocino
390 Kasten Street
(707) 937-4323
Inexpensive

Follow Main Street into Mendocino and turn right onto Kasten Street. The restaurant is on Kasten Street, at Albion.

Plan on light romance at lunch in this cozy, casual cafe, especially on a chilly, foggy day when firelight warms the room. This is the kind of place where the specials written on the blackboard can range from salmon smoked over apple wood to a saucy lasagne to an inventive quiche. Decadent desserts, such as the irresistible blackout cake, and gourmet coffees can make even a dreary day enjoyable when shared by two. The dinner menu offers the same types of imaginative dishes, and sparkling white lights trim the windows, warming the night.

◆ **Romantic Alternative:** If the sun is shining, choose a table on the patio of **THE MENDOCINO CAFE**, Lansing at Ukiah, Mendocino, (707) 937-0836, (Inexpensive). Standard fare of soups, salads, sandwiches, and light entrées are served along with a view of the crashing coastline beyond the village.

GRAY WHALE BAR AND CAFE, Mendocino
45020 Albion Street
(707) 937-5763
Moderate

As you turn west off Highway 1 onto Main Street, look for Lansing Street and turn right. The next block is Albion, where you turn left to the bar.

The epitome of North Coast dining and lounging is found here at the Gray Whale. The ambience is a careful combination of country Victorian refinement and laid-back California spirit. Whoever handled this renovation knew what they were doing. It takes a great deal of skill to meld the warmth of the past with the finesse of the present and yet create the illusion that nothing has changed in 100 years. A substantial cobblestone fireplace fills each of the dining rooms with a burnished light that flickers warmly against redwood paneling. The tables are placed far enough apart to provide for discreet conversation. A window-framed sun porch at the front of the lounge houses the cafe, which overlooks the bay and the street scene. Complementing this atmosphere is a menu of fresh fish, meats, and produce, all of which are exceptionally savory.

◆ **Romantic Note:** The Gray Whale Bar and Cafe is located on the ground floor of the **MACCALLUM HOUSE INN**, (707) 937-0289, (Inexpensive to Expensive), under separate management from the restaurant. This inn is, to say the least, one of the most unusual bed and breakfasts I've ever seen. The meandering array of rooms and suites ranges in style from overly rustic to unusually romantic. For kissing purposes, the best units are the Barn and the Barn Apartment. The Barn has a massive stone fireplace, cozy sitting area, and a large picture window overlooking the bay. The Barn Apartment is similar, with the addition of a very sensual, very large bathroom. For the most part, however, this is not what we would call the best kissing place in Mendocino.

MENDOCINO HOTEL DINING ROOM, Mendocino
45080 Main Street
(707) 937-0511, (800) 548-0513
Expensive
Wedding facilities are available for a maximum of 50 people.

On Main Street, between Lansing and Kasten.

Arrive early to ease yourselves back in time by the fire in the elegant lobby, with its tapestried settees and Persian carpets. Candles flicker on the tables in the dining room, casting a nostalgic glow on the rich, red wall coverings and faceted glass partitions. Share aphrodisiacal oysters or Brie baked in puff pastry, followed by such continental favorites as petrale sole or prime rib served with Yorkshire pudding. For lunch or an early dinner, the hotel's Garden Room provides a gloriously lush greenhouse setting, especially inviting when the sun streams in.

Outdoor Kissing

MENDOCINO COAST BOTANICAL GARDENS
18220 North Highway 1
(707) 964-4352
$5 adults

On the west side of Highway 1, just south of Fort Bragg.

Natural gardens unfold before you with ever-expanding layers of beauty, each one surprising and evocative. The entrance is little more than a rustic garden shop by a roadside cafe, but don't be fooled. Just beyond the gate, the beauty of 47 acres of botanical wonder awaits. You can stroll hand-in-hand past formal plantings of colorful annuals, following walkways festooned with rhododendrons, over hillsides laced with hydrangeas, and across meadows mellow with heather. No matter what time of year you visit, something will be in bloom. Wander to the farthest reaches of the garden to find a stunning seascape with welcoming benches perched high above the crashing surf. In the winter you may even see a whale pass by, its spout punctuating the vastness of the sea.

MENDOCINO HEADLANDS and
BIG RIVER BEACH STATE PARK

The coastal headlands and park surround Mendocino on all sides.

Perhaps more than any other attraction in Mendocino, the headlands and Big River State Park are the primary draws of this region. The protected, flawless curve of land is an easily accessible place to see, hear, and feel nature in all its magnitude and glory. On a calm, sun-filled day, the glistening ocean reveals hidden grottos, sea arches, and tide pools, as foamy white surf encircles the rock-etched boundary of Mendocino. If you happen to be here December through March, you may see a school of whales making their way down the coast. Even on days when the thick ocean fog enfolds the area in a white-gray cloak, this is still a prime place to explore and daydream. Bundle up and snuggle close—the cool mist tingling against your cheeks is chilly.

◆ Romantic Option: **RUSSIAN GULCH STATE PARK,** just north of Mendocino off Highway 1, (707) 937-5804, is a small campground with redwood-lined trails, rocky coves, lovely inlets, a quiet bay, and campsites at the water's edge. There aren't many tent spaces available here, so make reservations well in advance.

◆ Second Romantic Option: **MCKERRICHER STATE PARK,** three miles north of Fort Bragg off Highway 1, (707) 937-5804, holds a wondrous assortment of nature's most attractive features: waterfalls at the end of forested trails, grass-covered headlands overlooking the Pacific, white sandy beaches, rolling dunes, and haystack rocks where harbor seals spend the day sunning themselves. The most outstanding feature of this state park is its distance from Mendocino; the extra few miles make it less popular, giving it a definite kissing advantage.

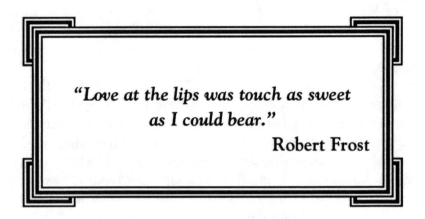

"*Love at the lips was touch as sweet
as I could bear.*"

Robert Frost

WINE COUNTRY

From San Francisco, take Highway 101 north to Highway 37 east. Highway 37 connects with Highway 12 (the Sonoma Highway), which heads north through the Sonoma Valley, and with Highway 29 (the St. Helena Highway), which accesses the Napa Valley.

The hills in this holiday countryside are given over to vineyards and the succulent grapes they produce. Once you visit this region you will understand the vivacious, impetuous temperament that is the hallmark of California's wine country, its robust regard for living life to its fullest. The boroughs and hamlets of the area are well stocked with an enormous selection of bed and breakfasts, restaurants, spas, wine tasting rooms, hot-air balloon companies, and the most remarkable picnic turf around. The roughest part of traveling here will be choosing where to concentrate your time.

◆ **Romantic Consideration:** The number of wineries scattered throughout these picturesque hills and valleys is staggering. Even if you were merely to sip your way in and out of tasting rooms for a week, you would make only a nominal, intoxicating dent in the possibilities that exist here. Because this book is about sentiment and not about choosing a vintage wine, we've chosen a handful of the lesser-known, out-of-the-mainstream wineries we found to be the most appealing for tasting and embracing, both the wine and each other.

Napa Valley

The heavily trafficked St. Helena Highway winds through most of the towns in the Napa Valley, detracting from the quiet splendor of the area. Nevertheless, the abundance of gorgeous wineries, restaurants, bed and breakfasts, and inns found in the beautiful surrounding countryside of the Napa Valley makes this area one of Northern California's most sensational places to pucker up.

Napa

It would be nice if the Napa Valley's namesake town were more impressive, but we found it too industrial to be a very romantic destination, especially when there are so many other quaint villages to recommend. Affectionate establishments do exist here, you just have to travel on busy streets to find them, and, unless otherwise stated, road noise can be a problem.

Hotel/Bed and Breakfast Kissing

BLUE VIOLET MANSION, Napa   ◆ ◆ ◀
443 Brown Street
(707) 253-BLUE
Expensive to Very Expensive
Wedding facilities available for a maximum of 100 people.

On Brown Street between Oak and Laurel.

Fantasy-inspired touches from all around the world will intrigue romantic spirits at the Blue Violet Mansion. The elaborate gold door frame, embossed leather wainscoting, Chinese carpets, and the modern sculptures and art that adorn the main foyer make it clear that this place is not your run-of-the-mill Victorian. Of the eight distinctive rooms here, all contain an international mix of antiques, three have gas fireplaces, two have two-person Jacuzzi tubs, and one has a deep Oriental soaking tub. There is a gazebo on the front lawn where, early in the morning, you can watch hot-air balloons float across the sky before you indulge in a full country breakfast.

◆ **Romantic Suggestion:** If playing lord and lady of the manor appeals to your *Masterpiece Theatre* side, the innkeepers will happily play along. A totally private, candlelit dinner in the formal dining room can be arranged; ask the innkeepers for complete details.

CHURCHILL MANOR, Napa
485 Brown Street
(707) 253-7733
Inexpensive to Expensive
Wedding facilities are available for a maximum of 150 people.

On the corner of Coombs and Brown streets.

Stately white columns are concealed from the street by the tall mani-cured hedges that cloak this grand mansion in welcome privacy. The 11 rooms are decorated in sort of a mismatched Victorian theme; some have claw-foot tubs and sitting areas, two have fireplaces. A shiny red and black Jacuzzi tub seems a little too slick in the "naughty but nice" Bordello Room, but matching decor will be the last thing on your mind as you luxuriate in the bath.

A tasty full breakfast is served in the marble-floored sun room or out-side on the spacious veranda that wraps around the front portion of the estate. Fresh-baked cookies in the afternoon, wine and cheese in the evening, and the use of several bicycles and croquet gear enhance your stay.

♦ **Romantic Note:** Churchill Manor is a popular place for confer-ences and weddings, which is outstanding if it's your own wedding but might be otherwise annoying.

THE HENNESSEY HOUSE, Napa
1727 Main Street
(707) 226-3774
Moderate to Expensive

On Main Street between Lincoln and Yount.

The Hennessey House, a gingerbread-trimmed Queen Anne Victorian, shines in this otherwise drab neighborhood. There are six lav-ishly decorated rooms in the main residence and four more in the adjacent Carriage House, each with a private marble-floored bath, European antiques, and handsome furnishings. High ceilings, fireplaces, comfy feather beds, canopy beds, stained glass windows, and claw-foot tubs are some of the features to choose from. The rooms in the Carriage House all have whirlpool tubs for two.

The full gourmet breakfast, served in the dining room beneath a hand-painted stamped tin ceiling, is an experience in itself. A different creative entrée is served every morning, along with homemade granola, fruit yogurt, and fresh baked goods such as orange scones, pineapple-ricotta muffins, and strawberry nut bread. We enjoyed a light raspberry-nectarine crisp, followed by "breakfast lasagne," a layered dish with French toast separating layers of applewood-smoked ham, cheddar cheese, pears, and granola, served with a sour cream-brown sugar sauce and a side of Southern-style grits with maple syrup. We wanted to lounge all day after such a satisfying repast, but the wineries were calling.

◆ **Romantic Alternative:** Abundant vintage and contemporary stained glass enhances **LA BELLE EPOQUE**, 1386 Calistoga Avenue, Napa, (707) 257-2161, (Moderate to Expensive). All six guest rooms are decorated in Victorian style with floral linens, all have private baths, and one has a wood-burning fireplace. Breakfast can be delivered to the Plumwood Room, which has its own sitting area; otherwise, the full gourmet breakfast is served on the sunny garden porch or at a large table in the dining room. Evening wine and hors d'oeuvres are served in the inn's own dark little wine cellar.

LA RESIDENCE, Napa   ◆◆ ◆◆
4066 St. Helena Highway (Highway 29)
(707) 253-0337
Moderate to Very Expensive
Wedding facilities are available for a maximum of 50 people.

Heading north on Highway 29, pass Salvador Avenue, turn right at the Don Giovanni Restaurant, and follow the drive to the inn.

In a pastoral setting, La Residence could be absolutely idyllic. Unfortunately, these two stately buildings, a Gothic brick mansion and a French barn, are right beside a four-lane stretch of Highway 29. Double-pane windows have been installed and a few trees in the front lawn help to conceal the neighboring highway, but it would take a lot more than shrubbery to totally muffle the incessant road noise. Getting a room that faces the backyard is the best way to ensure a good night's sleep.

If you do succeed in tuning out the road noise, you'll find casual refinement and great kissing potential here. Each of the 20 rooms is tastefully adorned with muted floral linens and wallpapers, a private bath, queen-size bed, and pine antique furnishings. The rooms in the French barn all have fireplaces; some have four-poster beds, some have French doors that open to a patio or balcony (make sure yours don't face the busy thoroughfare). Brick paths throughout the property invite you to admire the gorgeous, well-tended grounds, punctuated with roses trellises and grape arbors. A dip in the pool is a refreshing option on hot afternoons, but a moonlight soak in the Jacuzzi, where you can stargaze and sneak a kiss or two, is a much more affectionate option.

A plentiful wine and cheese buffet is served fireside each afternoon in the stylish, sun-filled dining room. In the morning, a savory full breakfast is presented here at tables for two.

◆ **Romantic Alternative:** The six rooms at **THE NAPA INN**, 1137 Warren Street, Napa, (707) 257-1444, (Moderate to Expensive), are decorated in typical Victorian fashion, but the commodious Grand Suite stands out. It takes up the entire top floor, and has vaulted ceilings, a king-size bed, a private balcony, and a gas log fireplace. The Eastlake Suite isn't as large, but the fireplace, solarium-style sitting room, and claw-foot tub are still inviting.

OAK KNOLL INN, Napa
2200 East Oak Knoll Avenue
(707) 255-2200
Expensive

Take Highway 29 north (just beyond the town of Napa) and turn right onto Oak Knoll Avenue. At the stop sign turn left onto Big Ranch Road and then turn immediately right onto East Oak Knoll Avenue. Continue one-half mile to the inn.

If you're headed to the Napa Valley specifically for romance, this is the place to kiss and kiss and kiss. The tree-lined drive and wrought-iron gates that welcome you to the Oak Knoll Inn only begin to suggest the remote splendor to be found here. The inn's location is as far removed from the madding crowd as you could ever hope for. Besides the handful of other guests, there is nothing else for miles around but the fertile vineyards, lush meadows, and quiet woodlands of the Napa Valley.

Once you enter the courtyard area, where two wings of suites overlook an aqua blue swimming pool and vineyards in the distance, you will realize that you have stumbled upon a one-of-a-kind retreat. The four guest rooms here are the most impressive I've seen anywhere. Each suite has a remarkable 17-foot-tall vaulted ceiling, floor-to-ceiling draped windows, a fireplace set into inlaid stone walls, a gorgeous bathroom with marble floors, and French doors that open onto the inner courtyard.

Not surprisingly, breakfast here is a mouthwatering gourmet's delight: baby banana splits in raspberry sauce with homemade strawberry, mango, and honeydew sorbet balls, followed by quiche with Anaheim chiles, served with chorizo, black beans, cilantro salsa, and corn muffettes. Heaven.

THE OLD WORLD INN, Napa
1301 Jefferson Street
(707) 257-0112
Moderate to Expensive

From Highway 29, take the Lincoln East exit to the Jefferson Street traffic light and turn right. The inn is a half mile down, on the right.

If the way to your heart is through your stomach, you'll be smitten by the Old World Inn. An afternoon dessert buffet with tea and a bountiful assortment of homemade treats will more than satisfy your sweet tooth, and the evening wine and hors d'oeuvres fest might encourage you to postpone dinner. After sampling these delectable creations, even the latest risers will be eager to get up the following morning for breakfast, served buffet-style at intimate tables for two.

In the stairwell that leads to your room, "WELCOME HOME, ROMANCE SPOKEN HERE" is stenciled on the wall, setting a loving, comfortable mood for your stay. Each of the eight rooms is unique, with features such as a complimentary bottle of wine, private decks, canopied beds, large bay windows, a private sun room with a Jacuzzi, skylights, stenciled walls, and comfortable furnishings. If you don't get the room with a private Jacuzzi, there is a huge outdoor one in the backyard for all to enjoy.

Restaurant Kissing

LA BOUCANE, Napa
1778 Second Street
(707) 253-1177
Expensive
Wedding facilities are available for a maximum of 50 people.

From Highway 29 north take the Central Napa exit. Turn right at the stoplight and left onto Second Street. The restaurant is located on the corner of Jefferson and Second streets.

The fresh strawberries drenched with red wine still make my mouth water when I think of our delicious experience at La Boucane. The setting, in an old Victorian home, with dark brown wallpapers and wood, is nothing out of the ordinary, but the service is attentive and the French cuisine exquisite. The simple but memorable strawberry dessert was the perfect finale to a satisfying meal of crevettes Provencale, avocado salad, and freshly pureed cream of vegetable soup. A different fixed menu is served every night, but you do get a limited choice for each course.

◆ **Romantic Note:** This restaurant serves dinner only and is closed on Sundays.

PETRI'S, Napa ◆ ◆ ◆
3342 Vichy Avenue
(707) 253-1455
Moderate to Expensive
Wedding facilities are available for a maximum of 45 people.

On the east side of Napa, Trancas Road ends and turns into Highway 121, called Monticello Road. As you head toward Lake Berryessa, look for Vichy Avenue on your right. The restaurant is at the corner of Monticello Road and Vichy Avenue.

Before you cast yourselves adrift on the backroads to find the sovereign wineries of this region, you may want to visit this amiable establishment filled with congenial charm and hearty pasta. The elfin cottage is so well camouflaged by flowering gardens that hug the vine-covered stone exterior that you could miss it completely. Two glass doors open into the main dining areas, where wood-beamed ceilings, tile floors, wood tables, and rough-hewn stone walls all make a charming backdrop for your meal. Sauce-laden pastas accompany continental dinners that are sure to please the most discriminating gourmets.

◆ **Romantic Note:** The restaurant is closed Mondays.

Outdoor Kissing

HESS VINEYARDS, Napa
4411 Redwood Road
(707) 255-1144
$2.50 tasting fee

Take Highway 29 north, turn left at the stoplight onto Redwood Road, and follow signs to Hess Winery. The winery is approximately six miles from Highway 29.

A fine wine should be savored, and so should this exceptional winery and art gallery. Located on a quiet side road, far removed from the rush of Highway 29, Hess seduces you into slowing your pace, taking time to stroll in the courtyard garden, taste a mellow vintage, and enjoy their small but superb collection of contemporary art. The airy, uplifting gallery showcases three floors of provocative pieces, interspersed with windows peeking into the sequestered winemaking operation, which, in this framework, appears to be a work of art in its own right. Sadly, picnic tables are not provided here, but you will find plenty of food for thought for a lively luncheon elsewhere.

NAPA VALLEY WINE TRAIN, Napa
1275 McKinstry Street
(707)253-2111, (800) 522-4142
$20 deli car, lunch train fare only (food not included)
$59 per person prix fixe lunch; $69 per person prix fixe dinner (price includes train fare, tax, and gratuity)

From Highway 29 north, take Highway 121 (Silverado Trail) toward Lake Berryessa. Bear left at a fork onto Soscol Avenue. Turn right onto First Street, then left onto McKinstry Street. The train depot is on your left.

The depot was buzzing with an undercurrent of expectation as the wine train pulled in. We left the station's tapestry sofas, souvenir shops, and small art gallery to board a line of beautifully restored 1915 Pullman cars. Once inside, we settled into plush, tufted gold velvet chairs that faced the picture windows but swiveled for an all-around view. Glowing wood paneling, stenciled ceilings, and etched glass partitions highlighted the elegant setting. After our chicken and mushroom terrine appetizer, we stepped through the back door to the sunny observation platform to watch the vineyards slowly roll by. Lunch in the dining car was served with the aplomb of yesteryear, from the pastry-encrusted soup to the filet mignon marinated in red wine to the decadent multilayered torte. Although the slow-moving trip lasted three hours, everyone sighed with reluctance as we pulled back into the Napa depot.

◆ **Romantic Option:** One car is devoted to wine tasting. For $5, you can try four wines from their extensive selection.

◆ **Romantic Note:** The view of the vineyards is the best part of the wine train experience, and it can't be seen after dark. If you want to ride a dinner train, which departs at 6:30 P.M. and returns at 10 P.M., go in the warmer months when the days are longer.

◆ **Romantic Warning:** Not everyone adores the wine train. Some locals have protested against it, citing noise, increased traffic congestion, and pollution. You may even see two or three "NO WINE TRAIN" signs, which to me is sour grapes.

THE SILVERADO TRAIL

This stretch of highway follows the east side of the Napa Valley, starting from the south, in the town of Napa, and going north to the town of Calistoga.

Only two major roads traverse the Napa Valley: Highway 29 and the Silverado Trail. At some points these roads are separated by only one or two miles, but in spirit and atmosphere they are eons apart. Highway 29 is just that, a highway, encumbered with cars, billboards, tourists, gas stations, and other "civilized" necessities. In contrast, the Silverado Trail is a meandering drive through nature at its most charming: contiguous, undulating hillsides endowed with a profusion of vineyards, forests, and olive groves. As you map your course through the wine country of Napa Valley, it would be a grievous mistake not to allow enough time to cruise along this absorbing roadway. The wineries tucked away in the network of backroads are less commercial and more personal than those that line the main road. Plus, when you do require provisions or restaurants, the towns of Napa, Yountville, Oakville, Rutherford, St. Helena, and Calistoga are practically across the street.

Yountville

Yountville is one of the few Napa Valley towns to veer off the St. Helena Highway. This fact alone endows Yountville with a distinctive quiet charm, and there are several very romantic locales here.

Hotel/Bed and Breakfast Kissing

CROSSROADS INN, Yountville
6380 Silverado Trail
(707) 944-0646
Expensive to Very Expensive

The inn is perched on a hillside above the Silverado Trail. Heading north, look for a sign on the right just before the Yountville Crossroad.

If your day of kissing in wine country has you walking on air, ascend to the lofty Crossroads Inn—a sprawling, contemporary wood house set high above the rolling, vineyard-laden hills. The view from its spacious, firelit living room and redwood deck is enchantingly mellow. Enjoy magnificent sunsets from the guest rooms' double whirlpools and private decks (views don't get much better than this). In the Puddleduck Room, the whirlpool is set in the outermost corner, with windows on either side looking over the valley to the west and a wild ravine to the north. Hiking trails climb up the forested hills to views that stretch as far as San Francisco on a clear day. Make your reservation early—you're not the only ones who want to kiss here.

OLEANDER HOUSE, Yountville
7433 St. Helena Highway
(707) 944-8315
Moderate to Expensive

As you head north on Highway 29 in Yountville, the inn is on your left.

What you see is what you get at this French country bed and break-fast, but what you hear is less pleasant. The brochure neglects to mention one thing: traffic. The sound of cars whizzing by on the adjacent highway is more than irksome, it's distracting. What a disappointment in an other-wise peaceful romantic find. A happy blend of old-fashioned decor and modern architecture and amenities accommodates guests inside. You can kiss by the fireplace in all of the upstairs guest rooms. The high peaked ceilings, private balconies, and uncluttered, softly hued decor lend a sense of simplicity and spaciousness to every room.

After a cup of morning coffee, guests often tiptoe to the backyard for a wake-up soak in the hot tub. (Traffic isn't the only noise out here: sometimes a strange *whoosh* pierces the morning and a brightly colored hot-air balloon floats overhead.) Later, guests meet in the dining room for healthy, hearty breakfast specialties like cinnamon-apple flan and locally made chicken sausage.

VINTAGE INN, Yountville
6541 Washington Street
(707) 944-1112, (800) 351-1133
Moderate to Very Expensive
Wedding facilities are available for a maximum of 200 people.

From Highway 29, take the Yountville/Veterans Home exit. Turn left onto Washington Street; the inn is on the left, just past the Vintage 1870.

Soft classical music breezes through the Vintage Inn's serene lobby, with its plum-colored chairs, brick hearth, and high peaked wood-paneled and -beamed ceiling. Fountains, reflecting pools, and flowers embellish the complex of numerous brick and blue clapboard buildings. Guest rooms are equally peaceful, enhanced by wood-burning fireplaces, neutral tones, jetted baths, and a complimentary bottle of wine to set the mood. Although the villas have two-room suites, I found the spacious

Deluxe and Superior rooms more conducive to kissing, especially those with marble fireplaces and contemporary padded and upholstered head-boards. In the afternoon, a dip in the inn's outdoor heated pool will reju-venate you for a night of romance.

Restaurant Kissing

CALIFORNIA CAFE AND GRILL, Yountville   ◆ ◖
6795 Washington Street
(707) 944-2330
Moderate to Expensive

In Yountville, follow Washington Street north. The restaurant is on the left.

Well, OK, maybe romantic isn't the word for this upbeat, casual cafe located in a shopping center, but the food is so tasty we couldn't resist giving it a mention. Pictures of flowers and mountain scenes decorate the peach walls, and the sound and aroma of sizzling seafood drift from the open, blue-tiled kitchen. You'll relish the angel-hair pasta puttanesca, with tomatoes, capers, olives, and oregano, or the cafe paella, with mus-sels, clams, shrimp, chicken, and andouille sausage on saffron rice. Dessert is a must, though it's hard to choose between the pumpkin cheesecake with fresh persimmons and toasted almonds or the vanilla crème brûlée with chocolate biscotti.

DOMAINE CHANDON, Yountville   ◆ ◆ ◆ ◖
1 California Drive
(707) 944-2892, (800) 736-8906
Expensive to Very Expensive
Wedding facilities are available for a maximum of 120 people.

Drive north on Highway 29 from Napa and take the Yountville exit to California Drive. Located next door to the California Veterans Home.

Domaine Chandon is considered by many to be the most beautiful place to dine in Northern California and it's no wonder. Secluded on the grounds of a country winery, this immense three-terraced dining room spares no expense in its quest for luxury. The inlaid stone walls, arched wood-beamed ceiling and doorways, murals, pink linens, and views of nearby vineyards combine to create a sensuous, elegant dining climate. If it weren't for the dining room's popularity, large size, and poor acoustics (it gets noisy here), we would have given this restaurant four lips without a second thought. It is still a stunning place to dine, though; the food is very good and often superb (especially the roasted Chilean sea bass), and the champagne is superior. Eat here before prime dining hours and you're likely to find the experience rapturous. Call for information regarding seasonal hours.

FRENCH LAUNDRY, Yountville
6640 Washington Street
(707) 944-2380
Expensive

Head north on Highway 29 and turn right onto Washington Street.

You need to look closely when searching for this restaurant or you will mistake French Laundry for a private country home. Housed in a lovingly renovated two-story brick building, this restaurant is reputed to be one of the finest in the Napa Valley. It is also one of the most charming, and consequently reservations are difficult to get, sometimes requiring weeks in advance for a weekend meal. Colorful modern art, fresh flowers on each table, and multicolored tablecloths add pizzazz to the provincial country setting. A superlative prix fixe meal changes nightly and can include an appetizer of artichoke with garlic mayonnaise, watercress and ginger soup, leg of lamb, and chocolate amaretto torte for dessert. Dinner here is a dream come true.

◆ **Romantic Note:** This restaurant has recently changed ownership and is scheduled to reopen after minor renovations in late spring of 1994.

MUSTARD'S GRILL, Yountville
7399 St. Helena Highway
(707) 944-2424
Moderate to Expensive

As you head north on Highway 29 in Yountville, the restaurant is on your left.

Mustard's popularity precludes it from being considered either intimate or romantic, so why are we sending you here? Despite the crowds and boisterous atmosphere, the extensive wine list and delicious seafood (steamy Thai mussels in coconut, basil, and mushroom sauce, for example) will appeal to those looking for a fun, relaxed luncheon or dinner spot. If you don't mind an audience, you might even want to sneak a kiss or two across the table.

Outdoor Kissing

**ABOVE THE WEST HOT AIR
BALLOONING, Yountville**
6744 Washington Street
(707) 944-8638, (800) 627-2759
Expensive to Very Expensive

Advance reservations required.

Nobody will argue that a hot-air balloon ride is the best vantage point for enthralling views of wine country. However, this adventure can feel a little too close for comfort when the two of you are squashed into a balloon basket with a large handful of other people. Above the West Balloon Company takes a special approach to ballooning, recognizing that crowds can be a deterrent to those who only have eyes for each other. By limiting the number of passengers allowed on every flight (their maximum is six), they cater to those who are looking for an intimate experience. True romantics can even reserve an entire balloon for just the two of them (extra, of course). What better way to celebrate your love?

S. ANDERSON WINERY, Yountville
1473 Yountville Crossroad
(707) 944-8642

Heading north on Highway 29, turn right onto Madison Street, which ends at Yount Street. Turn right onto Yountville Crossroad. The winery is one-half mile down on your right, just before you come to the Silverado Trail.

Aside from the fact that S. Anderson is situated on the corner of two fairly busy roads, the views from this small family-owned and -operated winery are unarguably magnificent. After you tour the vineyards, gardens, and wine caves, or sample delicious vintages in the charming, small stone tasting room, enjoy the gorgeous views from one of the umbrella-shaded picnic tables set near a splashing fountain on a stone patio hemmed with rosebushes.

Oakville

Outdoor Kissing

VICHON WINERY, Oakville
1595 Oakville Grade
(707) 944-2811

From Highway 29 north, in the town of Oakville, turn left onto Oakville Grade. The winery is one mile up on the left.

The view from up here is a gorgeous sylvan expanse of neatly arrayed vineyards blanketing sloping hills that surge down into the valley below. In the distance, forested peaks go on for as far as the eye can see. A picnic area on a knoll overlooks this bewitching landscape. As long as you're in this setting, you might as well indulge in a very California kind of afternoon and pack a picnic basket that includes a vintage bottle of wine, fresh cheeses, and sweet, ripe fruit. The winery is open seven days a week, from 10 A.M. to 4:30 P.M.

◆ Romantic Note: The picnic tables are only for people who purchase wine here, and you must reserve a table (on busy days, put your name on the list while you're tasting wines so you won't have to wait long). Speaking of gourmet California-style picnic lunches, the absolute best place for 100 miles around is the OAKVILLE GROCERY, on Highway 29 in Oakville. The intriguing pâtés, cheeses, olives, cured meats, and salads are all luscious to look at, delectable to eat, and outrageously expensive to buy. You can also grab a cappuccino at their newly opened espresso bar. This is gourmet heaven, but we hope the inflated price tags don't exist in heaven.

Rutherford

Hotel/Bed and Breakfast Kissing

AUBERGE DU SOLEIL, Rutherford
180 Rutherford Hill Road
(707) 963-1211, (800) 348-5406
Very Expensive to Unbelievably Expensive and Beyond
Wedding facilities are available for a maximum of 120 people.

From Highway 29, head north into the town of Rutherford. Take the first right onto Highway 128; follow this to the Silverado Trail and turn left. Turn right onto Rutherford Hill Road.

Besides running one of the best restaurants around (see "Restaurant Kissing"), Auberge du Soleil has some of the most well-known, heart-stirring, and certainly first-class accommodations in the area. In fact, the 50 exceptional rooms here are all outrageously expensive but also outrageously spacious and beautiful. Twelve of the rooms have Jacuzzi tubs, but all have fireplaces and terraces that overlook the Napa Valley. These stunning retreats look a tad like a suburban development on the outside, but not inside. Inside, everything is simply perfect.

RANCHO CAYMUS INN, Rutherford
1140 Rutherford Road
(707) 963-1777, (800) 845-1777
Moderate to Unbelievably Expensive
Wedding facilities are available for a maximum of 120 people.

Take Highway 29 north to Route 128 and turn right; the inn is 200 yards down and on your left.

Rancho Caymus Inn is a definite change of pace from most of the other bed and breakfasts and inns in the wine country—or anywhere else in Northern California. Each room is outfitted in a Southwestern Spanish motif. The tile bathroom floors, knotty hardwood floors, stucco fireplaces, and Native American-design blankets and throw rugs are part of the handsome individual decor. The spacious rooms are a bit on the dark side, but the spirit is definitely warm.

The 26 rooms, some quite large, come in five variations, including some with their own fireplace, wet bar, Jacuzzi, balcony, and full kitchen. This may not be the most romantic overnight stay in the area, but the location, architecture, and courtyards make it a good base camp for relaxing and touring the idyllic environs.

A complimentary continental breakfast is served in the Rancho Caymus Inn's Garden Grill Restaurant. The Spanish atmosphere and decor are congenial and inviting. The tiled floors, wooden tables, colorful tapestries, and gracious service are all a pleasure. A full breakfast is available for an extra charge. Be sure that one of you tries the Caymus eggs—scrambled eggs topped with creamy rich guacamole, cheese, and chiles, presented with a glass of bubbling champagne. The restaurant is open to the public for both brunch and lunch (dinner is not served).

Restaurant Kissing

AUBERGE DU SOLEIL RESTAURANT
AND LOUNGE, Rutherford
180 Rutherford Hill Road
(707) 963-1211, (800) 348-5406
Very Expensive
Wedding facilities are available for a maximum of 120 people.

From Highway 29, head north into the town of Rutherford. Take the first right onto Highway 128; follow this to the Silverado Trail and turn left. Turn right onto Rutherford Hill Road.

High above the Napa Valley, perched atop a ridge, Auberge du Soleil has a commanding perspective of the entire countryside. Ensconced in hills with flourishing olive groves, the restaurant and lodge are so well integrated with the landscape that they seem to be organically linked. Walls of cream-colored stucco, light pine-paneled ceilings, wooden tables, and a Spanish-style hearth all add to this effect. The dining room and lounge are designed to supply premium viewing pleasure from every nook and corner of the restaurant. The tables in the lounge are positioned near a fireplace large enough to generate ample warmth. A late-evening visit will allow you to drink in the watercolor hues of day yielding to night. Whether you indulge in a dining adventure here or simply toast each other in the bar, the potential for romance is more than likely—it's guaranteed. Breakfast, lunch, and dinner are served seven days a week, and each has its own affectionate appeal.

◆ **Romantic Suggestion:** Rising above Auberge du Soleil is the **RUTHERFORD HILL WINERY**, 200 Rutherford Hill Road, Rutherford, (707) 963-1871, (707) 963-7194 on weekends, just off the Silverado Trail and up Rutherford Hill Road. It is a heart-tugging spot to bring a picnic with your own tempting specialties for a leisurely lunch and private wine-tasting event. Spread your blanket under the shade of a sprawling tree to capture a splendid view of the valley. Or save your appetite and, as the cool of evening approaches, you can saunter down to Auberge du Soleil and toast the beginning of an amorous night.

St. Helena

This picturesque though sizable town embodies everything there is to love about wine country. The town's center is lined with art galleries, boutiques, cafes, and restaurants, while the town's country outskirts are laden with wineries and cozy bed and breakfasts. Of all the towns in wine country, St. Helena probably has the most abundant selection of places to explore, eat, stay, and (last, but never least) kiss.

Hotel/Bed and Breakfast Kissing

CHESTELSON HOUSE, St. Helena　　　　　　　　　　◆ ◀
1417 Kearney Street
(707) 963-2238
Inexpensive to Moderate

From Highway 29 north, turn left onto Adams at the first light in St. Helena. Take the second right onto Kearney; the inn is the second house on the left.

Located on a residential street two blocks from St. Helena's town center, this blue-and-white Victorian bed and breakfast has a flair for the old-fashioned. Firelight warms the parlor and adjacent dining area, where the innkeeper delights guests with gourmet breakfasts. Three of the four guest rooms here are on the main floor, and though they have crisp linens, brass beds, and beautifully restored antiques, they really don't compare to the lovely, private downstairs suite. Step through your private entrance into the inn's most romantic retreat: a cozy suite with the bright, airy feel of a cabana. Ceiling-high bay windows frame the bed's headboard, with sparkling white shutters that swing shut for private kissing. A large Jacuzzi tub also has shutters that open to windows overlooking the street.

HARVEST INN, St. Helena
1 Main Street
(707) 963-9463, (800) 950-8466
Moderate to Unbelievably Expensive

As you head north on Highway 29, the Harvest Inn is on the left.

Don't be fooled into bypassing the Harvest Inn because of the busy highway that fronts the property—you won't even know it's there once you've been embraced by the inn's 21 acres of manicured gardens and working vineyards. Brick walkways meander through the lovely grounds to each of the inn's 54 richly elegant guest rooms, found in clusters of English Tudor-style buildings graced with circular brick chimneys and turrets. Each room is a masterpiece of sensual luxury, complete with exquisite brick detailing, wood floors and ceilings, Oriental rugs, a brick fireplace, gorgeous floral fabrics and wallpaper, a newly tiled bathroom, and even a cushioned reading nook; some have large brick patios that overlook acres of vineyards. Savor the same views over a scrumptious buffet breakfast in the inn's cozy wood dining room, framed by stained glass windows and warmed by a large brick fireplace. Two outdoor swimming pools and Jacuzzis are also available for guests. Kissing in wine country doesn't get much better than this.

INK HOUSE, St. Helena
1575 St. Helena Highway, at Whitehall Lane
(707) 963-3890, (800) 553-4343
Moderate to Expensive

In St. Helena, head north on Highway 29. The inn is on the left at the corner of Whitehall Lane.

Authenticity is the hallmark of this grand, three-story, yellow Victorian built in 1884. (Some feel its real claim to fame is the fact that Elvis Presley filmed *Wild in the Country* here in 1959. If you're not partial to the King, don't panic—there's no paraphernalia in sight.) Black wrought-iron gates and landscaped gardens surround the home, lending privacy to the wrap-around veranda appointed with comfortable white wicker furniture (though the neighboring highway is still both visible and audible). Inside, the cozy common areas are brimming with antiques. The four upstairs guest rooms are also somewhat cluttered and mismatched, though charmingly Victorian with stuffed animals, carved wood beds, lace curtains, and Oriental carpets. For the best views (and the best kissing), climb upstairs to the sitting room perched at the top of the house. Surrounding windows allow ample light into this snug room furnished with comfortable white wicker chairs and a bookshelf full of books and games.

Conclude your stay with breakfast, an elaborate array of juices, coffee, tea, fresh fruit, freshly baked pastries, breads, and muffins served buffet-style in the dining room.

LA FLEUR, St. Helena
1475 Inglewood Avenue
(707) 963-0233
Moderate to Expensive

From Highway 29, turn west onto Inglewood Avenue. The inn is just past the Villa Helena Winery, on the left.

Intimacy and romance are La Fleur's raison d'être. From the moment we entered this enchanting 1882 Victorian, we knew we were in for a memorable encounter, even for wine country. Our royal retreat for the evening was the Prince Edward Room, with its majestic, billowing crown valance over the bed and a stunning floor-to-ceiling black marble hearth. Rococo gilt mirrors and wall sconces highlighted lavender walls, and a claw-foot tub awaited us in the bath. We were also impressed with the Antoinette Room: even Marie would toast its French-style femininity, its hand-painted shutters, bounteous ruffles and floral fabrics, red tile fire-place, and private veranda overlooking the vineyards. The Library Room is decidedly Victorian, with the original tile fireplace, cool green walls, shelves lined with books, and swag drapes crowning a bay window that looks out to the rose garden.

In the morning, linger in the sunny breakfast room over a glorious buffet of fresh baked goods, egg dishes, fruit, and more. *Bon appetit!*

◆ **Romantic Note:** Part of your intimate stay here is a private tour and tasting at the petite Villa Helena winery next door.

MEADOWOOD RESORT, St. Helena
900 Meadowood Lane
(707) 963-3646, (800) 458-8080
Very Expensive to Unbelievably Expensive
Wedding facilities are available for a maximum of 200 people.

From Highway 29, head north into St. Helena and turn right onto Zinfandel Lane. Go two miles to the Silverado Trail (just past a narrow stone bridge) and turn left. Follow this for one mile to Howell Mountain Road and turn right. Look for the Meadowood sign on the left.

If country clubs aren't your cup of tea, then skip this review. No matter what we say, you won't be impressed, because the somewhat pretentious air that is so common in exclusive resorts does exist here. Although it is tucked away in the forested foothills of wine country, Meadowood Resort could well be a grand old resort on some New England shore, with its tiers of gables, gray clapboard siding, and sparkling white trim and balustrades. Relaxation and rejuvenation are the essence of Meadowood Resort: it has its own manicured croquet lawns, a golf course, tennis courts, swimming pools, health club, and massage studio. The secluded guest rooms are scattered discreetly amongst the resort's 256 wooded acres. Private entrances, stone hearths, private balconies in the treetops, cathedral ceilings with skylights, and subtle, softly hued interiors create a sense of serenity. Even the bathroom's tile floors are heated, so as not to startle your toes.

VILLA ST. HELENA, St. Helena
2727 Sulphur Springs Avenue
(707) 963-2514
Expensive to Very Expensive

Head north on Highway 29 (the St. Helena Highway). Past the town of Rutherford and just before St. Helena, turn west onto Sulphur Springs Avenue.

Follow this road up and around to a wooden corral gate that may or may not be open, and continue up the drive to the villa.

If the owners of this expansive Mediterranean-style brick villa spent as much time and energy renovating their property as the original owner did building it, this would be the most remarkable destination in wine country. Unfortunately, Villa St. Helena has been sorely neglected over the years and almost feels eerily abandoned. The grounds and courtyard are overgrown, and the architecturally renowned Spanish mansion is in a state of disrepair. Why include a place that needs so much work? The outstanding setting and unique architecture are such a change of pace from the rest of wine country, we couldn't help ourselves.

The 20-acre estate is situated on a hillcrest overlooking Napa Valley. The grand interior of this villa becomes your own exclusive residence. The three spacious common rooms in the center of the house, appointed with antiques and sizable brick fireplaces, have the most romantic potential. There are only three functional guest rooms at this inn, located in opposite wings and set at the end of two echoing, glass-enclosed promenades. The rooms are simple and sparsely decorated, though like the rest of this property could be incredibly lovely and comfortable if given a little T.L.C.

VINEYARD COUNTRY INN, St. Helena
201 Main Street (Highway 29)
(707) 963-1000
Moderate to Very Expensive

In St. Helena, head north on Highway 29. The inn will be on your left.

Move this beautiful, newly built stone inn a little farther away from the highway and you couldn't ask for more. Other than its poor location, no detail has been overlooked here. All of the inn's 21 guest rooms are gracious two-room suites, situated in a complex of two-story stone buildings. Guest bedrooms have full baths, four-poster king- and queen-size beds, and sumptuous down comforters; the sitting areas are equally attractive and comfortable with wet bars, large brick fireplaces, rich color schemes, and private patios. A generous full breakfast is served at your two-person table in the lovely communal terra-cotta dining room that overlooks the inn's small roadside vineyard on one side and a brick courtyard with an outdoor pool and Jacuzzi on the other.

WINE COUNTRY INN, St. Helena
1152 Lodi Lane
(707) 963-7077
Moderate to Very Expensive

From Highway 29, head north into St. Helena and turn right onto Lodi Lane, north of downtown St. Helena. The inn is on your left.

Sometimes wine is best served with a splash. The outdoor pool at this unassuming inn set on a knoll above tree-hemmed vineyards is a perfect place to enjoy local vintages. Many of the 24 guest rooms in the three adjoining wood buildings share this placid view, including the parlor, where a continental breakfast is served each morning by the warmth of the wood stove in the winter or in the warmth of sunshine on the deck in the summer.

The rooms here are individually decorated with an old-fashioned (sometimes too old-fashioned) country flair. The fact that each of the rooms has a small private bath is a plus, though they're nothing special and give a motel feeling to the otherwise appealing inn. The mini-suite in the Brandy Barn was our particular favorite, with white wicker furniture in the sitting room and a private deck overlooking the manicured, terraced grounds.

ZINFANDEL INN, St. Helena
800 Zinfandel Lane
(707) 963-3512
Expensive
Wedding facilities are available for a maximum of 30 people.

From Highway 29 north, just before you reach St. Helena, turn right onto Zinfandel Lane.

The stone and wood exterior of this secluded Tudor home has the proportions of a mansion, enhanced by a spouting fountain set in the manicured front lawn. Guests will enjoy the forested surroundings that enclose two acres of gardens, an aviary, two gazebos, a swimming pool, a hot tub, and a fish pond and waterfall that overlook a lagoon.

The three guest rooms in this stately bed and breakfast are immensely comfortable, with an assortment of dazzling attributes: one has a large stone fireplace, wood-beamed ceiling, and sweeping bay windows that look out to the garden; another has a tiled Jacuzzi, private deck, and stained glass. All have snuggly down comforters and attractive antique furnishings.

Breakfast might include baked caramel French toast or baked eggs with cheese and basil, fresh croissants and muffins, and coffee and tea. The Zinfandel Inn provides a uniquely lovely alternative to the plethora of Victorian bed and breakfasts found in wine country.

Restaurant Kissing

THE RESTAURANT, St. Helena   ◆ ◆ ◆
900 Meadowood Lane, at the Meadowood Resort
(707) 963-3646, (800) 458-8080
Expensive to Very Expensive
Wedding facilities are available for a maximum of 200 people.

From Highway 29, head north into St. Helena and turn right onto Pope Street. Go two miles to the Silverado Trail (just past a narrow stone bridge) and cross it diagonally to the left onto Howell Mountain Road. Look for the Meadowood Resort sign on the left.

The restaurant at the Meadowood Resort exudes a rejuvenating serenity. A blazing fire warms the cozy lounge for appetizing kissing. The dining room is simultaneously spacious and intimate, with high peaked ceilings, plush private booths, and elegant table settings. The extensive wine selections, including 250 from the Napa Valley alone, will please any palate, as will the baked squab in a crust of eggplant and other entrées. Conclude with a dessert of poached pear with cinnamon and vanilla risotto or a dark chocolate sampling plate.

SHOWLEY'S AT MIRAMONTE, St. Helena   ◆ ◆
1327 Railroad Avenue
(707) 963-1200
Moderate to Expensive

In the town of St. Helena, just off Highway 29 going north, turn right onto Hunt Street. Just before the railroad tracks, turn left onto Railroad Avenue. Look for a white building on the west side of the street.

There are a handful of award-winning restaurants in the Yountville-Rutherford-St. Helena sector of the wine country. The international and regional crowds that flock to this part of the world keep a handful of chefs busy to almost distressed proportions. It is a feat to continually execute smashing meals that keep pace with the finicky palates of these visiting connoisseurs. Showley's, though not as in vogue as some of the other restaurants in the area, does a superior job of keeping up with the demand. In fact, since they are still considered the new kid on the block, they work even harder to impress you. Inside this large, unembellished white stucco building is a simple, subdued interior where you will find cordial service and a unique international menu that is as interesting as it is well presented. The Santa Fe lasagne with chiles and chèvre layered in flour tortillas with cilantro pesto, was great, and the shrimp etoufée was perfect.

SPRING STREET CAFE, St. Helena
1245 Spring Street
(707) 963-5578
Inexpensive to Moderate

Follow Highway 29 north into St. Helena. Turn left onto Spring Street, immediately after the Wells Fargo Bank. The restaurant is a block down on the left.

A very charming and affordable place for a casual lunch or dinner, this small, ivy-covered stucco house is harbored on a residential side street. The landscaped garden patio is especially romantic, with umbrella-shaded tables that are arranged around a burbling fountain. The menu includes healthy sandwiches, salads, burgers, and desserts; all are tasty, but the experience would be even better if the service were faster.

TERRA RESTAURANT, St. Helena
1345 Railroad Avenue
(707) 963-8931
Expensive
Wedding facilities are available for a maximum of 120 people.

In the town of St. Helena, just off Highway 29 going north, turn right onto Hunt Street. Just before the railroad tracks, turn left onto Railroad Avenue. Look for the stone front of the restaurant on the left side of the street.

Antiques and icons of the past do not automatically promote thoughts or actions that are conducive to kissing (or even hugging, for that matter). But blend the artifacts of days gone by with appropriate contemporary flourishes, and you have all the romantic atmosphere you could ever need. Restaurant Terra effortlessly achieves that heartwarming balance. The 100-year-old stone building has a noble yet unpretentious climate. As you enter, it feels as if you're setting foot in a miniature French castle. The wood beams that loom overhead, the burnt red tile floor, and the stone walls are complemented by contemporary paintings and fixtures. Here is a setting fit for award-winning dining. The menu lists an exotic assortment of fresh fish and game, accompanied by intriguing sauces and side dishes. The grilled quail with pecorino cheese and pumpkin ravioli, the grilled salmon with Thai red curry sauce, and the grilled squab with chanterelle mushroom and roasted garlic sauce are all exquisite.

◆ **Romantic Note:** Terra, which serves dinner only, is another hard-to-get-into place, particularly on weekends. Take kissing precautions and call ahead.

TRA VIGNE, St. Helena　　　　　　　　　　
1050 Charter Oak Avenue
(707) 963-4444
Moderate
Wedding facilities are available for a maximum of 80 people.

Just off Highway 29 at the south end of St. Helena, on the east side of the road.

Imagine a place so popular that they give confirmation numbers along with your reservation. The host informed us that giving out a number the way many hotels do "saves a lot of heartache when people insist they made a reservation, but we don't have them written down. People will do anything to eat here!" Why the intense competition for a table? The reason will be apparent the moment you glimpse the handsome burnt orange brick exterior of Tra Vigne. Passing through wrought-iron gates, you enter a tree-shaded brick courtyard dotted with tables for outdoor seating. Inside, the seductive interior with 25-foot ceilings, stunning oak bar, and towering wrought-iron French windows is all very impressive. The tables are individually spotlighted from above, which means the room is soft and subdued but you won't have to squint to look into each other's eyes. Every detail here is attended to with sophistication and panache, including the food.

Lobster tortellini and clams in a tomato-saffron broth; cracker-thin pizza with caramelized onions, thyme, and Gorgonzola cheese; and seared raw venison with chestnuts, dried cherries, and pecorino cheese are all tantalizing and beautifully presented. And the desserts are absolutely erotic. About that confirmation number they give you—get one of your own and don't lose it!

◆ Romantic Option: TRILOGY RESTAURANT, 1234 Main Street, St. Helena, (707) 963-5507, (Expensive), is a food lover's paradise. Inside this simple storefront location, a mere ten tables draped in white and peach are available for diners who wish to sample the delicate French cuisine served here. Sautéed duck with port and figs or grilled yellowfin tuna with lemon, capers, and dill butter are examples of the traditional lunch and dinner entrées you'll find here, always done to perfection.

Outdoor Kissing

**BALE GRIST MILL STATE
HISTORIC PARK, St. Helena**
(707) 942-4575
$5 day-use fee

The park is on the west side of Highway 29, a few miles north of downtown St. Helena.

You won't see any grape arbors at this cool, forested park a short drive and a world away from the area's sun-soaked vineyards. Stroll along restful paths that meander past a gurgling stream hemmed with wildflowers in early spring. One easy trail leads to a restored wooden grist mill with a 36-foot water wheel; tour it together on weekends to experience life in simpler times. Or follow the path through meadow and forest to a kissing spot that nature has saved just for you.

◆ Romantic Note: Nature-loving lovers will find tree-shaded campsites just up the road at BOTHE-NAPA STATE PARK, 3601 St. Helena Highway, St. Helena, (707) 942-4575.

BURGESS CELLARS, St. Helena
1108 Deer Park Road
(707) 963-4766

From the Silverado Trail going north, turn right onto Deer Park Road. As you wind up the mountain toward the town of Angwin, look on the left side of the road for the entrance to Burgess Cellars.

There are many reasons why you should visit one winery rather than another. If you are a consummate oenophile, you may be lured by the exceptional quality of the grapes at a particular vineyard or by the sterling reputation of an established estate. But it is also a treat when you become acquainted with the offerings of a small up-and-coming winery and can take pride in your secret discovery. All this and more are sublime reasons to seek out Burgess Cellars in the hills of Napa Valley. In addition to its winemaking craft, Burgess is famous for some of the most striking views of the Napa countryside. Your emotions and your taste buds will soar to new heights here.

◆ **Romantic Suggestion:** The drive up to Burgess Cellars along **DEER PARK ROAD** is stupendous. As you weave up this twisting road, enjoy marvelous vistas of the ravines and dells below.

JOSEPH PHELPS VINEYARD, St. Helena
200 Taplin Road
(707) 963-2745

One mile south of St. Helena, turn left off the Silverado Trail onto Taplin Road. Look for signs to the winery on the left.

Wind up and away from the busy Silverado Trail to this winery set on a verdant, secluded hillside. Large, impressive, and unpretentious, Joseph Phelps is one of the few wineries found along the Silverado Trail that escapes traffic noise entirely. Sip wine in the roomy tasting room or on the adjoining terraces that preside over views of a distant lake enclosed by vineyards and rolling hills.

ST. CLEMENT WINERY, St. Helena
2867 St. Helena Highway North
(707) 963-7221

From St. Helena, follow the St. Helena Highway north. The winery will be on your left.

Neatly cropped vineyards climb toward this picturesque, gabled Victorian perched at the crest of the hillside. The house's original living quarters are filled with antiques and serve as a quaint tasting room. Once you've filled your glasses, wander outside to the porch swing or to the picnic tables arranged throughout the terraced grounds and drink in lovely views of the surrounding countryside along with your wine.

V. SATTUI, St. Helena   ◆ ◆ ❮
1111 White Lane
(707) 963-7774
Wedding facilities are available for a maximum of 250 people.

From St. Helena, follow the St. Helena Highway south for about two miles; the winery will be on your left.

On a sunny weekend afternoon, it seems everyone in Napa Valley comes to picnic beneath the shade trees at this ancient-looking stone winery. This is one of Napa's most congenial spots, with a bevy of tables and a manicured lawn set aside for picnickers. Step into the inner recesses and you will discover a smorgasbord of delectables—some 200 cheeses, plus meats, breads, and desserts. The wine tasting room can be crowded, but press on. V. Sattui wines are sold only on the premises, and their Johannisberg riesling is especially luscious.

Angwin

Hotel/Bed and Breakfast Kissing

FOREST MANOR, Angwin   ◆ ◆ ◆
415 Cold Springs Road
(707) 965-3538, (800) 788-0364
Moderate to Expensive
Wedding facilities are available for a maximum of 100 people.

Go north on Highway 29 to Deer Park Road and turn right. Go about six miles to Cold Springs Road and turn right. Go to the end of the road, look for signs for the inn, and turn left at the large black mailbox.

Forest Manor is the ideal destination for a weekend sojourn. Located on the outskirts of Napa Valley, this English Tudor mansion is backed by more than 20 acres of woodlands and a neighboring 100-year-old winery. Inside, this special domicile has exotic furnishings from the Orient and an open staircase that ascends four flights to two of the three guest rooms. Your suite will have its own breakfast nook, a roaring fireplace, comfortable furnishings, and the relaxing quiet of nature all around. In the dewy morning or under the stars at night you can submerge yourselves in the outdoor whirlpool. During the heat of midday, dive into the 53-foot-long swimming pool for more invigorating recreation. A generous continental breakfast is graciously provided.

Calistoga

There is no place else in the United States quite like Calistoga, California. The entire town is dedicated to the rejuvenation of the body and spirit through an ingenious variety of treatments. We have added a special "Miscellaneous Kissing" section to highlight spas that offer services just for couples. In addition to spending a day at a spa, which you really should do, devote some time to exploring Calistoga, which has a laid-back atmosphere (even at the height of tourist season) and a fun mix of places to stay, eat, and shop in.

Hotel/Bed and Breakfast Kissing

CHRISTOPHER'S INN, Calistoga
1010 Foothill Boulevard (Highway 29)
(707) 942-5755
Moderate to Expensive

Follow Highway 29 north from St. Helena and look for a sales display of John Deere tractors on the right-hand side of the road (they're hard to miss!). The inn is 500 yards beyond this; if you've reached the red blinking light you've gone too far.

I nearly made the mistake of passing up Christopher's Inn because of its location near an intersection of jam-packed Highway 29. (Road noise is never romantic; in fact, it can kill romance as well as a good night's sleep.) Fortunately, the architect/innkeeper informed me that he had made special soundproofing efforts when he turned these three historic buildings into an English country inn, and the street sounds are hardly noticeable. Modestly decorated with Laura Ashley fabrics, some of the ten rooms have high ceilings, private entrances, and patios, and half of them have fireplaces. Large windows allow light to filter in, though the views aren't great. Mornings can be leisurely as an expanded continental breakfast is delivered to your door in a country basket, assuring complete privacy with your coffee.

THE ELMS, Calistoga   ❖ ❖
1300 Cedar Street
(707) 942-9476, (800) 235-4316
Moderate to Expensive
Wedding facilities are available for a maximum of 16 people.

From St. Helena follow Highway 29 north to the four-way stoplight and turn right into Calistoga, where Highway 29 becomes Lincoln Avenue. Drive for two blocks and turn left onto Cedar Street. The inn is the third building on the left.

If you want to wander around downtown Calistoga, the Elms is a good central location, right next to Pioneer Park. You can even borrow the inn's big, lovable dog for long, leisurely walks, in case you need an escort. The seven rooms are a bit on the small side, with the fluffiness of a feather bed and a billowy down comforter dwarfing the room even more, but these touches also mean that you'll be extra comfy at night. The rooms' decor ranges from Southwestern to Victorian. Five rooms have fireplaces; some have canopy beds, private balconies, and window seats. The Victorian Fantasy and Romantic Hideaway rooms both have authentic tin ceilings, pastel tile floors, fireplaces, spa tubs, and private entrances through French doors.

A full breakfast is served in the parlor, and later in the day a generous assortment of wine and cheese is offered beside the fire or outside on the patio.

FOOTHILL HOUSE, Calistoga
3037 Foothill Boulevard (Highway 128)
(707) 942-6933, (800) 942-6933
Moderate to Expensive
Wedding facilities are available for a maximum of 25 people.

Head north on Highway 29 into the town of Calistoga and pass through the four-way stoplight. Continue straight ahead and Highway 29 will become Highway 128. Foothill House is one and a half miles past the light on the left-hand side of the road.

When I first saw this country farmhouse, I drove right by it. My initial impression of this nondescript frame house with its highway frontage disappointed me. I thought, "This can't be romantic!" But lessons learned in the past made me turn around and go back. Once again I found that I must never judge a book by its cover. The outside of Foothill House gives no indication of the rapture and ease that wait inside.

The two sizable rooms in the main house overflow with everything your sentimental hearts could desire: a four-poster bed, a patchwork quilt, a private sun deck, a fireplace stacked with logs, perfect for a hearthside sip of sherry, and a Jacuzzi tub. If you go up the little hill in the backyard and pass the newly added gazebo, you'll find a separate cottage called the Quail's Roost, with a two-sided fireplace and a Jacuzzi tub for two beside a tall window that overlooks a waterfall cascading down the hillside. And wait, there's more! After a full day of sweeping your way through the wineries and health spas of this county, you'll return to find the bed neatly turned down, fluffy fresh towels, wine, and the piece de resistance—a ceramic canister of hot, chewy chocolate chip cookies. (Yes, cookies and wine sounds a bit odd, but taste these phenomenal little gems before forming an opinion.)

In the morning, depending on your mood, sit down to an attractively prepared gourmet breakfast in your room or in the glass-enclosed patio. As you linger over the last morsel of a pear tart soufflé, homemade biscuits, and fresh fruit soup, you will be revitalized for an encore performance of the day before. The super-hospitable innkeepers will gladly help you plan your day if you so desire.

◆ **Romantic Alternative:** Located in a neighborhood setting two blocks from the center of town, SCOTT COURTYARD, 1443 Second

Street, Calistoga, (707) 942-0948, (Moderate), is an attractive bed and breakfast. The white-trellised courtyard forms the boundaries of this hideaway, where a gated pool and hot tub also await. The peach-colored home and detached cottage look fresh and appealing, and inside the art deco-inspired rooms are very casual and spacious, with cane furniture and bright fabrics. Full breakfast is served family-style in the dining room.

LA CHAUMIERE, Calistoga
1301 Cedar Street
(707) 942-5139
Moderate
Wedding facilities are available for a maximum of 35 people.

From St. Helena take Highway 29 north to the four-way stoplight in Calistoga. Turn right onto Lincoln Avenue. From Lincoln, turn left on Cedar Street. The inn is two blocks down on the corner of Cedar and Elm streets.

La Chaumiere is a charming stucco home turned stylish bed and breakfast, located just four blocks from the town center. Draped in bountiful foliage, it feels more like a country hideaway than you would expect in this neighborhood location. The showcase here is a spacious two-tiered deck built around a massive redwood tree that shades an enormous hot tub, and I mean *enormous*. This setup has to be seen to be believed, but you can't see it unless you stay here: a six-foot-high fence keeps everything very private and secluded.

There are two nicely decorated rooms in this petite residence and the living room is wonderfully cozy, but the space is really too small to share with another couple that you don't know. My suggestion is to stay here when you are traveling the wine country with another romantic couple and have the entire house to yourselves. The owners don't live on the property, so you will be quite alone. Other amenities include a well-stocked wine and liqueur cabinet for your personal use. A two-course gourmet breakfast and hors d'oeuvres in the evening are beautifully presented.

◆ Romantic Alternative: The MEADOWLARK COUNTRY HOUSE, 601 Petrified Forest Road, Calistoga, (707) 942-5651, (Moderate), is simply decorated in neutral tones, with hardwood floors, Oriental rugs, and overstuffed sofas and chairs. The innkeepers give you what you need to be comfortable, and then leave you alone. That way you can intimately enjoy the house and its surrounding 20 acres with walking trails, a pool, and corraled horses (don't get excited, these two beauties are only for looking at).

Because of the close proximity of the four rooms here, we recommend that you bring along two or even three other couples that you'll be happy to share the property with. (Even the best romantic intentions can suffer if you are forced to socialize with strangers when you really want to just focus on each other.) The only drawback, regardless of who you share the house with, is that three of the bedrooms share the same hallway and the fourth is beneath them on the ground floor, which is probably a little too close for comfort even with the best of friends.

SILVER ROSE INN, Calistoga
351 Rosedale Road
(707) 942-9581
Moderate to Expensive
Wedding facilities are available for a maximum of 50 people.

From the Silverado Trail north, just outside of Calistoga, take a sharp right onto Rosedale Road. The inn is on the corner.

The Silver Rose Inn is located a discreet distance from Calistoga—far enough away from the spa scene, which can get a bit crowded, that you'll feel elated about staying here. This large estate is spread over an oak-studded knoll that has been lovingly landscaped to blend with the nearby foothills and leas. The hallmark of this place is an impressive rock garden with a flowing waterfall that spills into a huge stone-etched swimming pool adjoining the capacious Jacuzzi. And, of course, framing the entire backyard are hundreds of the striking rosebushes that give the inn its proud appellation.

The four rooms that have just been added to the already existing five are the best. Decorated in various themes, they each have a fireplace, tiled floor with area rugs, and a balcony or deck. The Southwest-inspired Western Room, sparsely decorated Oriental Suite, and pretty Garden Room all have two-person Jacuzzi tubs. Watch out for the Safari Room, though, which is only for lovers with a sense of adventure and humor. Be assured that all of the rooms here are quite comfortable and attractively furnished, and they all have views of the nearby vineyards.

A California-style breakfast of fresh fruits and muffins is served in the sitting area of your room or on your private balcony.

Outdoor Kissing

CHATEAU MONTELENA, Calistoga
1429 Tubbs Lane
(707) 942-5105
$5 fee for tasting

From northbound Highway 29, turn left onto Tubbs Lane. The inn is on the immediate right-hand side of the road.

Imagine kissing on your own private island, in the middle of a placid lake hemmed by vineyards, with a castle of a winery on the hill above you. This is Chateau Montelena, one of the wine country's ultimate picnic spots. Jade Lake, with its serene waters, family of ducks, and red-lacquered geometric bridges arching to two tiny islands, beckons to visitors emerging from the cool tasting room. As I strolled along the shore, a young couple embraced in the shade of the awning above their picnic table. They had been engaged here, I was told by the wine pourer, and now were celebrating their second anniversary. You can be the stars of your own love scene.

◆ **Romantic Note:** A picnic on your private island costs only foresight. Weekends are nearly impossible to secure, but call ahead to reserve a spot for a special weekday. Picnicking is allowed only on the two islands, which are reserved for the entire day.

CLOS PEGASE, Calistoga
1060 Dunaweal Lane
(707) 942-4981

Between the Silverado Trail and Highway 29, on Dunaweal Lane.

This dramatic, terra-cotta-colored winery is named after Pegasus, the winged horse of Greek mythology. As the story goes, Pegasus gave birth to wine and art when his hooves unleashed the sacred Spring of the Muses. The water irrigated the vines and inspired the poets who drank of them.

Today, Clos Pegase pays homage to the muses with classical Greek and modern sculptures that beautify the petite verdant grounds, appropriately dubbed the "shrine to wine." You will find many reasons to write your own poetry or sip a fine vintage here—whichever comes first.

SCHRAMSBURG VINEYARDS, Calistoga
1400 Schramsburg Road
(707) 942-4558

On the west side of Highway 29, two and a half miles south of Calistoga. Turn left onto Peterson Road and then take an immediate right onto Schramsburg Road.

It is no exaggeration to say that there are many wonderful wineries in the Napa Valley. One of the more distinctive and beautiful is Schramsburg. This 100-year-old estate, located in the highlands of Napa Valley, is full of historical and enological interest. The stone buildings of the winery are located far enough away from the traffic of the main road to provide quiet refuge. Because only private tours are allowed, your introduction to the world of champagne will be sparklingly intimate. After you roam through the labyrinth of underground cellars that were tunneled into the rocky ground years ago, be certain to leave enough time to stop at the wine shop. By this point, you will have learned almost all the secrets of *methode champenoise,* so purchase your own bit of effervescent history to share.

◆ **Romantic Warning:** You don't get to do any tasting here, and because of the limited number of people per tour group you must call far in advance to reserve a place.

ONCE IN A LIFETIME BALLOON
COMPANY OF CALISTOGA
The Train Depot, 1451 Lincoln Avenue
(707) 942-6541, (800) 722-6665
Very Expensive

Call ahead for reservations and directions.

Your excursion commences at sunrise, when the air is still and cool (yes, that means somewhere between 5 A.M. and 9 A.M.). As you step into the balloon's gondola, your eyes will gape at the towering, billowing fabric overhead, and your heart will race with wild expectation. Once aloft, the wind guides your craft above countryside blanketed with acres of grapes. Up here, the world seems more serene than you ever imagined possible. You will be startled by the sunrise from this vantage point; daylight awakens the hills with new vigor and warmth. After your flight, a gourmet champagne brunch awaits you at a nearby hotel. This isn't everyone's way to start an early morning. But for those who can handle the noise and heat from the overhead flame thrower that fills the balloon with hot air, it is a stimulating way to spend an early morning together.

◆ **Romantic Note:** There are many hot-air balloon companies in this part of the world. Once in a Lifetime also owns **NAPA'S GREAT BALLOON ESCAPE** and **ONCE IN A LIFETIME BALLOON COMPANY OF SONOMA COUNTY**. Check with your innkeeper or the telephone directory to find the balloon business nearest you.

Miscellaneous Kissing

INTERNATIONAL SPA, Calistoga
1300 Washington Street
(707) 942-6122
Prices vary depending on service.

Follow Highway 29 north from St. Helena and turn right at the four-way stoplight onto Lincoln Avenue. At the first stoplight, turn left onto Washington Street. The spa is at the corner of First and Washington. Turn right onto First and then turn left into the Roman Spa parking lot. The International Spa is right next door.

LINCOLN AVENUE SPA, Calistoga
1339 Lincoln Avenue
(707) 942-5296
Prices vary depending on service.

Follow Highway 29 north from St. Helena and turn right at the four-way stoplight onto Lincoln Avenue. The spa is situated kitty-corner from the old movie theater.

Besides offering services that range from a tranquilizing, peaceful massage to an invigorating rubdown that will knead away any anxieties you may have brought with you from the city, the staff at International Spa and Lincoln Spa are also skilled at foot reflexology and acupressure massage. Though both places took the time to explain the benefits of these two techniques, I can only tell you that it felt great and I didn't want them to stop.

My day at both spas went something like this: First I received an exceedingly tranquilizing massage, where every muscle in my body succumbed to relaxation. As time oozed by, I was taken to another room, where I was introduced to the organic mud baths. This is something you can do side by side with a loved one. If I fully describe the mud bath, you may decide not to try it; I know I didn't want to when I read about it. But take my word for it, sitting for more than an hour in something I used to get in trouble for sitting in as a kid was the most amazing physical sensation I have experienced. It's not even vaguely romantic, but afterwards you'll feel that all you want to do is melt into your loved one's arms.

You can experiment with other services at these spas, including facials, herbal blanket wraps (also a side-by-side service), enzyme baths, mineral baths, and on and on. The longer I was there, the more I came to understand the fascination of this place. I also realized how two people sharing such an experience could feel closer to each other than ever before. I think for the first time in my life every muscle in my body was in a blissful state. I'd go back and do this again—next time for an entire week.

♦ Romantic Suggestion: The LAVENDER HILL SPA, 1015 Foothill Boulevard, Calistoga, (707) 942-4495, affiliated with the International Spa, specializes in *spa pas deux*, an experience for couples only. It is a shame that the terraced garden they have created on a small hillside is so close to Highway 29; otherwise it would be a great place for an after-treatment picnic. The private little bath house is set away from the road though, so noise isn't a problem. Hardwood floors, a wood stove, side-by-side tables for body wraps or a massage, two claw-foot tubs, and two mineral-bath tubs create a calming atmosphere where you can soak all your cares away.

Sonoma Valley

Unlike the towns of Napa Valley, which are bisected by the St. Helena Highway, Sonoma Valley towns are set off the highway and consequently feel more rural, though less accessible. If you're in a hurry this might feel like an inconvenience, but slow down—the lack of nearby traffic creates a romantic climate that is more conducive to kissing.

Sonoma

Despite its tourist appeal and bustling popularity, the town of Sonoma is still a prime place for a romantic rendezvous. The village itself is wrapped around a park-like square shaded by sprawling oak trees and sculpted shrubbery. Weaving around this central area are flowering walkways, a fountain, a duck pond, and park benches. Beyond the square's perimeter, branching out in every direction, is an array of shops, restaurants, and wineries that have retained much of their original charm.

Consider starting your day at a local espresso shop or bakery to gather all of the necessities for a morning picnic breakfast on the square's cool green lawn. The rest of your day can be spent gallivanting through the wineries and tasting rooms that line the surrounding lush hillsides and valleys.

◆ **Romantic Warning:** Summer crowds in Sonoma can be overpowering all week long and unbearable on the weekends. Off-season is the best time to find a degree of solitude as well as comfortable weather conditions.

Hotel/Bed and Breakfast Kissing

TROJAN HORSE INN, Sonoma
19455 Sonoma Highway (Highway 12)
(707) 996-2430, (800) 899-1925
Moderate to Expensive

About one mile west of Sonoma Plaza. Where the Sonoma Highway (Highway 12) jogs north, look for the inn immediately on the left.

Weary wine-tasters will immediately feel rejuvenated upon entering this 1887 Victorian country inn. The spacious, sun-filled parlor appears to be abloom with bright spring flowers. Plaid sofas, floral accent chairs, and copious bouquets of silk flowers are at once homey and charming. In the evening, the hospitable innkeepers offer local wines, cheese, and conversation for all to enjoy before the glowing hearth. The six guest rooms have private baths and antique furnishings, with decor ranging from virginal in the Bridal Veil Room, with its billowing white lace canopy and curtains, and corner wood stove, to lusty in the Victorian Room, with its rich, Bordeaux satin bedcoverings. If your taste runs toward the less extravagant, try the placid Walden Pond, no-nonsense Jack London, or sunny Grape Arbor, which has a two-person whirlpool bath. In the morning, a full breakfast—perhaps asiago baked eggs and homemade boysenberry bread—ensures a hearty start to a full day of wine tasting.

VICTORIAN GARDEN INN, Sonoma   ◆ ◖
316 East Napa Street
(707) 996-5339
Inexpensive to Moderate

One and a half blocks east of Sonoma Plaza on East Napa Street.

Petite but extraordinary grounds envelop the Victorian Garden Inn, set in a peaceful Sonoma neighborhood. Fountains and white iron benches dot the glorious garden, and a trellised brick walkway leads to the front door. If the garden doesn't provide enough cooling shade on summer afternoons, a swim in the large pool behind the house should do the trick. This inn offers four comfortable overnight options, including a separate, very cozy cottage that features a high open-beam ceiling and a brick fireplace. Several rooms have private entrances, wicker furnishings, down comforters, sitting areas, and country-style antiques. Breakfast is a continental array of locally grown fruit, granola, fresh juice, and pastries.

Restaurant Kissing

PASTA NOSTRA, Sonoma
139 East Napa Street
(707) 938-4166
Moderate
Wedding facilities are available; call for details.

Less than half a block from Sonoma Plaza.

Take a cliche, add a dash of California freshness, and *voila!* you have this delightfully creative and comfortably casual Italian bistro. High peaked ceilings and a series of open rooms hint at the original framework of this former Victorian home. The restaurant is both airy and cozy, highlighted with little white lights and oil lamps flickering on the tables. The menu has both classic and more inventive dishes, such as succulently sweet veal marsala, homemade caramelized carrot pasta, and cream-cheese ravioli. My favorites were the specials: a Maui onion stuffed with sausage, then topped with cheese and baked, and the spinach fettuccine with sautéed tarragon chicken.

◆ **Romantic Alternative:** To maintain the spirit of a day spent stimulating your palates at wineries, indulge in a traditional European dinner. MAGLIULO'S, 691 Broadway, Sonoma, (707) 996-1031, (Inexpensive to Moderate), obliges with just that: incredible Italian cuisine and sensational desserts. Settle into a rustic Victorian setting of wrought iron and wood accented by pastel colors or dine on the garden patio. Lunch and dinner are served seven days a week, in addition to an enchanting Sunday brunch.

Outdoor Kissing

BUENA VISTA WINERY, Sonoma
18000 Old Winery Road
(707) 938-1266, (800) 926-1266
Wedding facilities are available; call for details.

From Sonoma Plaza, head east on East Napa Street. Turn left after the railroad tracks onto Old Winery Road. The winery is about one mile from the plaza.

We had gathered our picnic goodies in Sonoma Plaza: award-winning sourdough from the Sonoma Bakery, homemade deli meats and mustard from the Sonoma Sausage Company, and scrumptious pesto jack from the Sonoma Cheese Company. All we needed was a smooth chardonnay and a peaceful picnic spot, and we found both at Buena Vista. Tangled ivy over rugged stone walls lends an ancient feel to this winery, California's oldest. A bevy of picnic tables are set by the woodsy creek and on a hillside terrace, all shaded by sweet-scented eucalyptus trees. The cool tasting room offers a small selection of fine gifts to commemorate your time together; a mezzanine gallery showcases local art.

GLORIA FERRER CHAMPAGNE CAVES, Sonoma
23555 Arnold Drive (Highway 121)
(707) 996-7256
Wedding facilities·are available; call for details.

From northbound Highway 101, turn west onto Highway 37. At the intersection of Highway 37 and Highway 121, turn left onto Highway 121 and proceed six miles. The champagne caves are on the left side of the highway.

As the name suggests, the focus here is on champagne, an effervescent drink that almost always goes hand-in-hand with special occasions. Regardless of the occasion though, any afternoon here is sure to be special. Gloria Ferrer's stunning Spanish-style villa is set a half mile from the highway, at the base of gently rolling hills. After taking a tour of their unique caves and learning how fine champagne is created, stay and taste some. You are given a full glass of sparkling wine in the spacious tasting room, where plenty of two-person marble-topped tables sit beside a crackling fireplace. Or you can sit, sip, and smooch outside on the vast veranda that faces acre upon acre of grape arbors.

VIANSA, Sonoma
25200 Arnold Drive
(707) 935-4700, (800) 935-4740 in California
Wedding facilities are available; call for details.

Take Highway 101 north to Highway 37 (which is five miles down, toward Vallejo). From Highway 37, take the Napa/Sonoma turnoff to Highway 121 (a left turn). The winery will be on the right-hand side.

Viansa, a relatively new winery, offers not only fine wine, but an extensive Italian marketplace where you can purchase gourmet picnic necessities and plenty of edible mementos of your time spent in the wine country. Fresh herbs and vegetables complement pâtés, salads, and other tasty Italian treats, all made right on the premises. Try one of their freshly baked focaccia sandwiches and a luscious dessert followed by a smooth cappuccino (if you've already tasted enough wine). You can enjoy this small feast in the casual, brightly lit Italian marketplace inside, but the attractive grounds will beckon you outside. Numerous picnic tables are set beneath a grape trellis, overlooking young grapevines and a 90-acre waterfowl preserve that resembles a swamp. (But once you see how much the birds love it, you'll be glad it's there too.)

◆ **Romantic Note:** The picnic area is reserved only for people who purchase their picnic items from Viansa.

Glen Ellen

Glen Ellen is a quiet rural community located just off Highway 12. The town is so small that there isn't much to say about it except that the relaxed country atmosphere is a welcome change of pace compared to city life or even to life in one of the larger wine country towns. There are a few antique shops and a handful of wineries in Glen Ellen. Even if you can only spend an afternoon, driving through acres of grape arbors amidst gently rolling hills to get there makes the trip worthwhile.

Hotel/Bed and Breakfast Kissing

GAIGE HOUSE, Glen Ellen
13540 Arnold Drive
(707) 935-0237
Moderate to Very Expensive
Wedding facilities are available; call for details.

From Highway 37, turn onto Highway 121 and follow it to Highway 116, which turns into Arnold Drive (look for the sign to Glen Ellen). Gaige House is on the left.

The Gaige House, an impressive Italianate Victorian, seems to have taken root in this rural setting. You might want to do the same after staying the night here. An eclectic collection of antiques punctuated with an occasional art deco sculpture fills the fireplace-warmed double parlors and offers plenty of conversation pieces when the time comes for afternoon wine and cheese. The nine guest rooms are spacious and uncluttered, with comfortable, tasteful furnishings and private modern baths. Some bathrooms have claw-foot tubs and two rooms have fireplaces with a view of the garden. The Gaige Suite is the most grand, with its own vast wraparound deck, a king-size carved mahogany bed with a crocheted canopy, and an immense blue tiled bathroom with a whirlpool tub large enough for four, but much more romantic with just two. After a day spent wine tasting, refresh yourselves with a dip in the inn's pool or sink into the garden furniture and cool off on a shady section of the lawn. Breakfast is a two-course affair served on the commodious deck or in the sun room.

GLENELLY INN, Glen Ellen
5131 Warm Springs Road
(707) 996-6720
Inexpensive to Moderate

Driving north on Highway 12, turn left onto Arnold Drive (look for the sign to Glen Ellen). Take a right onto Warm Springs Road; the inn is located on the right in one-third mile.

This 1916 railroad inn is a legacy of Glen Ellen's heyday, when San Franciscans considered this woodsy town an invigorating getaway. The inn's setting is still enchanting, nestled at the base of a steep hill, shaded by the gnarled branches of century-old oak and olive trees. Now it is enhanced with a Jacuzzi and a brick courtyard in the lower rose garden, and a double hammock in the more naturally landscaped upper terrace.

Although the architectural design is from an era when standard rooms were smaller, the fresh, bright country decor, Norwegian down quilts, and claw-foot tubs make all of the eight rooms cozy. Wood-burning stoves in two of the rooms enhance the coziness. All of the rooms have private entrances, so there is no need to tiptoe in after a late-night dip in the hot tub or a moonlit swing in the hammock.

The full breakfast, served beside the fireplace in the spacious common room, always includes freshly squeezed juice, baked goods still warm from the oven, and granola. A tasty, more filling item such as lemon French toast or a sausage and spinach frittata varies from day to day.

◆ **Romantic Alternative:** The **BELTANE RANCH**, 11775 Sonoma Highway, Glen Ellen, (707) 996-6501, (Moderate), is a working farm, vineyard, and down-home bed and breakfast. Of the four rooms in this century-old home, the two upstairs are the best because you can sit outside your room on the wraparound deck, eat your hearty breakfast, and survey the lush front-yard garden. The rooms are slightly mismatched and on the small side, but you should still consider staying here because this ranch is set on 1,600 acres. The property is crisscrossed with hiking trails that are ideal for long afternoon walks. Wedding facilities are available; call for details.

Restaurant Kissing

MIEL RESTAURANT, Glen Ellen ◆ ◀
13648 Arnold Drive (Highway 121)
(707) 938-4844
Moderate to Expensive
Wedding facilities are available; call for details.

From northbound Highway 12, turn left onto Arnold Drive. The restaurant is the first business on the right.

Only ten tables fill this rather intimate French country dining room. Pale pink walls, flowers at each white linen-covered table, and low lighting add to an already pleasant atmosphere. If you like seafood, the homemade ravioli stuffed with lobster, scallops, and mussels, served in a tarragon cream sauce, or the fresh baked salmon served in a mint-butter sauce will be tempting options. For something different and delicious, try the wild boar served on a bed of red wine and onion confit. Romantic dining options in Glen Ellen are fairly limited, so you'll feel lucky to have found this little restaurant. Dinner is served Thursday through Monday, from 5:30 P.M. to 9:30 P.M.

Outdoor Kissing

JACK LONDON STATE HISTORIC PARK, Glen Ellen   💋
2400 London Ranch Road
(707) 938-5216
$5 per car, day-use fee
Wedding facilities are available; call for details.

From Glen Ellen's center, head west uphill on London Ranch Road.

Besides being a fascinating historical site, the Jack London State Historic Park offers some of the most pastoral picnic sites around, with lovely wooded paths for an old-fashioned country stroll after lunch. Sit at one of the picnic tables set amongst the trees, or bring a blanket and spread it out on the rolling lawn that overlooks the small cottage where London penned his famous adventures. A forested trail leads to the granite ruins of Wolf House, the castle that London was building for himself and his beloved wife, Charmian. Wolf House mysteriously burned down before they could move in, and London died shortly thereafter. Nearby is another grand stone structure, the House of Happy Walls, which Charmian built as a memorial to the love of her life. It holds memorabilia from their life and exotic travels together.

◆ **Romantic Warning:** In the summer, when tourism is at its peak and the kids are out of school, Jack London's "Beauty Ranch," as he called it, feels more like a zoo than a park.

◆ **Romantic Suggestion:** Stop at the **GLEN ELLEN WINERY,** 1833 London Ranch Road, Glen Ellen, (707) 935-3000, on your way up to Jack London State Historic Park, for wine tasting and a tour. Here you can get a brief lesson about winemaking and wander through lush, well-maintained grounds. Watch out for heavy equipment, though; this working ranch gets especially hectic around harvest time.

Kenwood

Kenwood is another modest village, located north of Glen Ellen on Highway 12. But don't let the small-town look fool you into just driving through. There are some places definitely worth stopping for in Kenwood.

Hotel/Bed and Breakfast Kissing

KENWOOD INN SPA, Kenwood   ◆ ◆ ◆ ◖
10400 Sonoma Highway
(707) 833-1293, (800) 3-KENWOOD
Very Expensive to Unbelievably Expensive
Wedding facilities are available for a maximum of 80 people.

From Highway 101 north, take the Highway 37 exit (Napa/Vallejo exit) and follow this to Highway 121, which turns into Highway 12 (Sonoma Highway) north. The inn will be on the left-hand side of the highway.

If an Italian count and countess were to greet you at the door of the Kenwood Inn, you probably wouldn't even flinch. This Tuscan-style villa is only a couple of years old, but it looks ancient, transplanted from a Mediterranean hillside. Ivy trails up the walls, a rose garden abounds with blooms, and tall hedges conceal the courtyard and its swimming pool and fountain.

Inside, 12 luxurious rooms await, each adorned with dark, rich brocade fabrics, faux marble walls, a feather bed, and a fireplace. Some rooms have whirlpool tubs for two and small ivy-framed stone balconies that face the lovely garden, pool, and, unfortunately, Highway 12 in the nearby distance. The Italian theme continues in the breakfast room, with its *trompe l'oeil* murals and tapestry-covered high-backed chairs. Here, a full gourmet breakfast is served at intimate two-person tables.

◆ Romantic Note: During the revision of this book, the Kenwood Inn was being renovated. A full-service spa and dining room were being added. If this project gets the same loving care as the rooms have, it should be absolutely fantastic.

Restaurant Kissing

KENWOOD RESTAURANT, Kenwood   ◆ ◆
9900 Sonoma Highway
(707) 833-6326
Moderate to Expensive
Wedding facilities are available; call for details.

On the west side of Highway 12, about ten miles north of Sonoma, two miles north of Glen Ellen.

Plan a sun-soaked luncheon or arrive before sunset for dinner at this lovely restaurant so you can beat the rush. The Kenwood Restaurant is elegant but not necessarily intimate once it fills up with devoted diners. The view of the pastoral fields and vineyards surrounding it is intoxicating, and the food is exquisite. A high peaked ceiling of rubbed wood paneling and exposed beams, whitewashed walls brushed softly with contemporary impressionistic paintings, bentwood rattan chairs, and white linen cloths set with silver and fine china adorn the dining room. The service is friendly, and the continental menu, featuring escargot, duck, salmon, and sweetbreads (or a club sandwich, if you prefer), is enhanced by an extensive selection of Valley of the Moon wines.

◆ **Romantic Note:** The restaurant is closed Monday, but serves lunch and dinner the rest of the week

Outdoor Kissing

CHATEAU ST. JEAN, Kenwood
8555 Sonoma Highway
(707) 833-4134, (800) 332-WINE

On the right-hand side of Sonoma Highway (Highway 12).

Getting stuck in a huge tour group is never romantic, which is why we loved Chateau St. Jean, an elegant winery estate where you take a self-guided tour at your own leisure. During harvest time you can witness the winemaking process, but no matter what time of year you visit, climb up to the observation tower. From this perspective you have a wonderful view of the expansive vineyards, rolling green hills, and beautifully manicured property. Pick a prime picnic spot on the lush green lawn, then kiss everyone in your intimate, two-person tour group.

Santa Rosa

Kiss the grape arbors, rolling hills, and sweet, fresh air goodbye, because this is the city. If you're still in a provincial mindset, Santa Rosa can be a disappointment. Not only is it a detour from the country, it is also California's largest city north of San Francisco. Despite this fact, Santa Rosa provides a handful of very distinctive romantic locales—several of which are located on the city's outskirts, so you can almost pretend it's the country.

Hotel/Bed and Breakfast Kissing

THE GABLES, Santa Rosa ◆ ◆ ◆
4257 Petaluma Hill Road
(707) 585-7777
Moderate to Expensive
Wedding facilities are available; call for details.

From Highway 101, take Rohnert Park Expressway east. In two and a half miles, where it dead-ends at Petaluma Hill Road, turn left. The inn is about four miles up on the left.

If it weren't for the busy highway that runs alongside this gabled Victorian Gothic Revival home, we would call this the country. Acres of farmland surround the inn, stretching as far as the eye can see. And you won't even notice the highway if sweets are the way to your heart—you'll be won over by the homemade cappuccino bars and herb tea set out by the Italian marble fireplace in the antique-filled parlor.

Once you've satiated your sweet tooths, sweep up the curving mahogany staircase to the refined yet unpretentious guest rooms. The unusual architecture of this beautifully restored home features 15 gables crowning keyhole-shaped windows that have become part of the rooms' decor. The Sunrise Room's eye-catching ceiling forms an eight-sided semicircle; the Meadow Room has five corners. All of the rooms have been lovingly decorated with floral wallpapers, country linens, soothing prints, and attractive antique furnishings; some rooms even have fireplaces to warm up your kissing.

In the morning, a country gourmet breakfast of fruit, home-baked breads with homemade jam, an egg dish, sausage, and strudel is served near the marble fireplace in the formal dining room.

The Gables' newest (and possibly most enticing) guest accommodation is the self-enclosed cottage located next door. Country wallpaper and beautiful hand-worked wood add cozy charm to this small but airy cottage, complete with a loft bedroom and full kitchen.

♦ **Romantic Note:** Although we felt it necessary to mention the cars whizzing along the adjacent busy highway, the Gables is remarkably soundproof and traffic noise is not a problem.

VINTNER'S INN, Santa Rosa
4350 Barnes Road
(707) 575-7350, (800) 421-2584
Moderate to Very Expensive

From Highway 101, take the River Road exit west (four miles north of downtown Santa Rosa). Take the first left onto Barnes Road. The inn is on the left-hand side of the road.

Driving toward Vintner's Inn past well-groomed rows of grapevines, I felt as though I had passed through a magic portal and landed in southern France. A fountain splashes in the central plaza of this complex of sand-colored buildings with red tile roofs; the inn seems more like a vintner's private estate than a hotel. The spacious, uncluttered guest rooms have antique pine and contemporary furnishings, and French doors that open to patios or iron grillwork balconies overlooking 50 acres of surrounding vineyards. Upper-story rooms have high peaked ceilings, and their oversized oval tubs invite long soaks. You can savor a mellow cabernet by the fireplace in many of the rooms or sink into one of the overstuffed sofas by the fire in the library.

A full buffet breakfast is served in the main building; enjoy home-baked breads and fruit in the bright sun room overlooking the lawns or savor a Belgian waffle together by the wood-burning hearth with a skylighted cathedral ceiling above.

Restaurant Kissing

JOHN ASH & CO. RESTAURANT, Santa Rosa
4330 Barnes Road
(707) 527-7687
Expensive

From Highway 101 north, take the River Road exit west (four miles north of downtown Santa Rosa). Take the first left, onto Barnes Road. The restaurant is adjacent to Vintner's Inn.

The view of the vineyards surrounding this elegant restaurant is almost as enticing as the fruit of their vines. Clusters of candlelit linen-covered tables overlook panoramic country views through floor-to-ceiling cathedral windows. In the evening, an inviting fire casts a warm glow inside this showcase for Sonoma Valley foods and wines. The menu changes seasonally, but is as contemporary and fresh as the decor, with choices such as a locally grown duck appetizer, Sonoma rabbit braised in red wine, or roasted local lamb in a walnut, thyme, and wild honey sauce. Wine for every taste is offered, from private reserves to a chardonnay made from grapes from the surrounding vineyards to cognacs blended by John Ash himself.

JOSEF'S RESTAURANT, Santa Rosa
308 Wilson Street, at Hotel La Rose
(707) 579-3200
Moderate
Wedding facilities are available for a maximum of 120 people.

From northbound Highway 101, take the downtown Santa Rosa exit. Turn left onto Fourth Street, then right onto Wilson Street. The hotel is on the corner of Wilson and Fifth Street.

The locally quarried granite exterior of this 1907 depot hotel wears a somber face, but inside the parlor and dining room are warmly inviting. An ebony grand piano, played by a computer, greets diners with clear, bell-like melodies. The mauve, green, and sand color-scheme is restful; the tables are elegantly laid out with white linen, fine china, and silver. Relax with an aperitif on the love seat in front of the wood-burning fire, then sit down to savor almond-encrusted baked Brie, breast of chicken stuffed with leeks and served with pistachio-orange sauce, or eggplant and almond crêpes.

◆ **Romantic Note:** Rooms in this old establishment don't compare with the restaurant for kissing ambience, but are a real bargain at less than $50 midweek.

Healdsburg

You might assume that if you've seen one small town in wine country, you've seen them all. Guess again. Amazingly enough, each town in this area has a character and disposition of its own, which makes traveling through wine country a continuing surprise. Healdsburg was one of our favorite towns in the Sonoma Valley for several reasons: its charming town plaza and park green are lined with interesting boutiques and restaurants, and the gorgeous surrounding countryside harbors numerous bed and breakfasts and wineries secluded on quiet, winding roads—perfect for kissing.

Hotel/Bed and Breakfast Kissing

BELLE DE JOUR INN, Healdsburg
16276 Healdsburg Avenue
(707) 431-9777
Moderate to Expensive

Drive 65 miles north of San Francisco on Highway 101, take the Dry Creek Road exit, and turn right toward Healdsburg. At Healdsburg Avenue turn left and go one mile to the inn.

Get back to nature at one of Belle de Jour Inn's four white cottages, situated on six acres of rolling hills lined with vineyards and profuse greenery. It's hard to choose between the cottages—all of them are exceedingly comfortable, with modern furnishings, wood floors, sumptuous linens, and private entrances. We were especially partial to the cottage with a fireplace, whirlpool tub, and French doors that open to a trellised deck. Our second favorite has high vaulted ceilings, a wood-burning stove, and a whirlpool tub.

Breakfast in the morning is a cornucopia of fresh fruits, crab quiche, Gorgonzola polenta, apple turnovers, and fresh muffins. Enjoy this feast on the garden deck or in the privacy of your own room.

CALDERWOOD INN, Healdsburg
25 West Grant Street
(707) 431-1110
Moderate to Expensive
Wedding facilities are available for a maximum of 35 people.

Drive north on Highway 101 and take the Dry Creek Road exit. At the bottom of the exit, turn right (east), go to the first stoplight, and turn right onto Grove Street. Stay on Grove, which becomes Grant Street. After a curve to the left, the inn is the third Victorian on the north side of the street.

The inscription on the Scottish crest hanging at Calderwood's back entrance says it all: "RIVIRESCO" ("I flourish again"). Thanks to the present owners, nothing could be closer to the truth. This Queen Anne Victorian inn is nestled in a quiet residential neighborhood, secluded behind cypress and spruce trees. Sip a cool glass of lemonade with your hors d'oeuvres as you relax in a porch swing on the front porch or examine the spacious parlor cluttered with period furnishings and knickknacks.

Custom-designed Bradbury and Bradbury silkscreened wall- and ceiling papers enhance the Victorian mood in each of the six guest rooms upstairs. Cozy alcoves, attractive linens, private baths with claw-foot tubs, and period antiques highlight the rooms; one even has a Jacuzzi.

Your hosts take cooking seriously and present guests with an opulent full breakfast in the dining room. The tasty special of the day, accompanied by home-baked breads and seasonal fruits, puts the finishing touch on a romantic interlude.

CAMELLIA INN, Healdsburg
211 North Street
(707) 433-8182
Inexpensive to Moderate

From Highway 101 north, take the second Healdsburg exit (Central Healdsburg). Follow Healdsburg Avenue past the plaza to North Street and turn right. The inn is two and a half blocks up on the left.

The Camellia Inn knows just how to get you in the mood. Start with a sip of wine or a sample of cheese in the double parlors of this 1869

Victorian trimmed with intricate leaf-motif plasterwork and decorated with Oriental carpets, floral sofas, and tapestried chairs. The bouquet of nine uniquely decorated guest rooms will appeal to almost any bed-and-breakfast connoisseur. Our favorites include one with a massive half-tester bed from a Scottish castle; one with a Mexican brass sink, gas stove, and double whirlpool; and one with a cutwork lace canopy and white wicker accent furniture. Guests who can bear to leave their room can refresh themselves in the backyard pool.

THE GRAPE LEAF INN, Healdsburg
539 Johnson Street
(707) 433-8140
Inexpensive to Moderate

From Highway 101 north take the Central Healdsburg exit and follow this off the freeway for three-quarters of a mile. Turn right onto Grant Street and drive two blocks to the corner of Grant and Johnson. The inn is on the right.

If you've never kissed in a purple house, here's your chance. It's hard to miss this conspicuous refurbished Queen Anne-style bed and breakfast set in an otherwise ordinary suburban neighborhood. The inn, a winsome and welcome combination of eccentricity and solace, has seven suites done up in seven personalized styles. From the outside it's hard to imagine that there is room for more than one, much less seven, but the accommodations are more than ample. Amenities include skylights, multicolored windows, separate sitting areas, five whirlpool baths for two, and hardwood floors covered with Oriental rugs. Breakfast in the morning is a substantial array of egg dishes, fresh baked breads, fresh fruit, and juice. An overnight stay here is a surprising combination of fun and good old-fashioned romance.

HAYDON HOUSE, Healdsburg
321 Haydon Street
(707) 433-5228
Inexpensive to Expensive
Wedding facilities are available for a maximum of 50 people.

From Highway 101 north, take the second Healdsburg exit (Central Healdsburg). Follow Healdsburg Avenue to Matheson, at the plaza. Turn right onto Matheson, then right onto Fitch, then left onto Haydon. The inn is the third house on the left.

Write your own happy ending at this high-gabled Victorian house and storybook cottage harbored on a quiet residential street. The two guest rooms in the cottage are utterly romantic: cathedral ceilings crown both upstairs rooms and skylights shed moonlight into double whirlpools. The Pine Room is awash in white, with a stunning Battenburg lace canopy, crocheted spread, and subtly scented dried-flower wreath above the headboard. Ralph Lauren accents in paisleys and plaids lend a more masculine feel to the Victorian Room.

Six guest rooms in the main house are smaller and less private, though also romantic, with antique beds, cozy down comforters, floral accents, and skylights. The Attic Suite is the most unusual, with a bed and a claw-foot tub both tucked into the sloping eaves. Breakfast is a delicious full country affair.

HEALDSBURG INN ON THE PLAZA, Healdsburg
110 Matheson Street
(707) 433-6991, (800) 491-2324
Inexpensive to Moderate
Wedding facilities are available for a maximum of 20 people.

In the town of Healdsburg, just one block east of Healdsburg Avenue, on the park green.

Yes, you're in the right place. In order to get to the inn, you must pass through the art gallery and gift shop located on the ground floor. (On your way, be sure to stop and peruse the work of the talented local artists featured here; you might even find a token memento to take home with you.) A staircase leads to the bed-and-breakfast area on the second floor, where nine guest rooms adjoin a mezzanine. Several suites were undergoing renovations when we were here. (I hope they install better lighting—our room was so dim we could hardly see each other.) Every suite has a private bath, some have fireplaces and bay windows, and the most recent addition has a full kitchen and private entrance. All are affectionately, though sparsely, decorated with American antiques, down comforters, firm canopied beds, and cozy sitting areas trimmed in pastel colors and textured country fabrics.

The best feature of this inn is the rooftop garden and solarium, set above the plaza—a charming setting for a hearty, savory breakfast and afternoon tea served with richly decadent cake and cookies.

MADRONA MANOR, Healdsburg   ❂ ❂ ❂ ❂
1001 Westside Road
(707) 433-4231
Moderate to Very Expensive
Wedding facilities are available for a maximum of 130 people.

From southbound Highway 101: Exit onto Westside Road and go west one mile. The inn is at the intersection of West Dry Creek and Westside Road. From northbound Highway 101: Take the Central Healdsburg exit. At the first traffic light, take a sharp left onto Westside Road and proceed for three-quarters of a mile; the inn is on the right.

A royal crest adorns the gates that welcome you to this landmark bed and breakfast and restaurant—considered to be one of the finest in the area. The beautifully landscaped and maintained gardens and woods surrounding this stately mansion estate create a setting that can only be described as romantic. Make a reservation and see for yourselves what true country luxury is all about.

Nearly all of Madrona Manor's 18 rooms have something to offer. Guest rooms in the three-story Victorian mansion are warmed by fireplaces and appointed with period furnishings (unfortunately, some of them look a little too time-worn). The renovated Carriage House also features rooms with fireplaces, though the decor here is newer and somewhat Oriental. The Garden Suite and the Meadow Wood Complex overlook the gardens; some rooms have private, sheltered decks.

With so many choices, how do you decide? In our opinion, it doesn't get much nicer than Suite 400 in the Carriage House, with French contemporary furniture, king-size bed, private deck, and Jacuzzi tub with shutters that open to views of the fireplace.

After an evening of romance, a scrumptious breakfast is served exclusively to guests in the main house's elegant dining room.

Restaurant Kissing

MADRONA MANOR RESTAURANT, Healdsburg
1001 Westside Road
(707) 433-4231
Moderate to Very Expensive
Wedding facilities are available for a maximum of 130 people.

From southbound Highway 101: Exit onto Westside Road and drive west one mile. The inn is at the intersection of West Dry Creek and Westside Road. From northbound Highway 101: Take the Central Healdsburg exit. At the first traffic light, take a sharp left onto Westside Road and proceed for three-quarters of a mile; the restaurant and inn are on the right.

Be sure to arrive 10 or 15 minutes before your dinner reservation so that you can wander through the handsomely landscaped grounds of this estate. If it's raining, even better: sit by the fire on an overstuffed sofa in the cozy parlor. The manor's dining room is characterized by high ceilings, rose wallpaper, lace curtains, and intimate tables covered in white linens and scattered throughout the house's original living and dining rooms. Given the ambience, it's no surprise that the food here is divine. Prix fixe menus include specialties like Dungeness crab mousse with scallops and sole, served with a sauce of tomatoes, leeks, saffron, basil, and orange zest; honey-glazed pheasant with wild rice, fresh corn, and polenta on a bed of spinach served with pomegranate sauce; and, for dessert, wild huckleberry puffs with lemon verbena and honey-roasted sunflower seeds baked in phyllo and served with tangerine ice cream. (We'd award four lips for their creative selections alone, not to mention the impeccable flavor and presentation.)

TRE SCALLINI, Healdsburg
241 Healdsburg Avenue
(707) 433-1772
Expensive
Wedding facilities are available for a maximum of 50 people.

From Highway 101 north, take the Central Healdsburg exit, which puts you directly on Healdsburg Avenue. The restaurant is on the left-hand side after the stoplight.

This small Italian eatery overlooks a busy street, but its gold interior is demure with white sconces, mirrors, and handfuls of intimate tables arranged in two dining rooms. An appetizer of roasted garlic and black truffle custard with sweet red pepper sauce will rouse your appetite for dishes like braised Pacific Coast salmon with fresh herb crust. Delicious. Dinner is served Monday through Saturday.

Outdoor Kissing

RUSSIAN RIVER WINE ROAD
Highway 128 to Chalk Hill Road

From Healdsburg, follow Healdsburg Avenue north until it becomes Alexander Valley Road. Follow this road to Highway 128 and turn south. Highway 128 branches off to the east; to the west is Chalk Hill Road.

The handful of wineries along this backwoods road are set apart from the rest of the Napa Valley by their isolation and beauty. Coiling through the hillsides and ravines, your path crisscrosses the tributaries and creeks of the Russian River. Along the way, the vineyards, redwoods, and forests take turns revealing their distinctive virtues and profiles. Whenever you see a sign along here that says "WINERY," it means you're invited to stop and rest for a bit under the shade of a tree or in the coolness of a cellar tasting room.

RUSSIAN RIVER AREA WINERIES
(707) 869-9212, (800) 253-8800 for tourist information

More than 50 wineries grace the Russian River area, which stretches from the Pacific Coast inland to Healdsburg, then north through Geyserville. Many are family-run operations that are far off the beaten path and a pleasure to discover together. The following wineries offer quiet, romantic picnic spots for the price of the wine you'll savor with the repast you've packed in your basket. *Salud!*

A. RAFANELLI WINERY, 4685 West Dry Creek Road, Healdsburg, (707) 433-1385, set deep in the heart of the country, is a departure from many of this area's chic and somewhat pretentious wineries. Although there are no picnic areas to speak of here, you'll enjoy sipping wine in the barn tasting room or wandering through the grounds, which are hemmed with grape arbors.

BELLEROSE VINEYARD, 435 West Dry Creek Road, Healdsburg, (707) 433-1637, is reached via a winding farm road and a long gravel drive. Two picnic tables set next to an old red barn overlook rolling vineyards with mountains on the horizon. Roaming chickens and weater-worn antique farm equipment emphasize the rural setting. Open Tuesday through Thursday from 1 P.M. to 4:30 P.M., and Friday through Sunday from 11 A.M. to 4:30 P.M., in summer; Friday through Monday from 11 A.M. to 4:30 P.M. in the winter.

DRY CREEK VINEYARD, 3770 Lambert Bridge Road, Healdsburg, (707) 433-1000, is situated on a flatland surrounded by vineyards and sloping hills, deep in the countryside. Stained-glass windows flank ivy-covered stone barns that serve as tasting rooms. When you've selected your wine, head outdoors to the picnic tables, set under shade trees on a manicured lawn framed by flower gardens.

HOP KILN WINERY, 6050 Westside Road, Healdsburg, (707) 433-6491, offers one of the most romantic picnic spots in the area. Sun-soaked picnic tables border a pond that is hemmed with vineyards and home to a family of mallards. More tables are in the cozy, shaded garden. Wine tasting takes place in the impressive stone historic landmark that was once a hop kiln and now doubles as a small gallery for local art. Open daily from 10 A.M. to 5 P.M. Wedding facilities are available for a maximum of 200 people.

KORBEL CHAMPAGNE CELLARS, 13250 River Road, Guerneville, (707) 887-2294, is farther west than most of these wineries, but a superb stop for romance if you're heading to the coast. The tasting room is one of the grandest in the land—a spacious, elegant chamber, complete with crystal chandelier, in a castle-like stone building. Before tasting, take a bubbly tour of the winery or the stunning gardens, April through October. Colorful flowers and towering shade trees enhance the picnic area, but noises from the busy street aren't conducive to vintage kissing.

ROBERT STEMMLER VINEYARDS, 3805 Lambert Bridge Road, Healdsburg, (707) 433-6334, provides cafe tables on a shaded redwood deck overlooking sun-soaked vineyards, plus several picnic tables beneath the trees with plenty of shade but not much view. Open daily from 10 A.M. to 4:30 P.M.

ROCHIOLI VINEYARDS AND WINERY, 6192 Westside Road, Healdsburg, (707) 433-2305, equals Hop Kiln in its intoxicating picnic setting. Spend a lazy afternoon lingering at a table on a shaded patio with an ambrosial view of rolling vineyards backdropped by mountains.

Geyserville

Geyserville felt like a ghost town as we drove in; we hadn't expected it to be such a tiny, lackluster village, and I must admit that we were disappointed. Once we decided to make the best of it, though, we realized that someone looking for a genuine rural getaway might love this northernmost destination in Sonoma Valley.

Hotel/Bed and Breakfast Kissing

HOPE-MERRILL HOUSE, Geyserville
21253 Geyserville Avenue
(707) 857-3356, (800) 825-4BED
Moderate to Expensive
Wedding facilities are available for a maximum of 35 people.

From Highway 101 north, take the Geyserville exit and continue north on Geyserville Avenue one mile to the inn on the left-hand side of the road.

Staying in one of the 12 rooms at this faithfully and elaborately restored turn-of-the-century Victorian is like stepping back in time. The Eastlake Stick-style home showcases Victorian intricacies alongside modern amenities. Stunning silkscreened Bradbury and Bradbury wall coverings and ceiling papers add the proper flourish to the white linen cutwork comforter and white wicker accent pieces in the Vineyard View Room, and to the floral sofa and flouncy draperies around the bay window in the Bradbury Room. Contemporary indulgences in some rooms include gas fireplaces, whirlpool tubs, and showers for two, not to mention the beautiful outdoor pool available to guests.

♦ Romantic Suggestion: For $30, the inn will prepare a gourmet picnic lunch for two. This includes an appetizer, entrée, salad, dessert, fruit, and a bottle of the innkeeper's wine, all packed in a keepsake wicker basket. Reserve ahead to enjoy this delicious experience.

◆ **Romantic Alternative:** Country cousin of the Hope-Merrill House is the **HOPE-BOSWORTH HOUSE**, 21238 Geyserville Avenue, Geyserville, (707) 857-3356, (800) 825-4BED, (Moderate), located across the street. All four rooms in this Queen Anne-style Victorian have a cozy country feel and queen-size beds, and one room has a whirlpool bath. Guests staying here have access to the Hope-Merrill House's pool and are served the same gourmet country breakfast.

Restaurant Kissing

CHATEAU SOUVERAIN, Geyserville
Independence Lane
(707) 433-3141
Moderate to Expensive

From Highway 101 north, exit at Independence Lane. The winery is on the left side of the freeway.

No matter which wine country town you are spending the night in, make sure you head north to Geyserville to dine at Chateau Souverain at least once. A stately stone and wrought-iron archway sets the mood as you approach the elegant chateau, set atop a vineyard-laden knoll. Swirl up the regal stone steps to the main dining room, where picture windows on three sides frame a view that is as intoxicating as the nearly 100 fine wines offered here. A massive fireplace, magnificent bent brass chandeliers hanging from a cathedral ceiling, and soft, neutral tones enhance the ambience. In the warmer months, tables are set on the grand terrace overlooking the vineyards of the Alexander Valley. The cuisine is equally wonderful, with appetizers like ahi tartare or white truffle risotto with smoked salmon, and entrées including roasted Sonoma chicken with sage and caramelized onions, or macadamia nut-encrusted sea bass. One of the desserts is tira misu, Italian "lift me up" cake, but by then you'll already feel you've been lifted to heaven.

◆ **Romantic Note:** Wine tasting is offered in the Cafe, Chateau Souverain's more casual and less pricey alternative to the restaurant. The Cafe is refreshingly modern, with geometric murals gracing the walls and live jazzy music on Friday and Saturday nights.

◆ **Romantic Warning:** Chateau Souverain's hours are limited: lunch is served Friday through Sunday, dinner is served Friday and Saturday evenings only. Reservations are highly recommended for every meal.

◆ **Romantic Alternative: HOFFMAN HOUSE,** 21712 Geyserville Avenue, Geyserville, (707) 857-3264, (Expensive), is another one of Geyserville's surprising finds. It isn't nearly as slick as Chateau Souverain, but this charming restaurant serves creative gourmet dishes in a delight- fully casual setting with just a touch of elegance. In the warmer months, tables are set on this Victorian's wraparound porch, where sweet-scented wisteria flows over its trellis, or on the front lawn. In winter, a gas fire warms the cozy parlor of a lounge and the dining room, graced with hard- wood floors, cane-back chairs, and pastel floral cloths topped with white linen. Such appetizers as home-smoked salmon or cream of wild mush- room soup with a blend of shiitake and oyster mushrooms will tempt your palate. Seasonal dinner entrées may include pork chops stuffed with pears, apples, raisins, and walnuts, and topped with bourbon and apple syrup. Wedding facilities are available for a maximum of 50 people.

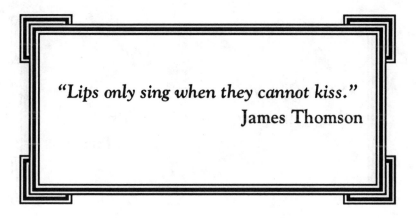

"*Lips only sing when they cannot kiss.*"
James Thomson

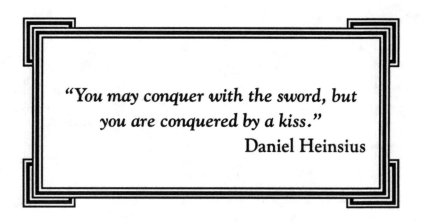

"*You may conquer with the sword, but
you are conquered by a kiss.*"
Daniel Heinsius

SAN FRANCISCO

Shrouded by fog and harbored between the Pacific Ocean and San Francisco Bay, the city of San Francisco pulsates with an electricity unlike any other metropolis. Colorful Victorian-style townhouses crowd together in lively hillside neighborhoods, and the landmark arches of the Golden Gate Bridge ascend above the clouds hovering over the bay. There is something for everybody in this city that thrives on cultural diversity. A single weekend isn't enough time here if you want to see it all (and believe me, you'll want to see it all).

Love flourishes here in intimate restaurants where world-renowned chefs display their talent, and romantic overnight accommodations abound. Whether you choose to visit the architecturally renowned Opera House or Palace of Fine Arts, or go shopping or dining in the bustling international districts, San Francisco's sights and sounds are sure to inspire some of the best kissing around.

◆ **Romantic Warning:** Parking in San Francisco, especially in crowded areas like Union Square or Chinatown, can be a real hassle. Don't let the frustration of searching for a space spoil the day or evening before it begins. If you are downtown or nearby, do yourselves a favor and catch a cab, a cable car, or walk (but go on foot only if you're prepared to climb some hills).

Hotel/Bed and Breakfast Kissing

ARCHBISHOP MANSION   ◆ ◆ ◆ ◆
1000 Fulton Street, at Fulton and Steiner
(415) 563-7872, (800) 543-5820
Expensive to Unbelievably Expensive
Wedding facilities are available for a maximum of 100 people.

The outside world melts into oblivion once you enter this haughty mansion turned bed and breakfast. As you cross the threshold, you can see what makes the Archbishop so magnificent. The massive foyer, the hand-painted ceiling in the parlor, the stained glass dome crowning the formidable three-story staircase, and Noel Coward's grand piano in the elaborate hallway are a few of the more notable appointments.

Each of the 15 lavish guest rooms is superbly designed for intimacy. In one, a white claw-foot bathtub sits next to one of the mansion's 18 carved-mantel fireplaces. In another, the room's centerpiece is a four-poster bed from a French castle. All of the rooms are decorated with choice antiques, and all have intimate detailing, embroidered linens, and graceful sitting areas; a few even have city views, and three of the rooms boast Jacuzzis. A gracious staff serves wine in the parlor, and in the morning a generous continental breakfast is brought to your door. Alamo Square (see "Outdoor Kissing") is right across the street if you care for a morning walk. The surroundings and the service at the Archbishop Mansion allow guests to revel in the noble, gilt-edged style of the rich and famous.

By the way, the Archbishop Mansion survived the 1906 earthquake. That tremor-worthiness alone should rate a high kissing score.

BED AND BREAKFAST INN
4 Charlton Court, at Union Street between Laguna and Buchanan
(415) 921-9784
Inexpensive to Expensive

Leave behind the urban pace of Union Street and immerse your senses in the countrified surroundings of this snug, hobbit-like hideaway. Formerly a neighborhood carriage house, the picturesque Bed and Breakfast Inn is nestled on a side street, and its 11 eclectic rooms provide an ideal city escape. Only six have private baths, but all are surprisingly comfortable and quaint, appointed with antiques and overstuffed down comforters. A select few even open onto their own hidden rooftop garden. The penthouse flat with a spiral staircase and the self-contained Garden Suite with a solarium, whirlpool tub that looks onto a garden patio, loft bedroom, and full modern kitchen, are both wonderfully luxurious and private.

Breakfast is served in the main house's small country-style dining room at cozy two-person tables and is included with every room except the Garden Suite. (People who opt for this suite don't mind; they can take advantage of their private full kitchen and make a romantic breakfast at their secluded leisure.)

◆ **Romantic Suggestion:** The multitude of cosmopolitan shopping and dining establishments on Union Street are steps away from the Bed and Breakfast Inn's front door. Browsing hand-in-hand around this area is a one-of-a-kind elite shopping extravaganza. From the western edge of the Presidio to Telegraph Hill on the east side, there is an endless parade of stores with everything a curious consumer could ever want.

CAMPTON PLACE HOTEL
340 Stockton Street, between Sutter and Post
(415) 781-5555, (800) 426-3135
Very Expensive to Unbelievably Expensive

Imagine a valet service that unpacks your baggage, brings fresh bouquets to your room, and provides shoe shines. There is only one word for the Campton Place Hotel: aristocratic; and only one word for you while you stay there: spoiled. From the marble lobby with Oriental accents to the rooftop garden and extravagant dining room, this hotel has spared no expense. Except, that is, for the guest rooms. Though attractively decorated with tasteful peach tones, fresh flowers, and thick down comforters, the bathrooms and furnishings are fairly standard and not nearly as posh as you might expect.

EDWARD II BED AND BREAKFAST
3155 Scott Street, on Scott at Lombard
(415) 922-3000, (800) 473-2846
Inexpensive to Moderate

The endless procession of cars whizzing by on Lombard Street is enough to make you want to pass this one up. Don't. If you're willing to overlook the traffic noise, this is one of San Francisco's best kissing bargains. The creative accommodations are colorfully bright, cheerful, and have been recently renovated. Six of the 31 rooms are luxury suites (some are full-size apartments) with canopy beds, soft down comforters, whirlpool tubs, and English country decor; 16 of the standard rooms have private baths and similar country-style appointments.

Continental breakfast is served in the morning at the inn's next-door bakery, where the lattes and baked goods are some of the best in town. (Even if the rooms weren't so affable, the bakery would be worth a mention in and of itself.)

FAIRMONT HOTEL
950 Mason Street, at the corner of California and Mason
(415) 772-5000, (800) 527-4727
Expensive to Unbelievably Expensive
Wedding facilities are available for a maximum of 900 people.

You might recognize the legendary Fairmont Hotel even if you've never been there—it's one of the most photographed hotels in the country. Built in 1907, it is also one of San Francisco's oldest standing hotels. The spectacular lobby, replete in red, sets the stage for romance, from the deep red carpet to the red velvet couches and settees, flanked by marble columns and exotic floral arrangements. Of the 596 rooms here, the Tower Rooms are the most inviting, with large picture windows showcasing stunning views of the distant bay, plus attractive antique furnishings and lovely linens. The remaining guest rooms are rather mediocre. An interesting note: The Fairmont's renowned Penthouse Suite was featured in the *Guinness Book of World Records* for being the most expensive in the world (just uttering the price will take your breath away). By comparison, the prices for the other rooms are much more reasonable, though still not inexpensive.

◆ **Romantic Suggestion:** The Fairmont Hotel's **NEW ORLEANS ROOM** and **MASON'S RESTAURANT** (see "Restaurant Kissing") are both wonderful places to dine and listen to jazz.

FOUR SEASONS CLIFT HOTEL
495 Geary Street, at Taylor
(415) 775-4700, (800) 332-3442
Expensive to Unbelievably Expensive

Is there anything about the Four Seasons that isn't romantic? Well, if there is, we sure couldn't find it. Whether you're savoring a glass of chardonnay in the exquisite Redwood Room, encompassed by velvet patina walls and grand burl redwood columns, or dining in the equally posh French Room (see "Restaurant Kissing"), every surrounding detail shines with a polished finesse. Not surprisingly, the guest rooms here are almost as extravagant, with deluxe furnishings, lavish swagged valances, marble baths, and, in the case of the Deluxe Suite, a spaciousness that may well be unmatched in the city.

HOTEL TRITON
342 Grant Avenue, at Bush
(415) 394-0500
Moderate to Expensive

If, after Alice went through the looking glass, she had needed a hotel room, she might have stayed at the Hotel Triton. This one-of-a-kind hotel offers all-out sensory stimulation. The interior is a combination of surrealistic and unconventional details: the chairs have S-shaped backs, the divider screens are painted bright yellow with floating pastel figures, the walls are either white-and-taupe checked or sponge-painted pink and iridescent gold. Crisp white bedspreads are strewn with oversized navy blue throw pillows, and the furniture has an art deco flair. In spite of the imaginative concept, all of the 140 rooms have up-to-date amenities to make your stay exceedingly comfortable, albeit amusingly eccentric. You can even rent in-line skates from the front desk. As you will see, anything goes here.

THE HUNTINGTON HOTEL
1075 California Street, between Taylor and Mason
(415) 474-5400
(800) 652-1539 (in California), (800) 227-4683 (in the U.S.)
Expensive to Unbelievably Expensive
Wedding facilities are available for a maximum of 80 people.

We are the first to admit it when we make a mistake, and not including the elegant Huntington Hotel in the last edition of this book was a big one. The 140 luxuriously appointed rooms here offer some of the best places to kiss in all of San Francisco. Other hotels located in the heart of the city are grand, but they lack individuality and romantic flair, and focus instead on their corporate clientele. At the Huntington Hotel, this is not the case.

Originally built as a luxury apartment building, the Huntington has commodious, wonderfully quiet rooms, each one adorned with sumptuous fabrics and ornate furnishings. Rich tones such as burgundy, forest green, and gold help to create a thoroughly regal atmosphere. The one- or two-bedroom suites fall in the Unbelievably Expensive price category, the other rooms are in the Very Expensive range, but as the saying goes, you get what you pay for. The gracious staff ensures that your stay here will be a private and comfortable one.

◆ **Romantic Note:** The Huntington prides itself on playing host to visiting nobility, dignitaries, and celebrities. At the risk of sounding like we're name-dropping, we must mention that we ran into Fabio, the famed romance novel model, in the elevator. If the so-called King of Romance stays here, need we say more?

◆ **Romantic Suggestion:** The Victorian mahogany walls and dark green leather chairs in **THE BIG 4 RESTAURANT** on the Huntington Hotel's main floor look like they belong in a men's club, which isn't particularly romantic. However, the same decor takes on new life when warmed by a crackling fire in the cozy lounge. In this alluring location, listen to a softly played piano and enjoy a nightcap before retiring to your choice accommodations.

THE INN AT THE OPERA
333 Fulton Street, between Gough and Franklin
(415) 863-8400, (800) 325-2708
Moderate to Very Expensive
Wedding facilities are available for a maximum of 50 people.

If you're not an opera buff, a single evening here might incite your cultural passions and encourage you to become one. It's hard not to get caught up in the excitement of the brilliantly dressed crowds returning from a night at the opera, with their binoculars and programs in hand.

Artists, patrons, and opera lovers alike seek refuge after the final curtain at this luxurious inn, conveniently located across the street from San Francisco's legendary opera house. The inn's softly stated elegance spoils guests at every turn with inviting, overstuffed pillows and comforters, bedside chocolates, and terry-cloth robes. The 48 guest rooms here, designed with intimacy in mind, feature canopy beds, subtle pastel color schemes, wet bars, and beautifully restored antiques.

A fireside dinner at the inn's sumptuous **ACT IV LOUNGE** (see "Restaurant Kissing") is a romantic must, though guests can also admire the handsome surroundings while enjoying a complimentary continental buffet breakfast.

THE MAJESTIC HOTEL ◆ ◆ ◆
1500 Sutter Street, at Gough
(415) 441-1100, (800) 869-8966
Moderate to Expensive
Wedding facilities are available for a maximum of 200 people in the
Cafe Majestic.

Several million dollars were spent transforming this mansion into a
designer masterpiece, and it shows. A mirrored marble entrance leads
into a plush lobby area brimming with antique tapestries, etched glass,
and French Empire furnishings. You may want to stop here and sip a
cocktail at the genuine 19th-century mahogany bar, but don't linger too
long—the real romance is waiting for you upstairs. The focal point of
each of the 59 rooms is a large, hand-painted, four-poster canopied bed
dressed in plump feather pillows, fine linens, and plush down comforters.
Small chandeliers hang from the ceiling of every room, and gas fireplaces
lend a warm glow to suites with marble bathrooms. Our only complaint is
the drab color schemes displayed in most of the rooms (they might be
authentic, but they're also a little too somber for our romantic tastes).

◆ Romantic Note: For a very convenient romantic repast, consider
dining at CAFE MAJESTIC (see "Restaurant Kissing"), located downstairs adjacent to the lobby.

◆ Romantic Option: LAFAYETTE PARK, located at the corner of
Octavia and California, three blocks up from the hotel, is a beautiful oasis
with remarkable views and well-tended gardens. Romance novelist
Danielle Steel just bought one of the mansions across the street from this
inspiring park. Enough said?

MANDARIN ORIENTAL HOTEL—(see Silks, "Restaurant Kissing")

THE MANSIONS HOTEL
2220 Sacramento Street, between Laguna and Buchanan
(415) 929-9444, (800) 826-9398
Inexpensive to Unbelievably Expensive
Wedding facilities are available for a maximum of 120 people in the
stained glass dining room.

From a distance, the two illustrious mansions enfolded by fertile jungle landscaping look similar to other properties in this prestigious San Francisco neighborhood. Once you've stepped inside the Gothic doorway of the Mansions Hotel, however, you realize this hotel is truly one-of-a-kind. In fact, its strange combination of flamboyant flourishes and fun almost makes it feel like a curiosity shop. The main floor is outfitted with a billiard room, a stage area where a magician entertains on weekends, and, finally, tucked around the corner, a thoroughly idyllic, crystal-chandeliered dining area where continental breakfast and dinner are served to guests.

All of the rooms in the first mansion have a crystal decanter of sherry set next to a queen-size bed embellished with attractive linens, and feature a marble fireplace or a private terrace. The second mansion, connected to the first through a breezeway, is definitely more traditional and subdued. The four-story redwood mansion successfully blends formal sophistication with relaxed country charm. A grand fireplace in the library, yellow brocade Queen Anne-period furnishings, an outdoor sun deck and garden patio, and inviting, generous-sized rooms all make for ardent accommodations.

♦ **Romantic Note:** Rumor has it that the first of these two mansions is haunted, but we didn't notice anything out of the ordinary (other than the peculiar surroundings).

PETITE AUBERGE
863 Bush Street, between Mason and Taylor
(415) 928-6000
Moderate to Expensive
Wedding facilities are available for a maximum of 30 people.

A deluge of stuffed teddy bears and the smell of freshly baked cookies will greet you in the lobby of this winsome yet practical downtown hotel. It doesn't matter which of the 26 cheerful guest rooms you choose; even those without fireplaces are endowed with the gracious charm of a French country inn. Creamy lace window treatments, thick comforters, and private baths ensure comfort and pleasure during your stay here.

As the smell of baked goods in the lobby suggests, the continental dining service is first-class here. The kitchen prepares both thoughtful breakfast buffets and late-afternoon samplings of hors d'oeuvres followed by a glass of wine. You can enjoy them at one of the dining tables situated adjacent to a small garden or on a love seat next to a roaring fireplace.

◆ **Romantic Option:** Just down the street the **HOTEL VINTAGE COURT**, 650 Bush Street, (415) 392-1666, (800) 654-1100, (Moderate), has one of the cozier hotel lobbies in San Francisco. A crackling fire inspires guests to kick off their shoes and relax; pretty floral bouquets and comfortable furnishings complement the tranquil atmosphere. Each of the guest rooms at the hotel is named for a California winery, but all basically look the same. The rooms have been recently updated and some feature wonderful bay windows, but the furnishings still appear aged. If you plan to spend a lot of time out and about in the city, or downstairs by the roaring fire, you can probably overlook the fact that the appointments aren't very romantic, especially since the rates are so reasonable. Plus, continental breakfast and an evening wine and cheese tasting are both included with your stay.

◆ **Romantic Warning:** Bush Street, home to both the Petite Auberge and the Hotel Vintage Court, is a busy one-way thoroughfare. Rooms close to the ground floor on the street side tend to get a lot of traffic noise, while those off the street or on upper levels seem quiet. If you don't want to deal with the sounds of the city, ask for a room that won't echo with screeching brakes and honking horns early in the morning.

THE PRESCOTT HOTEL
545 Post Street, between Taylor and Mason
(415) 563-0303, (800) 283-7322
Expensive to Very Expensive
Wedding facilities are available for a maximum of 40 people.

The Prescott is too large to be considered a charming European-style hotel, but that doesn't keep the management from trying to make things feel that way. The roaring fire is the focal point of what the hotel refers to as its "living room." Located to the left of the lobby, this warm area is filled with cozy furniture and early California arts and crafts. It's an ideal spot for relaxing and enjoying the hotel's hospitality, or listening to fireside storytelling on Sunday evenings. Complimentary coffee and tea are served during the day, and wine and cheese are offered in the evening.

All of the rooms in the hotel are attractive, albeit hotel-like, with hunter green bedspreads with hints of burgundy, cherry-wood tables and chairs, bowfront armoires, and brass accents. The suites with sitting rooms are elegant in style and comfortable. Every modern hotel convenience is provided: each room is equipped with a color television with remote control, a stocked bar and refrigerator, terry-cloth robes, a hair dryer, and, in the suites, VCRs and single whirlpool tubs. Those who stay on the Club Level (rooms and suites on this floor are slightly more expensive) also receive a complimentary breakfast, a cocktail reception in the evening, and use of the exercise facilities.

◆ **Romantic Indulgence:** The Mendocino Penthouse at the top of the Prescott may be the most extraordinary suite in the city. This luxurious escape seduces guests with two wood-burning fireplaces, hardwood floors, rich Edwardian furnishings in the parlor and bedroom, beautiful artwork, a grand piano in the formal dining room, and a rooftop deck with a Jacuzzi and garden. Staying here is the height of romantic pampering. It's unbelievably beautiful, unbelievably expensive, and absolutely worth it if you can make room in your romantic budget!

◆ **Romantic Note:** POSTRIO (see the Compass Rose, Romantic Alternative, in "Restaurant Kissing"), located just off the hotel's lobby, is an upbeat, chic eatery with sensational cuisine.

THE RITZ-CARLTON   ◆ ◆ ◆ ◆
600 Stockton, at California
(415) 296-7465, (800) 241-3333
Very Expensive to Unbelievably Expensive
Wedding facilities are available for a maximum of 800 people.

How could we not include the Ritz, known worldwide for impeccable service? If you're in the mood to be waited on, catered to, and simply spoiled, book a night here. Before the opening in 1991, Ritz-Carlton restored this stately building's Neoclassical exterior to its original splendor, added an expansive courtyard rose garden with manicured hedges and a fountain, and completely renovated the interior. From the Persian carpets to the Bohemian crystal chandeliers, everything is first-class.

All 336 choice rooms feature Italian marble bathrooms with double sinks, plush terry-cloth bathrobes, pale silk wall coverings, antique-style furnishings, and richly upholstered furniture. The 44 spacious suites are the most grand, with separate dining, living, and sleeping rooms, and private balconies that overlook the city. In the Ritz-Carlton Club guest rooms that fill the eighth and ninth floors, special amenities like complimentary continental breakfast, midmorning snacks, afternoon tea, cocktails and hors d'oeuvres, and late-evening cordials and chocolates are provided. If you don't stay in one of these rooms, you can get meals downstairs in the Terrace or the Dining Room (dinner only).

On warm days, the Terrace offers courtyard seating at white wrought-iron chairs and tables with peach-colored umbrellas. Both dining options are too large and formal to be considered romantic, but the food is wonderful and they couldn't be more conveniently located, unless, of course, you opt for room service.

If you've overindulged (or plan to), visit the workout facility, complete with a heated indoor pool, whirlpool, and spa. Massage therapy is also offered in case you climbed one too many of San Francisco's infamous hills. Basically, everything you might need is at your fingertips when you stay at the Ritz.

SHERMAN HOUSE   ◆ ◆ ◆ ◆
2160 Green Street, at Webster
(415) 563-3600, (800) 424-5777
Very Expensive to Unbelievably Expensive
Wedding facilities are available for a maximum of 100 people.

Kissing here may turn your heart inside out, but so will the bill unless you're on the Forbes 100 list. An Absurdly Expensive category is more appropriate for many of the rooms in this exquisitely restored, 1876 French-Italianate mansion. Still, this is San Francisco's most aristocratically intimate hotel and restaurant. Each of the 14 lavish guest rooms is individually decorated. One room is akin to a king's chamber, with a full canopy bed of heavy velvet-lined tapestry draperies, a plush window seat with a plethora of pillows and billows of drapes above, and an immense bath with a deep, black soaking tub. Another room, in the Carriage House, is strikingly different, with a chic cabana look of latticed walls, slate floors, teak-trimmed jetted tub, and free-standing fireplace. Others are equally stately, with canopied queen-size beds, wood-burning fireplaces, and luscious fabrics.

If you're hesitating because of the price tag, keep in mind that the sumptuous surroundings are unparalleled anywhere else in San Francisco. You might want to save up to celebrate a special occasion at this extraordinary place.

SPENCER HOUSE
1080 Haight Street, at Baker
(415) 626-9205
Moderate to Expensive

The Spencer House has little need for advertising. In fact, there isn't a "SPENCER HOUSE" sign to be seen anywhere near the grand, multicolored gabled Victorian, set behind wrought-iron gates. It isn't even listed in the phone book. So how do guests find out about this extraordinary bed and breakfast? Word of mouth from satisfied customers and repeat business. This fact alone gives you some idea of the kind of intimacy guests experience here. Although the Spencer House has all the trappings of a noble Victorian—spacious firelit parlors, wood floors, Oriental carpets, and period antiques—its real focus is on comfort. All of the six guest rooms have feather beds, rich fabrics, and private baths; some have large bay windows that offer glimpses of the Golden Gate Bridge peeking over the city rooftops. Bradbury and Bradbury silk-screened wall and ceiling coverings, crisp linens trimmed with antique lace, gas and electric chandeliers, and a collection of gorgeous antiques blend to create an authentic but fantastically comfortable Victorian climate. And the hospitality doesn't stop there. A delicious breakfast of eggs ranchero with salsa or Belgian waffles topped with warm strawberries is served in the wood-paneled dining room. It's no wonder they don't need to advertise!

WARWICK REGIS HOTEL
490 Geary Street, at Taylor
(415) 928-7900, (800) 827-3447
Moderate to Expensive

Set in the heart of San Francisco's theater district, the Warwick Regis couldn't be more conveniently located. Its reputation for romance, however, has more to do with its enticing, luxurious atmosphere. The Warwick combines old-fashioned charm with modern amenities to create an exceedingly comfortable yet elegant climate. The 80 regal guest rooms here are decorated with choice fabrics in muted tones, comfortable antiques, lace curtains, and textured wallpaper, and feature black marble bathrooms. Some of the exceptionally romantic suites have canopied beds, balconies, and fireplaces. Complimentary continental breakfast is served downstairs at the chic **LA SCENE CAFE**. Once you've satiated your romantic inclinations, you'll appreciate the fact that the Warwick is a short walk from much of what San Francisco is famous for: Union Square, the cable cars, galleries, good shopping, great dining, and, of course, the theaters.

♦ **Romantic Note:** The Warwick offers several different romantic packages (including theater packages) that can include valet parking, continental breakfast, dinner at La Scene Cafe, red roses on your pillows at turndown service, and mementoes.

WASHINGTON SQUARE INN   ◆ ◆ ◆
1660 Stockton Street, on Washington Square
(415) 981-4220, (800) 388-0220
Inexpensive to Expensive

Location is everything at the Washington Square Inn, which is situated in the heart of North Beach, San Francisco's vibrant Italian district. The inn looks out (across a busy street) onto verdant Washington Square and the magnificent Gothic cathedral of Saints Peter and Paul. A fire warms the cozy parlor, where complimentary continental breakfast and late-afternoon wine and hors d'oeuvres are served. Guest rooms are modestly adorned with a simple blend of French and English antiques, floral draperies, canopied beds, fresh flowers, and contemporary paintings by a local artist. In several rooms, you can pledge your *amore* on a window seat as the sun sets over San Francisco's little Italy.

WHITE SWAN INN   ◆ ◆ ◆ ◆
845 Bush Street, between Mason and Taylor
(415) 775-1755
Expensive to Very Expensive
Wedding facilities are available for a maximum of 25 people.

Magically, the White Swan Inn brings the English countryside to life in the heart of downtown San Francisco. Each of the 26 rooms is masterfully done, with stately antiques, floral and striped wallpaper, and bay windows. Personal touches like dried flower arrangements, bath salts, canopied beds, and tiled fireplaces make this one of the most special bed and breakfasts in the city.

As wonderful as the rooms are, you will also enjoy sharing high tea (served every afternoon) in the handsome fireside living room downstairs or lingering over a full buffet breakfast in the inn's intimate dining room.

◆ **Romantic Warning:** As much as we loved the White Swan Inn, we must mention that the windows are not soundproof. City noise is a problem unless you reserve a room away from the street.

◆ **Romantic Alternative:** The lasting impression of your stay at **THE INN AT UNION SQUARE**, 440 Post Street, (415) 397-3510, (Moderate to Expensive), will be one of cozy comfort and dedicated service. All 30 rooms are outfitted with sitting areas, Georgian furnishings, and tasteful pastel fabrics. Each of the six floors has a small tranquil lounge with a crackling fireplace where morning breakfast, afternoon tea, or hors d'oeuvres can be enjoyed (or taken back to the privacy of your own room). Most of the rooms are a bit on the small side, except for the choice (Unbelievably Expensive) Penthouse Suite on the top floor, which has its own sauna, deep Oriental soaking tub, fireplace, and wet bar.

Restaurant Kissing

ACORN TEA AND GRIDDLE
1256 Folsom Street, between Eighth and Ninth
(415) 863-2469
Moderate

The word "griddle" might lead you to believe that the Acorn is little more than a diner, but don't be fooled. Despite its name and its obscure location in a dingy neighborhood, the Acorn is chock-full of romantic possibilities. From the street you'd never guess that the two dining rooms here could have a view of anything other than a city alley, but guess again. Both charming dining rooms overlook a verdant garden and a fire escape draped in greenery. In the summer, guests can fully enjoy this unique setting at several tables arranged outside on the patio. The dining rooms' interiors are set off by luxurious fabrics that have been twisted and draped over the windows, country murals framed by dried branches, and cozy tables set along the walls. The menu here is nearly as surprising as the surroundings: cornmeal-crusted oysters with spinach and pancetta; Vietnamese shrimp cakes; grilled pork loin on rice noodle salad with mint, chili, and lime; and house-made scrumptious desserts.

ACQUERELLO
1722 Sacramento Street, between Van Ness and Polk
(415) 567-5432
Expensive

Given that *acquerello* is the Italian word for "watercolor," you'd expect to see more vibrant colors here. Nevertheless, everything about this cozy Italian restaurant is as pretty as a painting. A small handful of tables topped with candles, white linens, and pale pink china are surrounded by cream-colored walls softly illuminated by wall sconces and graced with simple artwork. An exquisite pastel floral arrangement at the front entrance adds a dash of color to the otherwise unassuming surroundings.

While the setting alone might whet your romantic appetite, Acquerello offers an innovative selection of Italian dishes flavored with the freshest ingredients of each season. If it's available on the night you dine, don't miss the pumpkin gnochetti with black truffles and sage, or the homemade green onion fettuccine with salmon in spumante sauce. The wine list is extensive, and the courteous staff is always willing to help you select the perfect wine to accompany your meal.

◆ **Romantic Alternative: IL FORNAIO**, 1265 Battery Street, (415) 986-0100, (Moderate), is one link in a chain of restaurants, and something about that almost precludes romantic encounters. Almost. If rules can have exceptions, and we believe they can, Il Fornaio is certainly one of them. This restaurant is very contemporary inside, with black, white, terra-cotta, and marble accents; high ceilings; an open kitchen; and art-work on the walls. Dining outside is more romantic: gas lamps warm the enclosed patio, pretty flowering plants add a burst of color, and a fountain flows just outside the glass walls. A second Il Fornaio in the city is located at 101 Spear Street, (415) 777-0330. In Marin County, a third Il Fornaio is at 233 Town Center, Corte Madera, (415) 927-4400. All of the restaurants are similar in design and ambience.

ACT IV LOUNGE
333 Fulton Street,
between Gough and Franklin, at the Inn at the Opera
(415) 553-8100
Moderate to Very Expensive
Wedding facilities are available for a maximum of 50 people.

After an exhilarating night at the opera, pamper your senses a little further at the Inn at the Opera's Act IV Lounge, a bastion of refinement and gourmet cuisine. The handsome interior is accented by a marble fireplace, mahogany pillars, and muted lighting that gently illuminates the walls and furnishings. Seated at one of the handful of tables sprinkled about the room, you and your companion will be perfectly situated to enjoy the delights of the ensuing meal—from appetizers to after-dinner drinks. The menu changes frequently, but we were thrilled with the duck and pheasant in caramelized onions served in a puff pastry shell, and the angel-hair pasta with prawns, scallops, and caviar. You'll be kissing before you know it. While Act IV is open for breakfast, lunch, and dinner daily, dinner is by far the most romantic interlude.

♦ Romantic Suggestion: The upstairs guest rooms at the INN AT THE OPERA (see "Bed and Breakfast Kissing") are equally sumptuous and romantic.

AMELIO'S
1630 Powell Street, between Green and Union
(415) 397-4339
Very Expensive
Wedding facilities are available for a maximum of 80 people.

From the street, Amelio's might not beckon to you, but your second thoughts won't linger very long once you step inside this intimate dining room. The deep-colored walls are softened by oil paintings and the delicate light of gilded chandeliers. Tapestry-covered booths, designed so couples can sit next to each other, line the walls, with a few additional tables in the center of the room. An exotic floral arrangement provides the focal point of the restaurant. More fresh flowers and candles are placed at each elaborately set table.

The French cuisine is divine—perfectly prepared and beautifully presented. You have a choice of ordering from an à la carte menu or selecting the fixed-price dinner. Amelio's is not the kind of restaurant you decide to dine at late in the day; usually, reservations are required in advance. Dinner is served Tuesday through Saturday.

BIX   ◆ ◆
56 Gold Street, an alley between Pacific
and Jackson, and Montgomery and Sansome
(415) 433-6300
Moderate

You will feel as though you've been transported back to the '40s once you step across the threshold of Bix's back-alley entrance. That's the point. This two-story restaurant and jazz club is highlighted by Corinthian columns, cathedral ceilings, and an expansive mural of a '40s dance floor. Jazz is the theme here, and if you're looking for great entertainment to accompany an excellent meal, you've come to the right place. While you're partaking of well-prepared dishes accented with a few unusual ingredients (the bananas Foster with vanilla ice cream and rum was heavenly), you can also listen to a torch singer, saxophone player, or jazz pianist. Though sometimes the volume of the music makes soft, romantic conversation impossible, it doesn't prevent you from snuggling up close in the cozy, cushioned booths set along the upstairs wall.

CAFE MAJESTIC   ◆ ◆ ◆
1500 Sutter Street, at Gough
(415) 776-6400
Moderate to Expensive
Wedding facilities are available for a maximum of 200 people.

Local polls have named Cafe Majestic one of San Francisco's "most romantic" cafes more than once, and we're not surprised. More a restaurant than a cafe, the Majestic's tasteful interior is characterized by lofty ceilings, Corinthian columns that separate its three dining rooms, and muted pink and green tones. To enhance the mood, a pianist in the evenings takes special requests. Don't be shy—he's willing to play just about anything! The kitchen strives hard to please at any time of day and is open for breakfast, lunch, and dinner seven days a week (except lunch on Monday). Sautéed crab cakes with roasted bell pepper aioli, and the salmon fillet stuffed with prawn mousse and baked in puff pastry are two of the tempting items you can choose from.

CAFE MOZART
708 Bush Street, between Powell and Mason
(415) 391-8480
Moderate to Expensive
Wedding facilities are available for a maximum of 40 people.

Thick red velvet and timeworn embroidered white curtains hang in the windows, secluding diners from the busy street. One of San Francisco's more intimate restaurants, Cafe Mozart has a mere ten tables, each draped with white linens and set with fine china, silver, crystal, and a single red rose. Antiques, artwork, and music by the restaurant's namesake enrich the interior.

The French cuisine is flavorful and beautifully presented. (The warm chocolate cake with roasted banana sauce is a lip-warming production.) This is a remarkably romantic place for a special occasion, even if the occasion is simply that the two of you are together. Open for dinner only, Tuesday through Saturday, from 5:30 P.M. to 10:30 P.M.

CAMPTON PLACE DINING ROOM
340 Stockton Street, at Sutter
(415) 955-5555
Expensive

Campton Place is an exceptional culinary landmark where the elite come for very serious dining and very intense romancing. Its elegance and refinement are dazzling. Extravagant floral arrangements and gilded mirrors surround tables set with crystal and freshly cut flowers. I would think fast after dropping a fork or napkin at this establishment—better to kick it under the table next to yours than admit to a faux pas. (Well, perhaps I'm exaggerating just a bit.) The American cuisine is sublime and, as you would expect, rather costly.

If you wish, you can also visit Campton Place for a regal morning repast. The atmosphere is less stuffy in the morning: you could drop your napkin twice and no one would blink an eye.

◆ **Romantic Note:** For the same formal style in accommodations, consider splurging and making overnight reservations at the deluxe CAMPTON PLACE HOTEL (see "Hotel/Bed and Breakfast Kissing").

THE CARNELIAN ROOM and BAR
555 California Street,
at Montgomery, in the Bank of America Building
(415) 433-7500
Very Expensive
Wedding facilities are available for a maximum of 320 people.

Fifty-two floors above it all, the distinctive glass-enclosed lounge at the Carnelian Room offers a mesmerizing view of San Francisco. For this stellar experience, you will want to arrive just before sunset. The last light of day will cast striking shadows across the city. This heavenly grandeur makes a heart-felt backdrop to the lounge's opulent interior. The view is accessible from both the restaurant and the bar, with the bar being an economical kissing windfall. Over an espresso or a glass of wine, the wonder of the city spreads out before you with a radiance that needs to be shared.

The Carnelian Room's service is, to say the least, gilt-edged, and the food is very good. On Sunday a bountiful brunch is served.

◆ **Romantic Indulgence:** For $50, you can have your own private room, complete with a table for two, a cushy love seat, and a green/red light outside of the room that you control, summoning your own personal waiter only when you require service. Otherwise, this is your place alone, for the entire meal, suitable for proposals of any kind.

THE CLIFF HOUSE
1090 Point Lobos Avenue
(415) 386-3330
Moderate
Wedding facilities are available for a maximum of 135 people.

Take Geary all the way to the ocean, where it dead-ends at the Cliff House.

All right, I know this is a tourist attraction. I also know it is hard to ignore the busloads of tourists that arrive here almost hourly to take in the stunning view from this landmark. But note that word "almost." In late afternoon or early evening, the place may be practically empty, and you'll be glad you took the risk. The Cliff House offers an incomparable view of the forceful, roaring ocean and the prolific sea life on Seal Rock below—a feast for the soul and the eyes. The weather conditions won't affect anything adversely either. Whether the sun is boldly sizzling above the sea or hiding behind a curtain of fog, the waves colliding against the jagged black rocks at the base of the restaurant will compose a rhapsody you can call your own.

◆ **Romantic Note:** By the way, the sandwiches, seafood, and desserts here are good. The Sunday buffet brunch in particular is a great idea if you go early enough or don't mind waiting for a table.

CLUB 36   ◆ ◆
345 Stockton Street,
between Post and Sutter, in the Grand Hyatt
(415) 398-1234
Inexpensive to Moderate

Hovering 36 airy floors above the city, this cocktail lounge overlooks the bay facing Fisherman's Wharf and Coit Tower. Club 36 doesn't open until 4 P.M., but after a day of working, shopping, or sightseeing, it is a good place to sit back and gaze at the city from afar. Sink into one of the burgundy leather chairs to soak up the casual atmosphere, stunning view, and soothing piano music played nightly from 9 P.M. to 1 A.M. This is a wonderful place to begin or end your evening out together in San Francisco.

THE COMPASS ROSE   ◆ ◆ ◆ ◆
335 Powell Street,
between Geary and Post, in the Westin St. Francis Hotel
(415) 774-0167
Inexpensive to Moderate

The Compass Rose is a plush, stunning place for afternoon high tea. While a string trio performs, you can relax in this rich room with high ceilings, accented with dark wood and black marble, Oriental touches, and rare antiques. Tea service is offered from 3 P.M. to 5 P.M. daily, and includes finger sandwiches, scones, berries with Grand Marnier cream, and petit fours. Lunch and cocktails are also served, and the dimly lit atmosphere is warm and sensuous any time of day.

◆ **Romantic Alternative: POSTRIO,** 545 Post Street, (415) 776-7825, (Moderate to Expensive), is an upbeat dinner option for those who are looking for a good time rather than quiet ambience. Everything about Postrio reminds me of a theatrical production. Diners make an entrance down a sculpted iron and copper staircase to the main dining room. This "set" is an artistic array of colors, textures, and lighting designed to stimulate the senses. Plush fabric-finished booths alternate throughout the room with striking tables draped in white linen and accented with black chairs. Modern art hangs on the walls, lamps hang from the high ceiling, green plants and exotic flowers add even more color. The "producers" in the large, open kitchen turn out flavorful, award-winning California cuisine, and the dishes are served by a "supporting cast" that wants to assist your performance. It's up to you to decide how to play out the evening. Breakfast and lunch are served Monday through Friday, and dinner is served daily.

The upstairs bar at Postrio serves gourmet pizzas and lighter fare until 1:30 A.M. It's the perfect place for a bite to eat and a quick kiss or two after a real night at the theater! And if you have trouble getting a reservation for lunch or dinner (they are difficult to come by), breakfast or Saturday and Sunday brunch are also possibilities.

DOIDGE'S   👄
2217 Union Street, between Fillmore and Steiner
(415) 921-2149
Very Inexpensive

Ask most people what their idea of a romantic meal is, and they will probably tell you it takes place at night in a wonderful restaurant glowing with candlelight. They might even mention violins. But those who believe romance can be found only in the evening are missing out on a fabulous opportunity. A leisurely breakfast with your loved one can be quite compelling.

You won't think much of Doidge's as you enter. The first thing you'll see is a diner-style counter, complete with cooks in the background flipping pancakes. But you'll also notice the music—classical, maybe even violins. Inside the dining room you won't find candles, but crisp linens and fresh flowers do adorn the tables. That's all. That's plenty. Doidge's serves up bountiful country breakfasts and leaves the romance up to you. Usually, customers are happy to oblige.

◆ **Romantic Note:** Doidge's is open seven days a week, between 8 A.M. and 1:45 P.M. Monday through Friday, and from 8 A.M. to 2:45 P.M. Saturday and Sunday. On the weekends it is crowded, but the restaurant does accept reservations in advance.

EMPRESS OF CHINA   ◆◆
838 Grant Avenue, between Clay and Washington
(415) 434-1345
Moderate
Wedding facilities are available for a maximum of 700 people.

Those who know the Chinatown area understand that it can be too noisy and crowded for a romantic rendezvous. But don't completely overlook the possibilities of an intriguing evening in Chinatown—there is romance to be found here, after all.

When you step off the elevator at Empress of China (the restaurant is six stories above the hustle and bustle), you step into a distinctly mysterious setting. The soothing sound of Oriental music wafts through an interior fashioned after ancient Oriental architecture. The restaurant boasts a priceless assortment of antiques and temple artifacts that are coveted by museums. Big windows along the exterior walls look out onto the lights of the city after dark.

Empress of China is a frequent award-winner for its cuisine. The chefs highlight fragrance, color, and flavor in their preparation of such Chinese favorites as almond chicken, Mongolian lamb, and lobster in garlic sauce. The opulent atmosphere, great food, and gracious service make dining at Empress of China an exciting adventure. The restaurant is open for lunch and dinner seven days a week.

◆ **Romantic Alternative: THE IMPERIAL PALACE,** 919 Grant Avenue, (415) 982-8889, (Moderate), is also known for its quiet elegance and superb cuisine. Chinese lanterns frame closely arranged (too closely arranged in many cases) faux marble tables, creating an amiable setting for sampling minced barbecued duck, Mongolian beef, or fresh Pacific crab baked with ginger, scallions, and Chinese wine, among other tasty menu items.

ERNIE'S
847 Montgomery Street, between Pacific and Jackson
(415) 397-5969
Expensive to Very Expensive

Ernie's is the kind of restaurant you save for special occasions because it is one of the most elegant dining establishments in the city. The lobby looks like a parlor in a Victorian mansion, and the lounge is built around a dark wooden bar with mirrors and stained glass. The main dining room is rich with tapestries, exotic flowers, and silver and crystal gleaming in the candlelight.

Ernie's accommodating wait staff serves fine French cuisine (we especially liked the lobster-stuffed cabbage and julienne of vegetables in a ginger-lobster broth), and the wine list is considered to be among the best in the country. The most compelling thing about Ernie's is a feeling of warm sentimentality you might call inspiration. Ernie's puts you in the mood for romance, and provides the perfect atmosphere for reveling in it.

◆ **Romantic Note:** Dinner is served Monday through Saturday. Men are required to wear a jacket.

FLEUR DE LYS
777 Sutter Street, between Jones and Taylor
(415) 673-7779
Expensive to Very Expensive
Wedding facilities are available for a maximum of 100 people.

There are some illustrious explanations why Fleur de Lys is consistently recommended as one of the most romantic restaurants in San Francisco. Legend would have us believe that Gypsies are romantic nomads, colorful wanderers who lead lives of passion and excitement. Whether or not the legends are correct, Fleur de Lys is the perfect place to spend an enchanted evening completely secluded from the busy street outside.

Fleur de Lys evokes the festive mood of a Gypsy encampment. Hundreds of yards of hand-printed red floral fabric drape the ceiling and walls of the main dining room, giving you the feeling you are in a big, beautiful tent. In the center of the room, a tall arrangement of exotic flowers is spotlighted by a Venetian chandelier hanging from the pinnacle of the fabric.

The food here completes the evening. It's fabulous! Fleur de Lys serves contemporary French cuisine with a flirtatious touch of Mediterranean flavor. Every dish is cooked to perfection, artistically presented, and served by a staff that truly wants you to delight in your dining experience. Dinner is graciously presented Monday through Saturday.

FOURNOU'S OVENS   ◆ ◆
905 California Street,
between Powell and Mason, in the Stanford Court Hotel
(415) 989-1910
Moderate to Expensive
Wedding facilities are available for a maximum of 550 people.

I'll admit Fournou's Ovens isn't exactly what you would describe as intimate or elegant. So why recommend this restaurant as a best place to kiss? Because sometimes simple and casual can be romantic if it's done right. Breakfast, brunch, lunch, or dinner, you can always expect a culinary treat at Fournou's Ovens. The restaurant is really a series of small dining rooms, and depending on your mood, you can select a setting that matches the kind of experience you want to have. The enclosed atrium overlooking Powell Street and the cable car line feels more like a cafe and is a lovely spot for breakfast or lunch. At dinner, choose between the Mediterranean-style dining rooms decorated with antiques and art, or the lower level where tables surround an open wood-burning oven.

The chefs here prepare continental cuisine that is best described as hearty and flavorful. The restaurant's wine cellar contains 20,000 bottles from all over the world, with an emphasis on California vintages.

THE FRENCH ROOM
495 Geary Street,
at Taylor, in the Four Seasons Clift Hotel
(415) 775-4700, extension 256
Expensive to Very Expensive
Wedding facilities are available; call for details.

Even if you're not a guest here, an amorous rendezvous in the French Room is a must for any romantic. Known to be one of the loveliest dining rooms in San Francisco, the French Room is accentuated with rich wood paneling, beautiful fabrics, elegant table settings, and classical pillars rising to lofty ceilings set off by stunning crystal chandeliers. The food is consistently good and the atmosphere is unceasingly heartwarming, especially the Viennese dessert buffet served Tuesday through Saturday.

◆ **Romantic Alternative:** The Four Seasons' dimly lit **REDWOOD ROOM** is similarly handsome, with high ceilings, polished dark wood paneling adorned with immense Gustav Klimt replicas, and plush lounge chairs arranged around coffee tables.

GARDEN COURT
2 New Montgomery Street,
between Second and Third, in the Sheraton Palace Hotel
(415) 546-5010
Expensive to Unbelievably Expensive

Crystal chandeliers drop from a leaded-glass dome ceiling and illuminate the mirrored doors, gold leaf sconces, marvelous flower arrangements, and marble columns that enhance the Garden Court. Overstuffed sofas and chairs provide relaxed, intimate seating in the back of the room; the front tables are more proper, draped elegantly in white and graced with fine china and fresh flowers. The ornate splendor of this palatial room might well surpass that of any other dining room in San Francisco, but unfortunately so do the prices. To best appreciate the gorgeous surroundings without spending a fortune, you might consider opting for high tea instead of dinner.

◆ **Romantic Warning:** Astonishingly, the white glove service here is the slowest we encountered in all of San Francisco. (For the prices you pay, this feels offensive.)

GAYLORD INDIA RESTAURANT
900 North Point Street, in Ghirardelli Square
(415) 771-8822
Expensive
Wedding facilities are available for a maximum of 250 people.

Perhaps Ghirardelli Square itself is too touristy to be considered total-ly romantic, but all the right ingredients are present at Gaylord's for an intimate dining experience. The ornate interior and attentive service are highlighted by huge bay windows that overlook the harbor and Fisherman's Wharf below. The view is what lends magic to Gaylord's, as well as the excellent East Indian cuisine. When an affectionate evening is at stake, every little bit helps.

JULIUS' CASTLE,   ❤❤
1541 Montgomery Street, north of Union Street
(415) 362-3042
Moderate to Expensive
Wedding facilities are available for a maximum of 160 people.

Yes, we know this is a tourist trap (and we also know tourist traps are antithetical to kissing), but the spectacular views from this castle are worth mentioning. Nestled on Telegraph Hill, the castle's upstairs dining room surveys unhindered views of San Francisco Bay and the Golden Gate Bridge. The dining room's Victorian-style interior is somewhat timeworn, though still pleasant, with mauve walls, dark wood paneling, and crystal chandeliers that shed soft light onto linen-cloaked tables. If you're still having trouble overlooking the crowds, turn your focus to the delectable French menu. You can't go wrong with the delicately sautéed abalone with a lime infusion and chives or the broiled swordfish with gar-lic, tomatoes, herbs, and peppers.

◆ Romantic Alternative: Another, less touristy dining option is the nearby SHADOWS RESTAURANT, 1349 Montgomery, (415) 982-5536, (Expensive), set on the easternmost flank of the hill, just a stroll's length down from Coit Tower. Here the crowds will seem to melt away as your emotions and taste buds come alive. This pastel, high-beamed restaurant overlooks the bay and has floor-to-ceiling picture windows, high-backed wicker chairs, apricot-colored tablecloths, pine paneling, and an open, airy atmosphere. As you relish the California cuisine, watch the mosaic patterns of the water and sky alter as day makes its transition into night. Wedding facilities are available for a maximum of 80 people.

KISS ◑ ◖
680 Eighth Street, between Brannan and Townsend
(415) 552-8757
Moderate

How could we pass up a name like this? Modeled after Gustav Klimt's famous painting called *The Kiss*, this restaurant has designed its own sensuous, citified version of his masterpiece. A white canopied ceiling and an expansive mural depicting a man and woman in an embrace atop a skyscraper enliven the mood of this otherwise stark, cafe-like restaurant. (Kiss's location among the warehouses in San Francisco's design district only adds to the spartan mood.) The menu changes weekly, but is typically quite good. We savored our tomato-herb pasta with crabmeat in a puff pastry shell covered with spinach puree, sun-dried tomatoes, and melted Swiss cheese; a breast of pheasant with black currant sauce; and, last but not least, a Grand Marnier soufflé.

◆ **Romantic Warning:** You'd think they'd know better with a name like Kiss, but the tables here are arranged a little too close together for comfortable displays of affection.

LA FOLIE ◑ ◖
2316 Polk Street, between Green and Union
(415) 776-5577
Very Expensive

The minute we saw it, we knew we'd like La Folie. A soft glow illuminates the mullioned windows and the boxes of flowering plants hanging from the second story. Inside, white billowy clouds are painted on the sky blue ceiling, and coral-colored faux marble walls provide a backdrop for some wonderful artwork. Lots of little tables for two are packed in the room; the half-curtained windows help conceal the bustling sidewalk and street outside. This eclectic yet charming mix truly exhibits the "folly" expressed in the restaurant's name. The food is fabulously French with striking flavors. The family-run restaurant exudes a friendly spirit and is open Monday through Saturday for dinner only.

LA NOUVELLE PATISSERIE
2184 Union Street, at Fillmore
(415) 931-7655
Inexpensive
Extensive catering services are available for weddings.

Now and then, rather than having a romantic destination, it's better to have a starting point and an open mind. If you find yourself feeling somewhat adventurous one morning and you decide to venture out in search of new places to kiss, we suggest you begin at La Nouvelle Patisserie. You can't miss this charming French bakery, partly because so many other people are headed there too. Inside, there are plenty of little marble tables filling the room, and the strong aroma of freshly brewed coffee complements the dozens of pastries, breads, fresh fruit tarts, truffles, cakes, and chocolates waiting for you.

Later in the day, lunch specials, salads, sandwiches, pâtés, and crêpes are also offered. This place is usually packed, but you can take your treats along on the next leg of your journey.

◆ **Romantic Alternative:** A few blocks down Union Street, you'll find another "little" place that has become a big success with couples looking for a choice rendezvous. **RISTORANTE BONTA**, 2223 Union Street, between Fillmore and Steiner, (415) 929-0407, (Moderate to Expensive), is a cozy storefront restaurant with a warm and inviting interior. The dining room is somewhat reminiscent of a trattoria in a small Italian town. Abstract art, fresh flowers, and candlelight combine to create a comfortable atmosphere. The food is superb and the service is very amiable. Ristorante Bonta can accommodate only about 30 fortunate diners, and sometimes the restaurant seems a little too crowded and noisy, but not so much that you can't focus your attention on each other. The restaurant is closed on Monday.

LA PERGOLA
2060 Chestnut Street, between Fillmore and Steiner
(415) 563-4500
Moderate
Wedding facilities are available for a maximum of 49 people.

Don't let La Pergola's casual atmosphere deceive you—there is nothing casual about this lovely Italian restaurant's menu. Round tables for two, track lighting, dramatic artwork on the walls, and a big picture window that looks out onto busy Chestnut Street make this attractive yet informal dining room a perfect place to savor black pasta filled with sea bass and fresh herbs in a sauce of leeks and sea scallops, or skewers of grilled prawns, sea scallops, and salmon with wild rice.

LASCAUX
248 Sutter Street, between Grant and Kearney
(415) 391-1555
Moderate to Expensive

It seems fitting that you must descend a flight of stairs to reach this wonderful underground dining room. Lascaux is named for the famous cave in France that contains some of the world's oldest paintings, reproductions of which grace the textured walls. Arched ceilings, resplendent hues, soft lighting, and a blazing fire in the huge stone hearth complete this present-day cavern.

The rustic theme continues in the food served at Lascaux. Many of the selections are based on old European recipes. Most prove to be treats, but those in the know always order the chicken or veal, spit-roasted on the rotisserie. The desserts are decadent, and certainly delicious enough to justify the temptation. You can share—there's something very sweet about one plate and two forks.

After dinner, a nightcap at the lively bar is a gratifying way to end the evening. A pianist or jazz ensemble provides the music; the rest of the evening's entertainment is left to your discretion. Lunch is served Monday through Friday, and dinner Monday through Saturday.

◆ **Romantic Option: BUCA GIOVANNI,** 800 Greenwich Street, at Columbus, (415) 776-7766, (Moderate), also has a cellar entrance and a cave-like setting. This brick-walled restaurant is more rustic in appearance than Lascaux, but that's part of its romantic allure. The dining room is modeled after an Italian trattoria, and the fresh bread and pasta entrées are authentically delicious. Our only hesitation is that the tables are very close to each other, so plan on sharing your romantic mood with others nearby if you dine here during prime time.

L'OLIVIER

465 Davis Street, a half block south of Jackson Street
(415) 981-7824
Moderate to Expensive
Wedding facilities are available for a maximum of 140 people.

By day, L'Olivier is popular with the business set and seems to lose some of its appeal and charm. But by night, L'Olivier is altogether a different restaurant. After nightfall it becomes an engaging setting in which to enjoy fine food and fine company.

The small two-tiered dining room, aglow with candlelight, can be likened to a country manor you might find in rural France. Floral wallpaper covers the walls, fresh flowers are placed on every table, there's always a large centerpiece arrangement in the middle of the room, French antiques add extra appeal, and chandeliers crown the room with soft light. All of these quaint touches combine to create an atmosphere that is inviting and intimate.

The traditional French menu includes favorites such as frog's leg soup, escargots de bourgogne, sautéed scaloppine of veal, and the house specialty, bouillabaisse. The wine list, devised to please connoisseurs, is a compilation of popular California wines, well-known French vintages, and a few surprises that may be worth sampling. And if wine is among your indulgences, partake, because you'll find L'Olivier inspires a night of romance that can be best described as intoxicating. Lunch is served Monday through Friday, and dinner Monday through Saturday.

THE MAGIC FLUTE

3673 Sacramento Street, between Spruce and Locust
(415) 922-1225
Inexpensive to Moderate
Wedding facilities are available for a maximum of 150 people in the restaurant or 350 in the gallery across the street. Call for details.

This angelic restaurant is a refreshing contrast to the affected style of many formidable highbrow dining establishments in San Francisco. Strands of tiny white lights ornament two dining rooms with warm peach walls embellished by dried vines and large watercolor paintings depicting San Francisco scenes. Italian wine bottles, placed at every table, serve as holders for long-stemmed candles, and white filigree chandeliers shed soft light throughout both charming dining rooms. Your sentiments will easily expand to blend with this engaging atmosphere as the evening slowly unfolds. It would be an error not to mention this restaurant's dedication to serving extraordinarily delicious desserts.

MAHARANI
1122 Post Street, between Van Ness and Polk
(415) 775-1988
Moderate
Wedding facilities are available for a maximum of 150 people.

It doesn't get more romantic than Maharani's pink Fantasy Room, where six private booths are secluded behind billowing fabric and surrounded by Oriental antiques. Make your reservations early—you're not the only ones who want to enjoy fabulous Indian cuisine, such as chicken curry or tandoor-baked fresh bread stuffed with raisins and nuts, served in the seductive intimacy of your own private nook.

MANSIONS RESTAURANT
2220 Sacramento Street,
between Laguna and Buchanan, at the Mansions Hotel
(415) 929-9444
Inexpensive to Unbelievably Expensive
Wedding facilities are available for a maximum of 120 people.

If you're looking for a little magic, you've come to the right place (although the magic you'll find here really has little to do with romance). Your dining experience at the Mansions Restaurant begins with a magic show, featuring a professional magician who mesmerizes dinner guests with disappearing acts in the parlor of a playful, museum-like mansion. After the show, guests are ushered to a handful of tables arranged in a stained-glass alcove overlooking a flower garden dotted with mosaic-tiled sculptures. The menu, or "Main Act," might include a fresh fillet of salmon roasted and wrapped in parchment paper or fresh jumbo prawns served in an ocean of garlic salsa. In accordance with the restaurant's unique surroundings, the "gold rush" desserts are equally unusual, and actually topped with 24-karat gold!

◆ **Romantic Note:** Accommodations at the **MANSIONS HOTEL** (see "Hotel/Bed and Breakfast Kissing") are comparably unique and definitely worth looking into.

MASA'S   ◉ ◉
648 Bush Street, between Powell and Stockton
(415) 989-7154
Very Expensive

Masa's is as formal as a French restaurant can be, and that's exceedingly formal. What the restaurant might lack in charm and coziness, it certainly makes up for in the stupendous quality of its cuisine. Masa's is, in the opinion of many, the best restaurant in San Francisco. From the foie gras with truffles and spinach to the white and dark chocolate mousse with raspberry sauce, Masa's makes every dish a masterpiece. The restaurant is handsomely decorated in rich, dark tones with an occasional accent of soft color and low lighting. Each table is elegantly appointed with crystal, china, and silver. The room is small and the staff is large, so each guest is assured the personal attention Masa's is famous for. If you find romance is best when you are catered to in every way, Masa's is definitely your style. Dinner is served Tuesday through Saturday.

/

MASON'S   ◉ ◉
950 Mason Street,
at the corner of California and Mason, in the Fairmont Hotel
(415) 392-0113
Expensive
Wedding facilities are available for a maximum of 300 people.

The prestigious Fairmont Hotel is more formal in its decor and more refined in its ambience than its dining room, Mason's, though this restaurant and jazz lounge does offer wonderful window tables that look out onto the cable cars of California Street. Attractive brass and blond oak furnishings and the allure of low lights and fresh flowers create an appealing ambience. A congenial staff serves delicious entrées like champagne-braised salmon or roasted Cornish hen stuffed with spinach, prosciutto, and sun-dried tomatoes.

Our favorite kissing attractions here are the cozy two-person tables and overstuffed sofas surrounding a grand piano in Mason's lounge, where jazz musicians entertain nightly. Now that's romantic!

MCCORMICK AND KULETO'S
900 North Point Street, in Ghirardelli Square
(415) 929-1730
Moderate to Expensive
Wedding facilities are available for a maximum of 200 people.

The fact that McCormick and Kuleto's is located in touristy Ghirardelli Square didn't much interest us—personally or for purposes of this book. But the wonderful view and showcase interior are worth a closer look. Huge picture windows accented with stained glass look out onto the bay; on a clear evening you can watch the water sparkle as the sun begins to slip away and ships roll by on their way to destinations unknown. You can easily disregard the tourists with a view like this. The restaurant is large and airy, with dark wood, brass accents, and abundant green plants. It's often crowded, but the tables are situated far enough apart that in some ways your dining experience here can be more intimate than in a smaller, more crowded restaurant. The menu offers an incredible selection of fresh seafood and an extensive wine list. The restaurant is open seven days a week for lunch and dinner.

◆ **Romantic Extra:** If it's already too late for the view or you haven't planned far enough in advance to have reservations by the window, try the **CRAB CAKE LOUNGE AND BAR** attached to McCormick and Kuleto's. A glass case presents ocean delicacies for your inspection. The chefs will prepare these or other snacks, including individual pizzas and baby back ribs cooked in an open oven. Booths and a counter are available.

◆ **Romantic Alternative:** Next door to McCormick and Kuleto's is the upbeat **LA PASTA,** 900 North Point Street, (415) 749-5288, (Inexpensive to Moderate), offering the same stunning view of the bay. The restaurant is decorated in art deco style. The menu is innovative, with Italian favorites. I liked the angel-hair pasta with walnuts, arugula pesto, and red bell peppers. The fresh seafood selections such as grilled scallops with spinach, chive, and champagne sauce also sounded (and smelled) wonderful. Wedding facilities are available for a maximum of 40 people.

NEW ORLEANS ROOM
950 Mason Street, at California, in the Fairmont Hotel
(415) 772-5259

The reasonably priced musical rhythms of the New Orleans Room make for a wonderful evening of tripping the lights fantastic. This is swing at its best, with smooth and intoxicating renditions that will make you sway to the beat like never before. The dimly lit lounge features a large stage surrounded by colorful art and cozy cushioned settees with just enough room for two.

NIEMAN MARCUS ROTUNDA RESTAURANT
150 Stockton Street, at Geary
(415) 362-4777
Inexpensive to Moderate
Wedding facilities are available for a maximum of 200 people.

Who would ever guess that we would find a great place to pucker up in a department store? Believe it or not, there really is a wonderful kissing place in Nieman Marcus. On the fourth floor, under a spectacular stained glass dome, the Rotunda Restaurant provides a respite from the shopping crowds and offers an invitation to romance. Select a table, draped in white linen and accented with a pale pink rose, near the floor-to-ceiling windows overlooking Union Square. The dining room serves lunch and light meals from 11 A.M. to 5 P.M. Monday through Saturday, but in my opinion afternoon tea at the Rotunda is the most ideal interlude. In a world where late-afternoon romance is too often overlooked because of busy schedules, you'll discover teatime can be a leisurely treat! You're sure to relish the selection of brewed teas, finger sandwiches, pastries, muffins, scones with cream and preserves, and an assortment of cookies.

PANE E VINO
3011 Steiner Street, between Union and Filbert
(415) 346-2111
Moderate

There's much more to Pane E Vino than the bread and wine its name salutes. Not the least is its quaint, authentic Italian atmosphere that invites devoted hearts to partake in the pleasures of an evening together. The restaurant comprises two small dining rooms. The one in back is more romantic, with a brick fireplace, a sideboard adorned with fresh flowers and aged cheeses, low lights, a beamed ceiling, and a clay tile floor. Accommodating waiters, most with thick Italian accents, are always happy to make recommendations if you're having difficulty deciding. The food is delicious (especially the pastas), the wines are wonderful, and the atmosphere is certainly for lovers. The restaurant really should be renamed Pane E Vino E Amore!

PLUSH ROOM   ◆ ◆ ❖
940 Sutter Street,
between Hyde and Leavenworth, at the York Hotel
(415) 885-2800
Expensive

Remember those late-night black-and-white movies from the 1940s, where hearts were lost, found, broken, and mended, all at a quiet table in the corner of a jazz club? There was always moving music in the background that would reach a crescendo just in time for the lovers to join in a torrid embrace. The Plush Room keeps alive this tradition of steamy jazz and soothing contemporary ballads in an appropriately classy, intimate setting. Whether or not you are a jazz connoisseur, you'll find one of the dark mauve cushioned booths set beneath a stained glass ceiling a tempting spot to share with your partner. You may be surprised to discover that words will be of no practical use all evening long (then again, maybe you won't).

SHERMAN HOUSE RESTAURANT   ◆ ◆ ◆ ◆
2160 Green Street, at Webster
(415) 563-3600, (800) 424-5777
Very Expensive to Unbelievably Expensive
Wedding facilities are available for a maximum of 100 people.

Even if you don't have the good fortune to be a guest at the Sherman House Hotel, the dining room here is the ultimate in intimacy for breakfast, lunch, or dinner. Copious bouquets of fresh flowers, elegant furnishings, and impeccable service are de rigueur. Sunlight streams through the diamond-paned windows of the solarium, embracing you with warmth during the day. Firelight warms the formal dining area, where seasonal specials such as lobster minestrone, squab salad, coq au vin of quail, and baked sea bass delight diners.

◆ **Romantic Note:** Just to remind you that you're not pinching pennies here, a 20-percent service charge is automatically added to your bill.

SILKS
222 Sansome Street,
between Pine and California, in the Mandarin Oriental Hotel
(415) 986-2020
Moderate to Expensive

To arrive at Silks, pass through the Mandarin Oriental Hotel's lovely lobby and ascend an elegant sweeping staircase. The centerpiece of this dining room is a splendidly ornate wood table plumed with a lavish floral bouquet. Surrounding this are clusters of tables set far enough apart to allow for a considerable amount of intimacy. The food at Silks is imaginative, combining French techniques with Oriental ingredients and California zest, but presentation is the specialty here. As its name suggests, Silks has a soft atmosphere that makes it a comforting place for tender time together.

◆ **Romantic Note:** The Unbelievably Expensive **MANDARIN ORIENTAL HOTEL, (415) 885-0999,** is an outstanding, albeit business-oriented, place to stay while you are in San Francisco. The guest rooms are located on the top 11 floors of the 48-floor twin towers of the California Center. Every room has an unbelievable view, and some have marble bathtubs with the same celestial perspective of the city.

TOMMY TOY'S
655 Montgomery Street, between Washington and Clay
(415) 397-4888
Moderate
Wedding facilities are available for a maximum of 130 people (weekends excluded).

There are no chopsticks at this ambrosial location. That's because Tommy Toy's is different—Chinese cuisine with French flair. I don't know of many restaurants that serve Peking duck with crêpes for the main course and a fluffy, smooth chocolate mousse for dessert. And "elaborate" is the only word to adequately describe the decor. The restaurant is patterned after the 19th-century Dowager Empress's reading room, and she obviously knew how to live. These ornate surroundings almost feel like a museum, filled with exquisite Oriental art pieces, fabrics, and tapestries. Hand-painted candle lamps and fresh, fragrant flowers accent each table. Menu items are no less detailed, from the pan-fried foie gras with sliced fresh pear and watercress in sweet pickled ginger sauce to the breast of duckling smoked with camphorwood and tea leaves served with a plum wine sauce.

UMBERTO RESTAURANT   ◆ ◀
141 Stewart Street, between Mission and Howard
(415) 543-8021
Expensive
Wedding facilities are available for a maximum of 350 people.

There are more than a few Umberto Restaurants in the world, but this one happens to be the most beautiful. Built to resemble an Italian villa, it is a perfect setting for a pasta extravaganza. Arched doorways, terra-cotta tiled floors, provocative Michelangelo and Botticcelli prints, and soft lighting create an eye-catching environment for conversation and *amore*.

VICTOR'S   ◆ ◆ ◆
335 Powell Street, in the Westin St. Francis
(415) 956-7777
Very Expensive

One of the most scintillating views of San Francisco is found at Victor's, 32 stories above the city. An outside, glass-walled elevator takes you to the restaurant, on the top floor of the Westin St. Francis Hotel. Here, floor-to-ceiling windows disclose what sitting on Cloud Nine is really like. The continental cuisine, such as baby salmon in dry vermouth and caviar cream sauce, is truly amazing, and the service is superior. Victor's only drawbacks are its popularity and the tourists, but the inspiring view ensures that you'll only have eyes for each other.

Outdoor Kissing

ALAMO SQUARE

At the corner of Fulton and Steiner streets.

One great thing about San Francisco is that numerous parks are scattered throughout in the city, in places where you would least expect a grouping of trees or lush green grass. Take time to enjoy one of these welcome patches of nature in quiet, tree-dotted Alamo Square. This park perches high above the city and offers a most remarkable view of San Francisco. On a sunny day, it's a lovely spot for a picnic.

ANGEL ISLAND
Ferries from San Francisco, Vallejo, or Tiburon
(415) 546-2810 (San Francisco and Vallejo)
(415) 435-2131 (Tiburon)
$5 to $10.50 for the ferry

Become castaways for a day on this angelic island in the middle of San Francisco Bay. The ferry ride alone is worthy of a windswept kiss. Once on the island, you can leave the lively little marina and ascend primitive trails to your private panorama of the San Francisco skyline or forested Marin hills. Bring along a picnic lunch to enjoy in a sun-soaked meadow. With its six-mile perimeter trail and rugged climb up to a 360-degree view of the Bay Area, Angel Island is sure to yield a secluded kissing spot.

GOLDEN GATE BRIDGE

Lincoln Boulevard, Park Presidio Boulevard, and Lombard Street all merge onto the Golden Gate Bridge. There is a parking area just east of the toll booths, where you gain entrance to the walkway across the bridge.

Walking over the venerable, symbolically soaring Golden Gate Bridge is an exhilarating, unforgettable journey. This monumental structure offers views that can only be described as astonishing. From this vantage point you can survey the city's physique while you balance high above it, unencumbered by buildings or earth. The Pacific Ocean, 260 feet below, is an endless blue apparition framed by the rugged curve of land north to Marin and south to San Francisco. As unbelievable as it sounds, the gusts of wind up here can cause the reinforced, Herculean steel cables to sway to and fro. This is the time and place where, without even kissing or touching, you can really feel the earth move—and it won't be from an earthquake, either. On a clear, sunny day, just once in your lives, put on your walking shoes and discover this one for yourselves.

◆ Romantic Option: GOLDEN GATE PROMENADE winds for three and a half miles around one of the most astounding scenic routes the Bay Area has to offer. This walkway extends from AQUATIC PARK at Fisherman's Wharf to FORT POINT under the Golden Gate Bridge. If there is a lover's lane to be found anywhere in San Francisco, it would be the projection of land at Fort Point. As you gaze out to the golden rocky hills, the vast lengths of the Golden Gate and Bay bridges, the glistening blue water, and the formidable cityscape, there is little else to do but move closer and kiss.

GOLDEN GATE PARK

Between Lincoln Way, Fulton Street, Stanyan Street, and the Pacific Ocean.

For those who know this vast acreage of city woodland and gardens, it is possible to imagine that Golden Gate Park and Romance are themselves an adoring couple. There is so much to see in this diverse three-mile-long park that even in a day you can only scratch the surface. Nevertheless, any of the park's varied attractions can provide a prelude to an enchanting day together. You can start at the STRYBING ARBORETUM, a horticultural wonderland of plants and trees from all over the world. Another remarkable city escape is the JAPANESE TEA GARDEN, where an exotic display of Japanese landscaping gives you a tranquil reprieve from anything having to do with urban life. While school is in session, the CHILDREN'S PLAYGROUND, with its extraordinary carousel, offers adults a grand backdrop for playtime. The CONSERVATORY OF FLOWERS is a stunning structure that houses many of the earth's most brilliant colors and plant life. Wherever you find yourselves, this magical San Francisco park is the foremost outdoor spot of the city.

PALACE OF FINE ARTS

Bordered by Lyon, Bay, Baker, and Jefferson streets.

Nothing in San Francisco compares to the European splendor of the Palace of Fine Arts. Erected in 1915 for the Panama Pacific International Exposition, it was not built to last. When the structure began to crumble in the late 1960s, San Franciscans, who had come to cherish the Palace, raised enough money to restore it, making it a permanent city landmark. Reminiscent of European architecture, the mock-Roman rotunda is supported by mammoth Corinthian columns and flanked by majestic colonnades. Walking paths lead beneath the dome and around the adjacent lagoon, where ducks and swans are often seen gliding. This setting is ethereal any time of day, but is especially romantic at night when the spellbinding architecture is lit up by spotlights.

♦ **Romantic Option:** A few blocks away, on Marina Boulevard, between the Yacht Harbor and Fort Mason (Cervantes and Buchanan streets), you'll find a grassy stretch of land called **MARINA GREEN** that hugs the bay. On warm weekends, if you don't mind crowds, it's a good place to watch sailboats, fly a kite, or simply sit and enjoy the sunshine.

PIER 39

At the foot of Beach Street, at Embarcadero.

OK, call me a kid; I won't be insulted. After all, sometimes it is easier to see the joy of life through the eyes of a child. In the case of Pier 39, if you don't use a younger viewpoint, all you're likely to see is a sizable tourist attraction. Try my approach and spend your time eating cotton candy on the carousel or riding the bumper cars. Or you can investigate the teddy bear store, home to more than 2,000 of these huggable creatures. Or watch mimes, magicians, and musicians perform while you wrinkle your nose at the smell of the sea and squint at the sparkling reflection of the sun on the ocean. On a nice day, you're sure to see sailboats whipping across the water with the wind.

On the tourist side of things, more than 100 specialty shops line the two-story boardwalk. There are at least a dozen eating spots for every taste and budget, and as an extra incentive many of the restaurants have views of the bay. Pier 39, if you're willing to adjust your biases and be young at heart, can be a pretty neat place.

◆ **Romantic Suggestion:** Take a cruise on exquisite San Francisco Bay. **THE BLUE AND GOLD FLEET,** (415) 781-7877, is docked at Pier 39's west marina; scenic, very touristy tours depart frequently. You won't be alone, but if you concentrate on the scenery the crowds will be much less apparent.

THE PRESIDIO

Bordered by the Pacific Ocean, San Francisco Bay, Lyon Street, West Pacific Avenue, and Lake Street.

It started in the 1700s with the Spanish settlers. Then, the Presidio was their northern military post. Now, the Presidio is home base to the U.S. Army's Sixth Division. Fortunately for those who are inclined to kiss in the great outdoors, the Presidio is not just a military installation. This beautiful corner of San Francisco contains hundreds of acres of lush lands and is open to the public. There's much more to the Presidio than you can see on foot, so start by driving around the grounds on roads that are lined with redwood and eucalyptus trees. Then, do yourself a favor, and park the car, take your companion's hand, and go for a walk. You might choose to stroll by some of the historical sites and displays. Maybe you'll opt for an open area with views of the Golden Gate Bridge and the Pacific Ocean. Or perhaps you'll select the residential area, where old yet immaculate base houses (still occupied) evoke the nostalgic feeling of days long past.

TELEGRAPH HILL

From Union Street, head east up Telegraph Hill.

If you live in or visit San Francisco regularly, there is probably one place that symbolizes for you what this city is all about. For some it's Fisherman's Wharf, for others it's Union Square, for some eccentrics it may be Alcatraz. For kissing, I nominate Telegraph Hill.

The top of Telegraph Hill is where the famous **COIT TOWER** presides over the city. This fluted, reinforced concrete column was built in 1933 and is noted for its interior murals that depict historic San Francisco scenes. An elevator takes visitors to the top of the tower, and from this vantage point you get a sense of the city's passionate personality and dynamic energy, as well as its orderly, well-contained physique. You will also be exposed to a lot of other sightseers, who may obscure the view and reduce your hope for a romantic measure of time. But then again, when you actually witness the sights and sounds from this pinnacle, you may find that the crowds around you don't seem to matter. It's worth the try!

◆ **Romantic Suggestion:** When you've finished admiring this hallowed view, make sure you have made nearby dinner reservations at either **SHADOWS RESTAURANT** or **JULIUS' CASTLE** (see "Restaurant Kissing"). If you haven't, the North Beach area is overflowing with Italian restaurants and Italian bakeries that tantalize the senses.

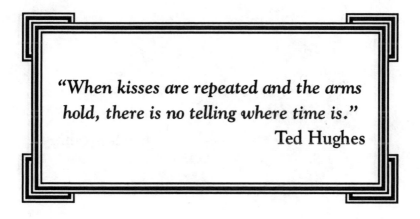

"When kisses are repeated and the arms
hold, there is no telling where time is."
Ted Hughes

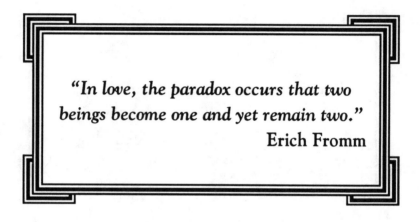

"In love, the paradox occurs that two
beings become one and yet remain two."
Erich Fromm

MARIN COUNTY

The famous Golden Gate Bridge connects San Francisco to the totally separate (but easily accessible) world of Marin County. From the picturesque waterfront towns of Sausalito and Tiburon to the woodsy hills of Mill Valley, Larkspur, and Greenbrae, Marin County offers a little bit of everything for just about everyone. The most wonderful thing is that an escape from the craziness of city life is only a bridge away.

◆ **Romantic Suggestion:** One way to get to Marin without getting stuck in traffic is to take the **GOLDEN GATE FERRY,** (415) 332-6600, which leaves from the San Francisco Ferry Building, located at the foot of Market Street, and makes its way across the bay every day of the week. The more romantic times are during off-peak hours most weekdays, but even when the boat is thick with commuters this is a genuinely San Francisco way to sightsee in the Bay Area.

Sausalito

I once heard someone refer to Sausalito as one big beautiful view of San Francisco, and it's true: this little waterfront town is one of the best vantage points from which to ogle the city skyline. Sausalito is also an enjoyable place to escape the citified hustle and bustle of San Francisco and browse through stylish boutiques, gift stores, and art galleries.

Hotel/Bed and Breakfast Kissing

CASA MADRONA HOTEL, Sausalito ◆ ◆ ◆ ❨
801 Bridgeway
(415) 332-0502, (800) 288-0502
Moderate to Very Expensive
Wedding facilities are available; call for details.

Heading north to Marin County on Highway 101, take the first exit (Alexander Avenue) after you cross the Golden Gate Bridge. This winding road proceeds downhill and automatically connects to Bridgeway. The hotel is located on the left side of the road, after the second traffic light in town.

Casa Madrona's Victorian-style property meanders up a residential hillside set above Sausalito Bay. As you climb to your accommodations on the tiered walkway, this multilayered hotel reveals every sort of style—from blushingly romantic to endearingly strange. Describing all of the 34 rooms at Casa Madrona would require a book in itself. The two of you need only to decide on the composite you want. You name it and you can find it here, in a variety of combinations: spacious to cozy, French country to contemporary, brilliant sunlit harbor views, skylights, fireplaces, and the list goes on. The rooms display the creative work of no fewer than 16 local designers, and each room is more interesting than the last. Continental breakfast, served in Casa Madrona's elegant dining room with surrounding panoramic views of the bay, is included in the cost of your room.

Restaurant Kissing

ALTA MIRA RESTAURANT, Sausalito   ◆ ◆ ◆
125 Buckley Avenue
(415) 332-1350
Expensive to Very Expensive
Wedding facilities are available; call for details.

Heading north to Marin County on Highway 101, take the first exit (Alexander Avenue) after you cross the Golden Gate Bridge. This winding road proceeds downhill and automatically connects to Bridgeway. Once you enter the town of Sausalito, turn right onto Bay Street. Go to Buckley Avenue, turn right, and follow the signs to the Alta Mira.

A more impressive location for brunch or an afternoon nosh would be hard to find. Tucked away on a hillside overlooking Richardson Harbor and the San Francisco skyline, this terraced restaurant is a prime spot for a leisurely meal together. The beautiful view from up here has become an integral part of the interior. Leave yourselves plenty of time to take in the entire panorama and relish entrées such as fricassee of fresh Maine lobster flamed with cognac and served with caviar (come on, be daring!) or poached Pacific salmon with ginger and black bean sauce.

♦ **Romantic Warning:** The Alta Mira is also well known for its hotel accommodations, though why anyone would want to stay here is beyond me: the hotel has been in desperate need of renovations since the 1960s. The rooms are tacky, the floors creak, the bathrooms aren't big enough for one person, let alone two, and the mildewy smell throughout is fairly unpleasant. Our suggestion is to stay elsewhere and enjoy the view from the restaurant during breakfast, lunch, or dinner.

CASA MADRONA RESTAURANT, Sausalito ◆ ◆ ◆
801 Bridgeway
(415) 331-5888
Moderate to Very Expensive
Wedding facilities are available; call for details.

Heading north to Marin County on Highway 101, take the first exit (Alexander Avenue) after you cross the Golden Gate Bridge. This winding road proceeds downhill and automatically connects to Bridgeway. The restaurant is located in the Casa Madrona Hotel, on the left side of the road, after the second traffic light in town.

Even if you can't stay overnight at the lovely Casa Madrona Hotel, a meal at the restaurant here is a heart-stirring alternative. The simply adorned dining area has a remarkable panoramic view of Sausalito Bay, and the visual refreshment outside the windows will complement your meal. All of the tables have glorious views, but the tables nearest the windows have it all. The eclectic cuisine, with Mediterranean influences, is beautifully prepared. After you've dined, take a stroll through the town of Sausalito. Or, if you are staying at the hotel, stroll back to your private, individualized haven at Casa Madrona.

♦ **Romantic Note:** Lunch is served Monday through Saturday, dinner nightly, and brunch on Sunday.

SCOMA'S, Sausalito
588 Bridgeway
(415) 332-9551
Moderate

Heading north to Marin County on Highway 101, take the first exit (Alexander Avenue) after you cross the Golden Gate Bridge. This winding road proceeds downhill and automatically connects to Bridgeway. Continue on Bridgeway to the restaurant, on the right side of the road.

The dynamite location on the shore of Sausalito is what makes Scoma's a sure spot for an enticing encounter. Classic seafood dishes are served in two nautical-inspired dining rooms. The tables in the glass-enclosed dining room promise a breathtaking view from every seat. After dinner, walk along the shore (the pace may depend on how much you ate) to watch the moon's reflection on the water, a spectacular way to end the evening.

◆ **Romantic Alternative: HORIZON'S,** 558 Bridgeway, Sausalito, (415) 331-3232, (Moderate), has a more casual atmosphere that offers the same outstanding, expansive view as Scoma's. The dark wood interior is fronted by a wall of windows that open onto a deck poised directly over the bay. From here you can survey the entire area, from the Bay Bridge to the home-covered hills of Tiburon. A hot cup of coffee or cocktails from this vantage point could turn out to be an inspiring affair.

THE SPINNAKER, Sausalito   ◆ ◆
100 Spinnaker Drive
(415) 332-1500
Moderate

Take Highway 101 north across the Golden Gate Bridge to Alexander Avenue. Follow Alexander Avenue to the east until it becomes Bridgeway. Continue following Bridgeway to Anchor Street and turn right. Anchor Street becomes Spinnaker Drive; the restaurant is at the end of the road.

Situated on a rocky point next to the Sausalito Yacht Harbor, the Spinnaker Restaurant enjoys the best views of Sausalito and the distant San Francisco cityscape. Windows span the entire length of one wall, from floor to ceiling, looking out onto the bay. During the day, you can watch sailboats and ships slip by on the horizon against the picturesque backdrop of the city skyline. At night, when it is clear, the city lights are dazzling. The varied menu includes seafood, poultry, and beef for dinner; salads, sandwiches, and light meals for lunch. The food is always satisfying, but also always secondary to the splendid setting, where couples can and should fill up on romance.

♦ **Romantic Alternative: THE CHART HOUSE,** 201 Bridgeway, Sausalito, (415) 332-0804, (Moderate to Expensive), may be a name you know. Most major cities have one. But I've never seen a Chart House with a better view than the one in Sausalito, which is right on the water. Huge picture windows frame the bay and the San Francisco skyline, the food is always good, and in my opinion the salad bar at the Chart House is the best in the Bay Area.

Outdoor Kissing

MARIN HEADLANDS
Northwest of the Golden Gate Bridge
(415) 331-1540

From the north: Heading south on Highway 101, take the last Sausalito exit. Follow signs to the park. From the south: Heading north on Highway 101, take the Alexander Avenue exit and follow San Francisco signs under the freeway, then follow signs to the park.

What is it about the Golden Gate Bridge that evokes passion in all who see it? Find out for yourselves by visiting the Marin Headlands. A precipitous road hugs the cliff above this graceful sculpture of a bridge. Several viewpoints are perfect for windblown kisses before the Golden Gate, with the San Francisco skyline as a backdrop. The scene is truly magical when fog rolls in, cradling the arching span and city skyscrapers in cottony billows of mist. Intrepid romantics can continue on the winding road to the edge of the Pacific, hike inland to secluded, grassy picnic spots, or comb rocky beaches for sea-swept caresses.

RODEO BEACH AT THE MARIN HEADLANDS
(415) 331-1540

Head north from San Francisco on Highway 101. Take the Alexander Avenue exit and follow San Francisco signs under the freeway, then follow signs to the Marin Headlands. At Bunker Road continue three miles to the beach.

This expanse of white sandy beach is not a secret among locals, but you can be effectively alone during most weekdays before summer vacation releases eager kids from the classroom. A more beautiful scenic area for rambling through surf cannot be found so near to San Francisco. Colored stones of jasper and agate are scattered along the shore. Bird Island, just a short distance from shore, is often blanketed with fluttering white seabirds. In the distance, rolling hills and jagged cliffs make distinguished tableaux against the bright blue sky. There are plenty of hiking trails nearby that lead over intriguing terrain to breathtaking overviews of the area. You won't be at a loss for ways to spend time here; you only need to be prepared for sun, wind, and long, loving hours together.

◆ **Romantic Note:** GOLDEN GATE NATIONAL RECRE-ATION AREA, (415) 331-1540, contains more than 70,000 acres of protected coastline, pristine woodland, mountain terrain, rugged hillsides, and meticulously maintained city parks. To say that there is a diverse assortment of places to discover here is at best an understatement. It is hard to believe that such a massive refuge can exist so close to San Francisco. Hiking, picnicking, swimming, or any other outdoor activity you can think of is possible in this awesome stretch of land with something for the most ardent wilderness lovers or tamest urban dwellers. It is simply there for your pleasure, provided by Mother Nature and the Golden Gate National Park Association.

◆ **Romantic Possibility:** Nearby **MUIR BEACH STATE PARK** is a well-frequented expanse of white sandy shoreline. While too much smooching is probably out of the question, you can still claim your own spot, lie back, listen to the ocean's serene rhythms, and concentrate on each other.

Mill Valley

Restaurant Kissing

EL PASEO, Mill Valley   ◆ ◆ ◆ ◆
17 Throckmorton
(415) 388-0741
Expensive
Wedding facilities are available for a maximum of 55 people.

Take Highway 101 north to the East Blithedale off-ramp. Follow East Blithedale about two miles to Throckmorton and turn left. The restaurant is tucked away in the back of the building.

The Spanish name is very misleading: El Paseo is anything but the cantina your mind conjures up. Instead, it's one of the loveliest, most intimate *French* restaurants in Northern California. The deep, rich decor and the dining room's brick walls reflect European elegance and style. A candlelight dinner at one of the cozy tables for two is an experience in indulgence. Among the fine offerings from the menu are escargots with blue cheese butter, roast baby rack of lamb with rosemary, and a dark and white chocolate mousse. The restaurant has won a number of culinary awards, and deserves them all. El Paseo also deserves a prize for romance. You'll find this delightful restaurant a wonderful environment for kisses and other expressions of love.

◆ **Romantic Alternative: PIAZZA D'ANGELO**, 22 Miller Avenue, Mill Valley, (415) 388-2000, (Moderate), is another great place for lunch, dinner, or brunch on the weekend, if you are in the mood for Italian. It's more modern in appearance, with red tile floors, track lighting, textured walls, and windows framed with blond wood. Open kitchens to the side allow the scent of Piazza D'Angelo's delicious individual pizzas, pasta specialties, and meat dishes to tantalize and entice you. And the food tastes as good as it smells. On warm days the restaurant sets up tables on the patio for dining in the sunshine.

MOUNTAIN HOME INN RESTAURANT, Mill Valley ❖ ❖ ❖
810 Panoramic Highway
(415) 381-9000
Moderate to Expensive
Wedding facilities are available, call for details.

Drive north on Highway 101 to Stinson Beach, take the Highway 1 exit, and turn left onto Highway 1. In three miles turn right onto Panoramic Highway and proceed to the inn.

Situated on the north side of Mount Tamalpais, the Mountain Home Inn Restaurant stands guard over the surrounding East Bay hills, the Tiburon peninsula, San Francisco, and Mount Diablo. In this handsome, refurbished lodge, with redwood vaulted ceilings and huge windows, excellent food and sublime views combine to create a rare treat among dining experiences. Soups, salads, and sandwiches are the specialties at lunchtime, and dinner continues in similar continental fashion with menu items like grilled filet mignon and pan-fried rainbow trout. The restaurant is closed on Mondays.

◆ Romantic Note: MOUNTAIN HOME INN, 810 Panoramic Highway, Mill Valley, (415) 381-9000, (Expensive to Very Expensive), has ten cozy guest rooms, several of which boast their own fireplace, whirlpool or large soaking tub, and deck. A mountain lodge motif is attempted in every room, with wood-paneled walls and views of purple mountain majesty. A full breakfast is included in your stay, but the rooms unfortunately have a somewhat standard, hotel-like feel.

◆ Additional Romantic Note: MOUNT TAMALPAIS and nearby MUIR WOODS are ideal for a variety of day hikes (see "Outdoor Kissing"). If a day outdoors, high above the city, sounds like fun, you're in close proximity after brunch or lunch at Mountain Home Inn. It also means that weekends are insanely busy there since all the other outdoor enthusiasts are out in full force and there are no other restaurants in the vicinity.

Outdoor Kissing

MUIR WOODS AND MOUNT TAMALPAIS   ◆ ◆ ◆ ◆
Panoramic Highway
(415) 388-2070
Wedding facilities are available; call for details.

Take Highway 101 north to Marin County. Turn off at the Stinson Beach Highway 1 exit and follow the signs for Muir Woods and Mount Tamalpais.

If you long to be secluded and near nature, you need only cross the Golden Gate Bridge into Marin County and drive along Highway 1 to the crest of Mount Tamalpais. This is without question one of the most absorbing drives in the area. The S-curved road coils along the edge of this windswept highland, and each turn exposes another vantage point from which to scan the scenery: the land cascading down to Marin; the pattern of overlapping hills. As you continue your excursion, you can choose to remain in the car or venture out into the hills with a *fete champetre* (picnic) in hand. Here, in the midst of earth's simple gifts, a loaf of bread, a jug of wine, and thou are all you need.

♦ **Romantic Suggestion:** The **STEEP RAVINE TRAIL**, which begins at the Pantoll Station on the Panoramic Highway, is a magnificent deep-forest journey to views of the ocean and bay. This one is my sister's romantic favorite, and she ought to know: the idea for this book was hers.

Tiburon

Tiburon has the bright distinction of being the sunny spot of the Bay Area. Not always, but on many days, when other parts of San Francisco and Marin County are veiled in fog, Tiburon is basking in sunshine. The main part of town is located along the water, where restaurants and shops provide plenty of things for you to see and do during your visit here.

Restaurant Kissing

CAPRICE RESTAURANT, Tiburon
2000 Paradise Drive
(415) 435-3400
Expensive
Wedding facilities are available for a maximum of 130 people.

Do not take the Paradise Drive exit from Highway 101. Instead, take the Tiburon Boulevard exit (Route 131), which turns into Paradise Drive once you enter the town of Tiburon. Follow this road along the water to the end of Waterfront Park; the restaurant is on the right.

The stone embankment that the Caprice is built into has been incorporated into the homey wood-frame architecture. The natural rock is now a massive stone fireplace on the lower level where, if you arrive early for your reservation, you can relax in a warm, hobbit-like setting. (If you plan to do this, make sure there isn't a function scheduled—the lower level doubles as a banquet room.) The dining room, warmed by a radiating fireplace, sits snugly above the gently swirling waters of Raccoon Strait. Large windows allow unobstructed views of Angel Island, San

Francisco, and the Golden Gate Bridge in the distance. Lunch here is a fairly casual affair, but dinner can be an enamored event. The creative international cuisine is wonderful. Just thinking of the sesame-crusted salmon with spicy shrimp raviolis and orange tamari glaze makes my mouth water. It would be difficult for you not to give in to the loving atmosphere this place generates.

◆ **Romantic Note:** The Caprice is especially popular on weekends, which means you must make reservations. Also, service can be slow when they are busy.

◆ **Romantic Suggestion:** After brunch or an early dinner, continue up Paradise Drive until you reach **PARADISE BEACH PARK**. This quiet, wooded little corner of the world overlooks the distant hills beyond the bay and the San Rafael Bridge. Depending on the time of day and season, this place could be yours alone, and there is enough strolling and picnicking turf here to make it a significant lovers' point of interest.

GUAYMAS, Tiburon   ◆ ◀
5 Main Street
(415) 435-6300
Inexpensive to Moderate

From Highway 101, take the Tiburon Boulevard exit (Route 131) and follow Tiburon Boulevard east about five miles to Main Street. Guaymas is on the corner.

In every way, Guaymas reflects a south-of-the-border feel and flavor. The restaurant, named for a Mexican fishing town, emphasizes authenticity instead of Americanized versions of Mexican food. Menu selections include tamales or pork wrapped in banana leaves, fresh fish served with guero chile-tomato butter, and green poblano chiles stuffed with chicken and raisins. Some dishes may sound more exotic than your taste buds would care to sample, but they are all truly delicious. You can choose a table in the contemporary adobe dining room, which is accented with bright colors and a corner fireplace, or one outside on the waterfront deck. The patios are heated with gas warmers, making them pleasant even on cool nights. During the day, the stunning view of the bay and San Francisco makes outdoor dining even more irresistible. In this casual setting you'll find that sitting back, enjoying the view, and relaxing is very easy to do. All this, and you get a great meal!

◆ **Romantic Note:** Guaymas is located next to the ferry landing, making it a nice excursion from San Francisco. Be sure to check the departure schedules both in the city and in Tiburon so you won't get stuck without a way back.

SAM'S ANCHOR CAFE, Tiburon
27 Main Street
(415) 435-4527
Inexpensive

From Highway 101, take the Tiburon Boulevard exit (Route 131) and follow Tiburon Boulevard east about five miles to Main Street. Sam's is to the right.

Deck dining is incredibly popular in this small community, and no doubt why people come from miles away to have lunch at Sam's. The waterfront deck is right next to a yacht harbor; miles beyond, the city of San Francisco is its backdrop. Casual fare—burgers, omelets, and salads—in a casual setting—blue-and-white-checked vinyl cloths and plastic chairs—are what you should expect here. In fact, this place is so casual, the sea gulls aren't shy about sharing your french fries if you aren't paying attention to your plate. But that comfortable atmosphere is just what makes kissing at Sam's so special. There is no proper etiquette to adhere to, no refined rules, just the sun, the sea, the breeze, and your desire to enjoy a warm afternoon together.

◆ **Romantic Note:** Sam's also has an inside dining area for cold days and the dinner hour. In the evening, the menu features pasta, seafood, and light entrées.

◆ **Romantic Alternative:** Several other restaurants offer deck dining along Main Street. **MR. Q'S**, 25 Main Street, Tiburon, (415) 435-5088, (Inexpensive to Moderate), has the advantage of a second story from which to enjoy the view, but its food, ranging from egg dishes to seafood and baby back ribs, is inconsistent.

◆ **Romantic Option:** Marin County is blessed with several outdoor sanctuaries. If you're in Tiburon, stop by the **RICHARDSON BAY AUDUBON CENTER**, 376 Greenwood Beach Road, Tiburon, (415) 388-2524. The charmingly restored Victorian house is picture-perfect in its setting by the gentle bay waters. A short loop trail leads you up to the crest of a hill for scenic kissing before a lofty panorama of Angel Island, San Francisco, Sausalito, and the coastal mountains.

Larkspur

Restaurant Kissing

LARK CREEK INN, Larkspur ◆ ◆ ◆
234 Magnolia Avenue
(415) 924-7766
Moderate
Wedding facilities are available; call for details.

Take Highway 101 to the Mount Tamalpais/Paradise Drive exit. Go west on Mount Tamalpais for about one mile, then turn right on Corte Madera Avenue, which becomes Magnolia Avenue. The restaurant is a half mile down on the right.

As you wind through the remote wooded neighborhoods of Larkspur, you may be surprised to see this yellow frame home on what would otherwise be another curve in an out-of-the-way country road. Though this place feels remote, it is one of the more renowned dining spots in the North Bay. Lark Creek Inn deserves its reputation, and, in spite of its popularity, the environment is still conducive to a romantic interlude. The interior is highlighted by a glass-domed ceiling shaded by lofty redwoods. When the weather warms, the restaurant's garden, situated near a babbling creek, serves as an extension to the dining room. The only thing left to mention is the food. Dishes like oak-grilled salmon steak with avocado-tomato salad and chèvre vinaigrette, and grilled double-cut pork chops with skillet cheddar potatoes, braised red cabbage, and plum butter combine the best aspects of traditional and contemporary American cooking. Sheer heaven most of the time, and merely excellent the rest of the time.

REMILLARD'S, Larkspur ◆ ◆ ◀
125 East Sir Francis Drake Boulevard
(415) 461-3700
Expensive to Very Expensive
Wedding facilities are available; call for details.

From the north: Take Highway 101 to the Sir Francis Drake Boulevard exit. Follow Sir Francis Drake Boulevard east. From the south: Take Highway 101 to the Richmond Bridge/San Anselmo exit. Follow the signs to the Richmond Bridge until you are on East Sir Francis Drake Boulevard.

The structure that houses Remillard's was built more than a hundred years ago. Back then it was the Green Brae Brick Kiln, and it supplied bricks for such San Francisco landmarks as Ghirardelli Square, the Cannery, and the St. Francis Hotel. Now, a century later, and after more than a million dollars in renovations, Remillard's retains its historic charm while offering all the contemporary advantages of a fine French restaurant. The dining room, constructed of solid brick walls and ceiling, is shaped like a large tunnel. As you'd expect in such a place, it's dark, but low light is reflected off the walls from sconces and from candles on the tables. White linens and exotic flowers brighten the room a bit more. Though the restaurant is rather large, the tables are situated to provide a cozy and quaint feeling. The French cuisine receives high praise from food critics and from customers. The kitchen creates fantastic sauces, and those who know the menu well suggest the fresh poached salmon in a chive sauce or the fillet of beef with green peppercorns and calvados sauce. The dessert soufflés are decadent, but to pass them over would be a shame. Instead, order one and linger for a while in a place where the past provides the setting for modern-day romance.

Greenbrae

Restaurant Kissing

JOE LOCOCO'S, Greenbrae
300 Drakes Landing Road
(415) 925-0808
Moderate to Expensive
Wedding facilities are available; call for details.

Take Highway 101 to Sir Francis Drake Boulevard. Follow Sir Francis Drake Boulevard west to Barry Way and turn left. Go one block and turn left onto Drakes Landing Road.

An irresistible aroma fills the air as you enter Joe LoCoco's. As you pass the open kitchen, you cannot doubt that you will be totally satisfied with your meal. And then, as you look ahead into the dining room, you will also be pleased with the thoroughly romantic atmosphere. The restaurant is bathed in the soft glow of candlelight and pastel hues. The decor is contemporary and artistic, with peach-colored walls adorned with paintings. Exquisite floral arrangements add another gentle touch of color. Large windows open to the water and views of Mount Tamalpais during the day. At night, the deep darkness outside contrasts beautifully with the pretty interior. The Italian dishes served here are hearty, not heavy. The kitchen turns out marvelous homemade pastas, delicious wild game, and fresh seafood dishes.

◆ **Romantic Note:** Because the restaurant has such a great reputation, reservations are almost always needed at dinner. Make yours well in advance when planning a special evening out. The restaurant is also open for lunch.

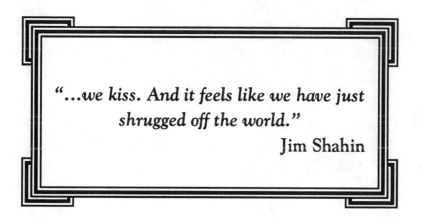

"...we kiss. And it feels like we have just shrugged off the world."

Jim Shahin

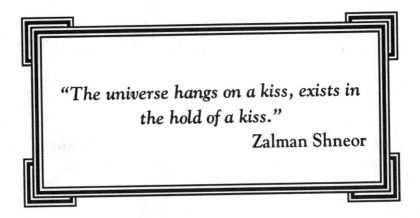

"The universe hangs on a kiss, exists in
the hold of a kiss."
Zalman Shneor

EAST BAY

Oakland and Berkeley

Hotel/Bed and Breakfast Kissing

THE CLAREMONT HOTEL
AND TENNIS CLUB, Oakland   ◆ ❖
Ashby and Domingo avenues
(510) 843-3000
Expensive to Very Expensive
Wedding facilities are available for a maximum of 250 people.

From San Francisco, take the Bay Bridge to Highway 24 east. Exit at Claremont Avenue, turn left at the bottom of the exit onto Claremont, and then right onto Ashby Avenue. The hotel is on the left after the fifth stoplight.

Nestled in the Berkeley Hills and enfolded by acres of deftly cultivated gardens and palm trees, this colossal plantation-style mansion is reminiscent of a European castle. Epic in scale and style, the hotel's exterior can appear overbearing and impersonal if you have something smaller and more intimate in mind. We usually shy away from recommending large flashy resorts—even when the large flashy resort has everything we want. The problem with resorts is that they lend themselves to conventions and tour groups. There's something about feeling like part of a software association's annual meeting that doesn't exactly make you feel like kissing. As you might have already guessed, this famous hotel and tennis club is an exception to that rule . . . in its own way.

The Claremont definitely attracts its share of businesspeople (87 percent of its clientele, in fact), but don't let this staggering statistic deter you from seeking romantic possibilities here. Guests at the Claremont have the opportunity to engage in any and all of the available indoor and outdoor activities, and there are many. Tennis courts, an Olympic-size swimming pool, a nearby golf course, saunas, hot tubs, a state-of-the-art exercise room, a fully equipped weight-training room, and a spa and fitness center offer invigorating ways to spend the day getting healthy together. (The best news is that the convention goers are usually more interested in business than in getting healthy—these amenities are often exclusively yours for the taking.)

Following a full day of athletic playtime, you can return to the comfort of your room. Most are fairly nondescript and hotel ordinary, though still attractive, with views of Berkeley's hills, the lovely garden grounds, or the distant San Francisco skyline.

◆ **Romantic Suggestion: THE PAVILION RESTAURANT** (see "Restaurant Kissing"), located downstairs next to the hotel lobby, is a convenient dinner option and offers spectacular distant views of the San Francisco Bay.

DOCKSIDE BOAT & BED, Oakland
77 Jack London Square
(510) 444-5858, (800) 4-DOCKSIDE
Moderate to Unbelievably Expensive

From Interstate 880 south, take the Jackson Street exit and turn right at the first light onto Jackson. At the second stop sign, turn right onto Third Street. Drive three blocks and turn left onto Webster Street. Enter the parking lot across the street from the Old-Fashioned Spaghetti House and bear left to Jack London Square.

Whether you fancy sailboats or luxury motor yachts, you can kiss like a millionaire (at least for an evening) on your boat of choice in this industrial, though surprisingly quiet, Oakland port of call. Our 35-foot sailboat would have been a dream come true if the intimate accommodations had been less rustic and confining. More spacious boats cruise into the Unbelievably Expensive category, but can still be a better way to go if you're willing to share the romance of the evening with another like-minded couple. Complete with several private staterooms, modern furnishings (including stereos), and private baths, a large yacht can provide ample space and privacy for two couples. If you wish, a candlelight catered dinner can be served on board, and continental breakfast, packed in a picnic basket, is delivered to your boat in the morning.

◆ **Romantic Suggestion:** The catered dinners are extra and can be quite expensive. Another option is to stroll through the picturesque marina to one of the many (less expensive) restaurants and cafes clustered along this waterfront.

GRAMMA'S ROSE GARDEN INN, Berkeley
2740 Telegraph Avenue
(510) 549-2145
Moderate to Expensive

From San Francisco, take the Bay Bridge east and then stay on Interstate 80 to the Ashby Avenue exit. Turn right onto Ashby and then left onto Telegraph Avenue.

A name like "Gramma's Inn" might not conjure up romantic images for you, but don't be too quick to judge. After all, what's in a name—beside letters?

This Tudor-style bed and breakfast actually comprises five restored mansions, cottages, and carriage houses set just off busy Telegraph Avenue, in a neighborhood that should take the hint and renovate itself. Though some of the rooms are a little worn around the edges, all of them have been lovingly enhanced with antique furnishings and thick hand-sewn quilts. Some of the suites overlook the garden, others have private decks or fireplaces, and one has stained glass windows that encompass the entire room. The only romantic warning here is that some of the rooms share baths. Be sure to ask for one with private facilities if that's one of your kissing requirements.

You won't find fault with the elaborate wine and cheese plate set out in the afternoon or the respectable breakfast of baked breads and homemade preserves.

◆ **Romantic Option:** Gramma's Rose Garden Inn is so close to the **UNIVERSITY OF CALIFORNIA AT BERKELEY** that you shouldn't miss the opportunity to see this beautiful campus, set beneath the Berkeley Hills. It is a lovely place for a picnic, particularly in the summer, when the student population dwindles significantly.

WATERFRONT PLAZA HOTEL, Oakland
Ten Washington Street, at Jack London Square
(510) 836-3800, (800) 729-3638
Expensive to Very Expensive

From Interstate 880 north, take the Broadway exit. Follow Broadway to the second light and turn left onto Washington Street. The hotel is at the end of Washington Street.

A romance package designed just for kissing is the year-round specialty at this recently opened hotel harbored along Oakland's industrial waterfront. Champagne and chocolate-dipped strawberries are the prelude to an amorous stay in a spacious waterfront view room. (Be sure to request a room with a view—not all of them have one.) For a little extra, you can also indulge in a suite with a gas fireplace. Bleached pine furnishings, televisions, VCRs, mini-bars, coffee makers, a fitness center, a sauna, and a pool are all provided to ensure that the only thing you need to make the scene complete is your love. In the morning, a continental breakfast is delivered to your room. You're also given two complimentary nightshirts, which, in this setting, are most likely to go home with you unworn.

◆ **Romantic Warning:** In spite of the romance packages offered here, this hotel draws an almost exclusively business-oriented clientele. You are likely to be the only two people here with something other than business on your mind.

Restaurant Kissing

CHEZ PANISSE, Berkeley
1517 Shattuck Avenue
(510) 548-5525
Expensive

From San Francisco take the Bay Bridge east; stay on Highway 80 until you reach the University Avenue exit and turn right. Drive for two miles and turn left onto Shattuck Avenue; drive for five and a half blocks to the restaurant on the right-hand side of the road.

Many restaurant reviewers say that if you eat out only once in San Francisco, Chez Panisse should be the place—even though it happens to be in Berkeley. Well, far be it from us to argue with the edible truth. If delicious French cuisine is your idea of a romantic meal and you happen to be on the other side of the bridge (and you can get reservations), the food and atmosphere are worth your while.

Chez Panisse offers two dining alternatives with two entirely different menus. The first is an upstairs cafe that offers a more casual à la carte menu (soups, salads, and a limited selection of entrées). Our favorite dining spot here was a cozy alcove set aglow with lanterns and filled with a handful of tables. The other choice is the downstairs dining room, which has similar decor but a much more elaborate prix fixe menu that might include an aperitif, a salad of prawns and wild mushrooms with saffron, artichokes and duck liver with a foie gras sauce, grilled guinea hen breast with riesling sauce, and citrus compote with Lavender Gem sherbet.

◆ **Romantic Warning:** Did we mention that you may have to book your reservations a month in advance, particularly if you want to dine on a weekend?

IL PESCATORE, Oakland ◗ ◗
57 Jack London Square
(510) 465-2188
Moderate
Wedding facilities are available on Mondays only
for a maximum of 150 people.

From San Francisco take the Bay Bridge east, look for Interstate 580 (which connects with Interstate 980 west), and head to downtown Oakland. Take the Jackson Street exit, drive to Oak Street, and turn right. Drive one-half mile to Embarcadaro Street, turn right, go another half mile to Franklin Street, and turn left. The restaurant is straight ahead.

While the twinkle of harbor lights is reflected on the water and yachts rock just outside the window, this Italian eatery serves up a touch of magic in the evenings. White linen tablecloths and crystal wine goblets add a dash of elegance, while the nautical theme and friendly, down-to-earth staff remain refreshingly unpretentious. Tender carpaccio (thin slices of raw beef served with sauce) provided the perfect start to our dinner, which continued with pasta topped with a scrumptious ground veal and prosciutto sauce. Seafood entrées featuring calamari steak, salmon, and scallops will tease your appetite for more waterfront romance.

KINCAID'S BAYHOUSE, Oakland
1 Franklin Street, Jack London Square
(510) 835-8600
Moderate

From San Francisco take the Bay Bridge east, look for Interstate 580 (which connects with Interstate 980 west) and head to downtown Oakland. Take the Jackson Street exit, drive to Oak Street, and turn right. Drive one-half mile to Embarcadaro Street, turn right, go another half mile to Franklin Street, and turn left. The restaurant is straight ahead.

A veritable waterborne parade of sailboats, tugs, motor yachts, and even a seal passed by on the estuary outside our window as we enjoyed yakisoba noodles with grilled chicken in this sunny lunch spot perched on the end of a wharf. Both the menu and decor are ultra-modern and eclectic, a blend of East meets West meets Caribbean.

◆ Romantic Warning: After dark, the loud music and singles atmosphere in the restaurant's swinging lounge seem to overwhelm the quiet waterfront ambience. We found it too distracting for a romantic dinner for two.

THE PAVILION, Oakland
Ashby and Domingo avenues,
at the Claremont Hotel and Tennis Club
(510) 843-3000
Expensive to Very Expensive
Wedding facilities are available for a maximum of 250 people.

From San Francisco, take the Bay Bridge to Highway 24 east. Exit at Claremont Avenue, turn left onto Claremont, then right onto Ashby.

Unless pink is your favorite color, the Pavilion's dining room might be too much for you. The designers got a little carried away with their art-deco theme and splashed pink everywhere they could, from the tablecloths to the pink flamingo art adorning the walls. Fortunately, stirring views of palm trees and San Francisco's distant skyline, visible from nearly every table, take your mind off the flamboyant decor. The menu is fairly limited, but the club sandwiches, seafood, pasta, and steaks are prime.

RESTAURANT METROPOLE, Berkeley   ◆ ◆ ◆ ❪
2271 Shattuck Avenue
(510) 848-3080
Moderate
Wedding facilities are available for a maximum of 90 people.

From San Francisco take the Bay Bridge east; stay on Highway 80 to University Avenue and turn right. Follow University Avenue to Shattuck Avenue. The restaurant is four blocks down on the left-hand side.

Now *this* is my kind of romantic. A fire crackles in the stone hearth of the cozy wood-and-brick dining room, reminiscent of a country chalet with its wood pillars and high open-beam ceiling. Lovely still-life paintings, colorful fabrics, and fresh potted flowers at every table add to the dining room's charm. High-backed cushioned booths offer the most privacy (you'll be kissing in a moment's time), but all of the tables are good places to enjoy such delicacies as crêpes bursting with prawns, scallops, spinach, and mushrooms. Save room for a rich slice of chocolate obsession cake set on a bed of raspberry sauce. Utterly delicious!

SKATES ON THE BAY, Berkeley   ◆ ◆ ❪
100 Seawall Drive
(510) 549-1900
Moderate

From San Francisco take the Bay Bridge east and stay on Interstate 80 north to the University exit. Make a (legal) U-turn at the first stoplight and head back in the opposite direction. You will come to a fork in the road at the marina. Stay to your left, and where the road dead-ends, turn right into the restaurant's parking lot.

San Francisco has one of the world's most stunning skylines. One way to really appreciate it is to go east across the Bay Bridge and look back across the water. From Skates on the Bay, you can observe the Golden City's dazzling profile, defined by the expansive blue bay and steep urban hills lined with steel-and-glass skyscrapers. The view from here is no secret—you're likely to find yourselves competing for reservations and dining among crowds. Thank goodness the food is good (we loved the Cajun fettuccine and fresh focaccia) and the ambience is a respectable blend of modern and quaint. You'll be tempted to stay for dessert so you can linger over the city's lights and revel in each other's company a little longer.

◆ **Romantic Suggestion:** After dinner, leave the crowds behind and walk along the water's edge to a nearby pier jutting out into the bay. Follow your instincts to the end of the dock, where the city skyline beckons to you from across the bay. This is one of the best places to kiss we've found yet.

Outdoor Kissing

BERKELEY MUNICIPAL ROSE GARDEN, Berkeley ◆◆◆◆

From San Francisco, take the Bay Bridge east and stay on Interstate 80 going north. Take the University exit and turn right. Go straight to Shattuck Avenue and turn left. At Hearst Street, turn right. From here your last turn is a left onto Euclid, which you follow to the top of the hill.

The Berkeley Rose Garden is an enchanting realm filled with color and fragrance. From its upper level you can gaze over an amphitheater of nature's splendor. As you make your way down the stairs, passing one rosebush after another, the scented air surrounds you. This is prime kissing territory (especially in the summer). The sedate setting is so expansive that even when others are around, you can almost always find an empty park bench. You can spend a few moments (or hours) enjoying views of acre after flawlessly beautiful acre of this earthly paradise.

LAKE MERRITT, Oakland

From San Francisco, take the Bay Bridge to Interstate 880 south, then take the Broadway exit east. From Broadway, turn right onto Grand, which eventually winds its way into the park.

Ask anyone in the East Bay area if downtown Oakland has any amorous potential and you'll probably hear the same answer: "No!" During my research, one person said, "Oakland is a pit," a response that was brief but to the point. If you ask about Lake Merritt, however, people tend to whistle a different tune. Surrounded by 155-acre Lakeside Park, Lake Merritt is located in, yes, downtown Oakland. Its surprising setting is ideal for picnicking, strolling, canoeing, or any of a myriad outdoor activities. Autumn, when the leaves slowly change and frame the lake in vibrant shades of gold and orange, is perhaps the best time to discover this city oasis.

Start an afternoon here with a picnic near the water, then try a sailing lesson or maybe take a tour on a miniature stern-wheeler. At **CHILDREN'S FAIRYLAND**, which attracts as many adults as kids, puppet shows, amusement rides, and scenes from your favorite fairy tales come alive and provide ebullient diversions. Don't be too disappointed when you find the afternoon has slipped away while many sections of this domain remain unexplored. You'll have to return a few times to see it all, but that leaves you with something to look forward to next time you happen to be near downtown Oakland.

TILDEN REGIONAL PARK, Berkeley Hills
(510) 525-2233
Wedding facilities are available for a maximum of 250 people.

From Oakland take Highway 24 through the Caldecut Tunnel. Drive to Fish Ranch Road and follow this to Grizzly Peak Boulevard. Look for entrance signs to Tilden on the right; several entrances are located along Grizzly Peak.

Nature's majesty is always close at hand in the Bay Area. Tilden, one of the most expansive and convenient of the region's earthy getaways, encompasses more than 2,000 acres of forested trails, gardens, and picnic grounds. A hand-in-hand stroll at the park's Botanic Garden is a fine first step to romance. Peaceful trails wind through terraced plantings of native California blooms and trees. Picnic spots abound throughout Tilden; just drive until you find one that suits your fancy. Ardent hikers will find private paradises along the park's paths, along with romantic respite from nearby civilization.

Lafayette and Walnut Creek

Hotel/Bed and Breakfast Kissing

LAFAYETTE PARK HOTEL, Lafayette   ◆ ◆
3287 Mount Diablo Boulevard
(510) 283-3700, (800) 368-2468
Moderate to Expensive
Wedding facilities are available for a maximum of 300 people.

From San Francisco take the Bay Bridge east to Highway 24 east, then take the Pleasant Hill Road exit to Mount Diablo Boulevard and turn right.

From the freeway the Lafayette Park Hotel looked like an impressive Swiss chalet, but because it was visible from the highway we were worried. After all, a love nest that borders a highway or a busy road is potentially a pigeonhole when it comes to romance. In this case, however, our skepticism was unfounded. The moment our weekend here began, we forgot the freeway even existed.

High above the lobby, skylights illuminate a hand-carved staircase that winds its way down three stories. A profusion of fresh flowers brought soft color and life to the elegant decor. Our brightly appointed room had a vaulted ceiling and a wood-burning fireplace, though we were disappointed with the thin bedspreads and standard furnishings. Exploring further, we found three charming courtyards: one was built around an Italian marble fountain, another surrounded a stone wishing well, and the third had a large swimming pool and a whirlpool spa. Adjacent to the lobby is the **DUCK CLUB RESTAURANT**, which offers an admirable dining experience. After dinner, a latte or cappuccino in the lounge, near the cobblestone fireplace, is a wonderful way to round out the evening.

THE MANSION AT LAKEWOOD, Walnut Creek
1056 Hacienda Drive
(510) 946-9075
Moderate to Very Expensive
Wedding facilities are available for a maximum of 80 people.

From Interstate 680, exit at Ygnacio Valley Road. Continue through seven signals to turn right onto Homestead. About two blocks up, turn left onto Hacienda.

Grand, immaculately white wrought-iron gates open to allow passage into this mansion's three-acre inner sanctum. Deer crafted of grapevines are set on the lawn beside the front entrance, and they are not the only creatures guests will happen upon during their stay. The abundant hand-crafted animals (rabbits in particular) are an integral part of the inn's country theme.

Inside, an impressionistic portrait of the inn hangs above the mantel in the grand Victorian parlor, where a plush settee and comfortable chairs are placed before a wood-burning fireplace. Guest rooms are entirely unique (our room had an original metal vault that now serves as a closet) and highlighted with romantic details, from billowing canopies to private balconies to a cupid fresco. Each of the seven suites has a special attraction. The Terrace Suite is warmed by a white brick hearth. The French doors of the Summer House open to a flowery porch where you can sink into a bubble bath in the claw-foot tub. The irresistible Estate Suite is warmed by a wood stove and has an immense bath with double whirlpools and fluted brass fixtures; after some good clean fun, climb a small platform to reach the four-poster bed, smothered in a goose down comforter. No detail has been overlooked. Over a delicious continental breakfast served in the airy dining room you'll notice that even the glasses are delicately etched with gold.

Restaurant Kissing

MAXIMILLIAN'S, Walnut Creek   ❤ ❤
1604 Locust Street
(510) 932-1474
Moderate to Expensive
Wedding facilities are available for a maximum of 100 people.

From Interstate 680 north take the South Main Exit, which puts you directly on South Main Street. Follow it to Mount Diablo Boulevard and turn left. Go one block and turn right onto Locust. The restaurant is four blocks down on the right.

Maximillian's is really two restaurants in one, and each sports its own dining room, menu, and style. Serious romantics dine upstairs, surrounded by oak paneling and brick walls, at a small handful of tables garnished with candles and long-stemmed pink roses. The French-influenced menu here is wide-ranging and excellent, and if you listen closely you might hear the faint melodies of the downstairs pianist. For better acoustics and a more casual dining atmosphere, many opt for the soft-hued downstairs dining room, where live music is featured Wednesday through Saturday nights. The contemporary California nouvelle cuisine served here is also quite good, particularly the grilled pork tenderloin with butternut squash pancakes and applewood-smoked bacon infusion.

TOURELLE, Lafayette
3565 Mount Diablo Boulevard
(510) 284-3565
Moderate
Wedding facilities are available for a maximum of 200 people.

From San Francisco take the Bay Bridge east and turn onto Highway 24. Take the Central Lafayette exit, turn right at the end of the off-ramp, then turn right again onto Mount Diablo Boulevard. The restaurant is on the left.

A stone path takes you to an ivy-covered tower and two brick homes that are enveloped by a charming courtyard. Here is an engaging place for a leisurely lunch or an intimate evening interlude. On one side of the courtyard is an informal, lively bistro with a glass roof and a big open kitchen; on the other is a beautiful, casually elegant dining room with towering vaulted ceilings, brick walls, and delectable European country cuisine. Selections from their smoker, grill, and oak-fired pizza oven are the specialties here. Dining at Tourelle is like relaxing in the south of France, a terrific feeling to share with someone special.

San Ramon

Restaurant Kissing

MUDD'S, San Ramon
10 Boardwalk
(510) 837-9387
Moderate
Wedding facilities are available for a maximum of 125 people.

From Walnut Creek take Interstate 680 south to the Crow Canyon exit west. Drive one mile and turn left onto Park Place; the restaurant is on the first drive-way on the left.

Neither the name nor the ambience is particularly romantic, but the food is some of the lightest and freshest we've had. Tables adorned with candle lanterns are scattered across two connecting dining rooms with arched wood ceilings and stone floors. While the atmosphere is relatively bland, the food is delicious. The garden lasagne and the charbroiled chicken served with black beans, rice, and spicy tomatillo sauce were enough to convince us to come back again (and again).

Danville

Restaurant Kissing

BRIDGES RESTAURANT, Danville
44 Church Street
(510) 820-7200
Moderate to Expensive

From Highway 24 south, turn onto Interstate 680 south. Take the Diablo Road exit and turn right onto Diablo Road. From Diablo, turn left onto Hartz Road, then turn left again onto Church Street. The restaurant is at the corner of Church and Hartz.

Bridges' Japanese food is so good that it draws overwhelming crowds (which, needless to say, are not the least bit conducive to kissing). The dining room's chic interior is ultra-contemporary and tables are arranged too close together for our romantic taste. You're better off outdoors (at least in the warmer months) on the garden terrace surrounded by trees, a burbling fountain, and strands of tiny white lights. As for the food . . . you've never tasted anything like their grilled Hawaiian opaka-paka with papaya-red pepper salsa and coconut-curry sauce or the three-tiered meal served in a traditional Japanese *bento* box (sautéed white prawns, chicken stir-fried with snow peas and oyster mushrooms, seafood samplers, and a trio of sorbets). After your first savory bite, you probably won't even notice the less-than-amorous crowded surroundings.

Livermore

Outdoor Kissing

LIVERMORE VALLEY   ❖ ❖

Take southbound Interstate 680, exit onto eastbound Interstate 580, and drive to the Livermore Avenue exit.

Escape the citified hustle of the Bay Area in the quiet Livermore Valley's historic wine region. Unlike the Napa and Sonoma valleys, this area has remained relatively undeveloped and serves as a refuge for numerous wineries nestled among rolling hills speckled with oak trees and cattle. A mere hour's drive from nearly anywhere in the Bay Area, the Livermore Valley makes for an ideal kissing excursion.

◆ **Romantic Suggestion:** If the weather makes picnicking impossible, **WENTE BROTHERS RESTAURANT**, 5050 Arroyo Road, Livermore, (510) 447-3696, (Moderate), located at the Wente Brothers Winery, is a recommendable lunch or dinner option in the Livermore Valley. Floor-to-ceiling windows offer views of the surrounding hillsides and vineyards; the service is affable, and the Italian food is quite tasty.

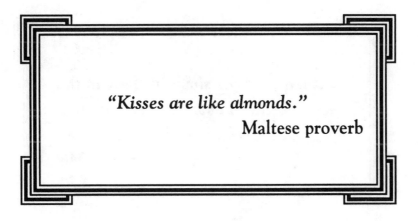

"Kisses are like almonds."

Maltese proverb

"...then I did the simplest thing in the world. I leaned down and kissed him. And the world cracked open."

Agnes de Mille

SOUTH OF SAN FRANCISCO

Palo Alto

Hotel/Bed and Breakfast Kissing

GARDEN COURT HOTEL, Palo Alto ❖ ❖ ❖
520 Cowper Street
(415) 322-9000
Expensive to Very Expensive
Wedding facilities are available for a maximum of 225 people.

From Highway 101 north, exit at University Avenue west; follow to Cowper Street and turn left. The inn is on the immediate right.

Escape downtown Palo Alto's street noise in a Mediterranean-style villa built around an enclosed courtyard. All of the 61 guest rooms here have balconies, many of which overlook the flower-filled courtyard below. Even the rooms that face the busy street are infused with sunlight and laden with luxurious appointments: canopied beds draped with luscious fabrics and plush down comforters, large arched windows, and contemporary furnishings. Four suites have fireplaces and six have Jacuzzis; all abound in romantic potential.

◆ **Romantic Note:** Though we were especially partial to the rooms with courtyard views, we must warn you that they directly face rooms on the opposite side of the hotel. It goes without saying that for the utmost privacy, you'll have to shut the curtains.

Portola Valley

Restaurant Kissing

IBERIA, Portola Valley   ◆ ◆
190 Alpine Road
(415) 854-1746
Moderate to Expensive

*One-fourth mile west of Interstate 280 on Alpine Road at the Country
Shopping Center.*

Don't reread your directions—you're *supposed* to be in a shopping
mall. We admit it's an unusual location for a romantic restaurant, but you
won't have any qualms about being here once the owner of this distinctive Spanish restaurant has greeted you and ushered you to the table of
your choice. Everything about this restaurant is authentically Spanish,
from the ambience to the menu to the wait staff. The dining room is
filled with European knickknacks and overlooks a small grove of trees.
Leaded-glass partitions lend privacy to cozy tables set with lovely hand-
painted dishes. The poached salmon in sweet vermouth sauce and the
interesting chicken and lobster dishes served in a sauce of saffron, chocolate, and nuts are both excellent.

Woodside

Restaurant Kissing

BELLA VISTA, Woodside   ◆ ◆
13451 Skyline Boulevard
(415) 851-1229
Moderate to Expensive
Wedding facilities are available for a maximum of 60 people.

*From Highway 101 or Interstate 280, take Highway 92 west to Skyline
Boulevard. Turn left and follow the road about five miles to the restaurant,
which is on your left.*

The winding scenic drive to Bella Vista is half the fun of dining here. Though the weathered wood paneling and worn carpets are as shabby in appearance as the restaurant's exterior, the floor-to-ceiling windows in two of the three dining rooms command endless views of a rolling procession of redwood trees and the distant blue outline of the bay. Arrive before sunset so you can have dinner as darkness begins to veil the area in velvety black. If you've timed things just right, you'll have finished your scallops sautéed in white wine and be taking your first exquisite bite of chocolate soufflé just as the lights of the towns below begin to twinkle in the distance.

Outdoor Kissing

FILOLI GARDENS AND ESTATE, Woodside
Canada Road
(415) 364-2880
$8 per person

Filoli Gardens is about 25 miles south of San Francisco. From Interstate 280, take the Edgewood Road exit west, then turn right onto Canada Road and drive 1.2 miles to the entrance.

This magnificent garden evokes passion in all who visit. The gardens are laid out in a sumptuous Italian-French design, with parterres, terraces, lawns, and pools that form a succession of garden rooms. More than 20,000 plants are added annually to ensure year-round splendor. The Chartres Cathedral Garden recreates a stained glass window with roses and boxwood hedges; the Woodland Garden is Eden revisited. The wisteria-draped mansion is akin to a European summer palace. Original furnishings and items from the Getty and de Young museums recall an era of grand luxury. If you feel a sense of deja vu, it may be because you have seen Filoli portraying the classy Carrington estate on television's *Dynasty*, or perhaps you kissed here in your most pleasant dreams.

◆ **Romantic Note:** Filoli is one of California's best-loved gardens. Because of this, reservations should be made as far in advance as possible.

Campbell

Restaurant Kissing

CAMPBELL HOUSE, Campbell
106 East Campbell Avenue
(408) 374-5757
Moderate to Expensive

From Highway 17 south, take the Hamilton Avenue exit and turn right onto Hamilton Avenue. Then turn left onto Winchester Boulevard and follow it until Campbell Avenue. Turn left onto Campbell Avenue; the restaurant is on the right, between Third and Fourth avenues.

Housed in a 60-year-old Spanish villa with arched windows and a lovely fireplace, this cozy restaurant provides a homey atmosphere, attentive service, and delicious food, all in just the right proportions. The cuisine is rumored to be some of the best in the South Bay area, and the rumor is well founded. Twelve intimate tables set off by dark wood paneling and dried flower wreaths provide a perfect setting for enjoying fresh seafood or grilled homemade Italian chicken sausage with blue cheese polenta. Lunch and dinner are served Tuesday through Friday, dinner only Saturday and Sunday.

San Jose

You might be wondering why anybody would go to the silicon capital of the world for anything other than computer software. We actually wondered the same thing until we stumbled across several very romantic finds . . . and, thankfully, there wasn't a computer in sight.

Restaurant Kissing

BELLA MIA RESTAURANT, San Jose ◆ ◆ ◖
58 South First Street
(408) 280-1993
Moderate to Expensive
Wedding facilities are available for a maximum of 100 people.

Take Interstate 280 south to the Guadalupe exit. From there, turn right onto Santa Clara and drive to Second Street; turn right and park behind Bella Mia.

Thirteen thousand square feet of romantic possibilities await you at this newly renovated turn-of-the-century restaurant, a diamond in the rough (as they say) set among the rundown storefronts of historic downtown San Jose. Wood and brick lend a handsome air to the downstairs dining room, though sounds drifting past the open kitchen can intrude on quiet conversation. If you're serious about wining and dining, head upstairs, where tables are arranged under skylights in the mezzanine or in a beautiful back dining room warmed by a fireplace and accentuated with candles and rich green wallpaper. The Italian menu has something for even the pickiest of palates—their fresh-baked focaccia and award-winning salmon ravioli with ricotta and herbs are both musts.

◆ **Romantic Note:** If only the owners of this fabulous restaurant would expend an equal amount of time and energy on Bella Mia's counterpart in Saratoga. Until they do, it's not really even worth mentioning.

EMILE'S, San Jose ◆ ◆
545 Second Street
(408) 289-1960
Moderate
Wedding facilities are available for a maximum of 100 people.

Call for reservations and directions.

Ultra-chic decor with track lighting, a massive floral arrangement in the center of the room, ornate ironwork on the ceiling, tapestry-covered chairs, and mirrors covering the walls distinguish Emile's. Proudly dubbed "San Jose's best," this newly opened restaurant offers a creative mix of contemporary European cuisines. Due to its extreme popularity and sleek atmosphere, it isn't very intimate, but the food is to die for! The menu changes weekly, but two of the delectable dishes offered are spinach and cheese ravioli with a compote of mixed mushrooms, and roasted peppered pork tenderloin served on roasted Granny Smith apples. Emile's is open for dinner Tuesday through Saturday and also serves lunch on Friday.

◆ **Romantic Alternative:** Just around the corner from Emile's is an exceptionally charming Italian eatery called **PASQUALE'S**, 476 South First Street, San Jose, (408) 286-1770, (Moderate). Stained glass windows line the entrance to the small brick dining room, which is cluttered with modernistic frescos and myriad knickknacks. You'll appreciate the cozy ambience, as well as the savory Italian fare.

LA FORET, San Jose   ◆ ◆ ◖
21747 Bertram Road
(408) 997-3458
Moderate to Expensive
Wedding facilities are available for a maximum of 140 people.

From Highway 101, take the Capitol Expressway to the Almaden Expressway and head south until you reach Almaden Road. Turn right and watch for the La Foret sign on the left.

Just a short drive away from the high-tech world this area is famous for, La Foret is touted as one of the prettiest restaurants in the South Bay. Located in the historic village of New Almaden, the restaurant sits next to a brook in what was the first two-story adobe hotel in California. The original wood paneling frames sizable windows that look out onto a wooded landscape. A sublime French menu offers a wide range of pheasant, chicken, duck, and pasta entrées, and the service is outstanding. Soft candlelight will cast a gentle spell as you lovingly share your evening here.

Saratoga

Everything about Saratoga is picture-perfect: the surrounding forest and parkland, the tall shade trees lining residential streets where much pride seems to be taken in well-tended gardens and homes, and the Victorian storefronts in the tradition of country shopping. The main street, **BIG BASIN WAY**, is ironically petite, but we had no trouble finding a fair number of award-winning restaurants that scored as high on the kissing-rating scale as they did on the culinary scale. Saratoga has more than enough romantic possibilities to fill a superlative afternoon or weekend interlude.

♦ **Romantic Warning:** Due to the growing popularity of the Paul Masson concert season, there are times when Big Basin Way is a traffic bottleneck, the likes of which are not supposed to happen outside the city. (At least not when I'm there.) Keep your schedule loose if you happen to be here at the end of a concert. Simply park your car and have a snack or cappuccino at any of the dining spots along Big Basin Way.

Hotel/Bed and Breakfast Kissing

THE INN AT SARATOGA, Saratoga   ◆ ◆
20645 Fourth Street
(408) 867-5020
Expensive to Unbelievably Expensive

One block north of Big Basin Way on Fourth Street.

The Inn at Saratoga strikes a perfect balance between the intimate warmth of a bed and breakfast and the comfortable practicality of a hotel (if you can overlook the prices, that is). It has the best of what makes some hotels distinctive and most bed and breakfasts quaint and cozy. Attractive, bright suites have all the amenities seasoned travelers require and romantics yearn for, including tiled Jacuzzis in several suites. For the purposes of this book, one of the most appealing details here is the fact that each room has its own balcony. These private viewpoints face a creek flowing through a small forest of sycamore, maple, and eucalyptus trees.

A buffet-style complimentary continental breakfast is served in the plush lobby downstairs, but there aren't always enough tables to go around. Consider taking breakfast up to the privacy of your own room.

Restaurant Kissing

ADRIATIC RESTAURANT, Saratoga
14583 Big Basin Way
(408) 867-3110
Moderate to Expensive
Wedding facilities are available for a maximum of 25 people.

On Big Basin Way, between Fourth and Fifth.

Chandeliers and candles cast soft light across the Adriatic's intimate French country-style dining room, aswim with deep blue fabric wall-covering and blue tablecloths. Dried flower wreaths and impressionistic paintings adorning the walls add to the room's countrified authenticity without making it feel cluttered. Though the ambience is sumptuously intimate and exceedingly romantic, the food was rather disappointing.

LA MERE MICHELLE, Saratoga   ❖ ❖ ❖
14467 Big Basin Way
(408) 867-5272
Moderate to Expensive
Wedding facilities are available for a maximum of 200 people.

One block west of the Sunnyvale-Saratoga Road on Big Basin Way.

When making reservations at La Mere Michelle, you will have to specify whether you want to eat indoors or outdoors (it's a difficult choice). The inside dining room is subdued and elegant, highlighted by sparkling crystal chandeliers, fine art, and mirrored walls. The outside patio is equally enticing, though more casual. The wooden deck over-looks the street and is encircled by a short brick wall blooming with peri-winkle blue flowers. Candles softly light the patio, which is decorated with blue-and-white accents. The traditional French menu and enchant-ing atmosphere of either dining room are sure to please. No matter where you choose to sit, the savory baked seafood mornay with fresh scallops, shrimp, crab, and prawns will taste divine.

LA FONDUE, Saratoga
14510 Big Basin Way
(408) 867-3332
Moderate
Wedding facilities are available for a maximum of 110 people.

On Big Basin Way, between Third and Fourth.

   La Fondue effortlessly lives up to its reputation as a unique restaurant. More unusual than it is romantic, the colorful dining room filled with moons, suns, and stars draws its theme from Greek mythology. Who would guess that the menu in an atmosphere like this would offer nothing but fondues? The air is laden with delicious aromas, and the fondue selection is limitless, from standard cheese or teriyaki sirloin fondue to white chocolate fondue. If you're wondering if fondue can be romantic, take notice of the restaurant's "fondue rules," which state: "If a lady loses her cube in the fondue, she pays with a kiss to the man on her right." Just make sure you're not seated next to strangers.

LE MOUTON NOIR, Saratoga
14560 Big Basin Way
(408) 867-7017
Moderate
Wedding facilities are available for a maximum of 90 people.

On Big Basin Way, between Fourth and Fifth.

   Le Mouton Noir is anything but the black sheep of Saratoga's restaurant row. The decor, a combination of pink and dusty rose paisley and Laura Ashley prints, gives a country feel to this very intimate Victorian dining room. French-inspired California cuisine and elaborate desserts are served with care, and the food is delectable. Whether you have lunch here, with sunlight streaming through the many windows, or bask in the glow of a candlelight dinner, Le Mouton Noir is a delightful romantic discovery.

THE PLUMED HORSE, Saratoga
14555 Big Basin Way
(408) 867-4711
Expensive
Wedding facilities are available for a maximum of 150 people.

On Big Basin Way, between Fourth and Fifth.

Each of the intimate dining rooms at the Plumed Horse has unique detailing and character. One is brimming with Victorian antiques and opulent, red velvet furniture; another has weathered wood walls encircled by stained glass windows. Appropriately, horse paraphernalia and horse-shoes are displayed everywhere. But best of all, the fine French food rarely disappoints. We recommend the toasted Cypress Grove goat cheese with a sun-dried tomato ratatouille, the lobster bisque, and the crisp baked salmon with poached oysters on a bed of spinach (wow!). Dinner (only) is served nightly.

◆ **Romantic Note:** The wild at heart can go dancing after dinner in the Crazy Horse Saloon, located next door.

Outdoor Kissing

HAKONE JAPANESE GARDEN, Saratoga
21000 Big Basin Way
(408) 741-4994

Take Big Basin Way through town; about a mile up the road you will see a turnoff sign on the left side of the street.

We missed it the first time we visited Saratoga, but after several friends who had been there admonished us for not checking out the Hakone Garden, we returned for what they said would be an unbelievable outing. We searched valiantly for the turnoff sign. Finally we spotted it and followed it to one of the most serene settings we've ever seen, a horti-cultural utopia, pure and simple and sublime.

Redwood trees stretch to the sky, sheltering a sculptured landscape of exquisite flora and fauna. In the center of the garden is a blue pond where sleepy carp, a Japanese symbol of love and longevity, languish in the still water, white water lilies float over the surface, and a cascading waterfall fills the air with mild, tranquilizing music. The garden is edged with wood-fenced walkways adorned by sweet-smelling flowers. The contem-plative mood of the area makes it prime territory for a walk with the one you love.

♦ **Romantic Note:** Food is not allowed in the garden, so a picnic is out. But if you truly want to experience the flavor of this exotic place, attend one of the authentic Japanese tea ceremonies performed on weekends. Reservations are required, so call ahead if you want to be served.

MOUNTAIN WINERY, Saratoga
14831 Pierce Road, at Highway 9
(408) 741-5181

From Big Basin Way, turn left onto Pierce Road and follow the signs to the main gate.

Spread above the idyllic town of Saratoga, up a steep and winding country road, the Paul Masson Vineyards cover some of the most august, sun-drenched earth in the entire South Bay. Everything here seems almost too picture-perfect. Graceful trees rustle in the soft, billowing breezes. Grapevines arc across the mountainside, disappearing from sight as the land curves to meet hill after hill. Perhaps the only flaw in this majestic setting is that the Paul Masson Vineyards are not open to the public except during special events. Then again, for most of the spring, summer, and part of fall, that's not a problem. Every year the winery presents a spectacular summer concert series featuring entertainers who appeal to almost every audience. Past concerts have showcased the soulful sounds of Ray Charles, classy jazz vocals from the legendary Ella Fitzgerald, the country stylings of Ricky Skaggs, and the soothing instrumentals of talented Kenny G. Regardless of what you choose to hear, there is something miraculous about listening to music in the mountains with a clear sky and the sweeping countryside as the only backdrop.

♦ **Romantic Warning:** On a summer day, sitting in an unshaded spot can be a melting proposition. Try to find protected seats or bring a sun visor, sunglasses, and towels. On the other hand, at night the mountain breezes can be cooler than you might expect. An extra sweater will keep shivers at a minimum.

♦ **Romantic Note:** If wedding bells are in your future, facilities and services for large groups are available here, through a separate company located adjacent to the winery. Call Chateau La Cresta Restaurant at (408) 741-5526 for details. This restaurant only does banquets or catering and is not open to the public.

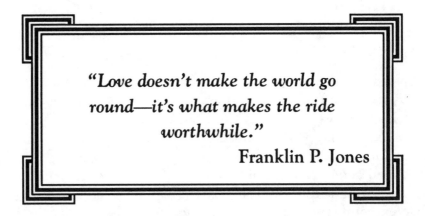

"Love doesn't make the world go round—it's what makes the ride worthwhile."

Franklin P. Jones

LAKE TAHOE AND ENVIRONS

Glistening in the foothills of the High Sierra, Lake Tahoe is 22 stunning miles long and 12 miles wide, the largest alpine lake in North America. The climate too is alpine in nature, which means summers are warm and dry and winters cold and snowy. Spring and fall can be a little of both. The area's breathtaking scenery, fishing, swimming, skiing, hiking, and, yes, even gambling lure tourists of all kinds—especially those looking for romance.

♦ **Romantic Warning:** During the off-season, when the weather is too cold for swimming in the lake but too warm for snow, many establishments are closed, especially on the north and west shores, where gambling does not keep visitors coming year-round. Always call in advance.

South Shore

South Lake Tahoe

If you want to elope, South Lake Tahoe is the place for you—as long as you don't mind pledging "I do" in a roadside chapel, surrounded by an endless sea of neon lights and casinos. Tahoe's south shore sits astride the California and Nevada state borders and is known for its economy hotels, gambling casinos, and wedding chapels. "No thanks," you say? Don't worry—there's something here for nature enthusiasts too. South Lake Tahoe's **HEAVENLY SKI RESORT** is America's largest ski resort, encompassing 20 square miles of terrain and dazzling panoramic views of Lake Tahoe.

Hotel/Bed and Breakfast Kissing

CHRISTIANA INN, South Lake Tahoe
3819 Saddle Road
(916) 544-7337, (800) 4-CAL-SKI
Very Inexpensive to Expensive
Wedding facilities are available for a maximum of 40 people.

From Highway 50, turn toward the mountains onto Ski Run Boulevard, then left onto Needle Peak, right onto Wildwood, and left onto Saddle Road.

Tucked beneath pine trees at the base of Heavenly Ski Resort, Christiana Inn is reminiscent of a European youth hostel. You can literally ski from the slopes (across the street) right to the door of this cozy lodge. Six guest rooms await you, ranging from simple bedrooms to full two-story suites, and each is appointed with a blend of contemporary and antique furnishings. You can warm your toes together in front of a fireplace in four of the suites, enjoy a dry sauna in Suite 5, a whirlpool in Suite 6, or cuddle up in Suite 4's loft overlooking the ski runs at Heavenly, which is just the word for the view.

◆ **Romantic Alternative:** The Christiana Inn Restaurant is also a great kissing spot (see "Restaurant Kissing").

EMBASSY SUITES, South Lake Tahoe
4130 Lake Tahoe Boulevard
(916) 544-5400, (800) EMBASSY
Moderate to Expensive
Wedding facilities are available for a maximum of 350 people.

On the California-Nevada state line, adjacent to Harrah's Casino.

This brand-new high-rise hotel is situated yards away from the Nevada state line and surveys neon casino country. If casinos aren't your thing, neither is this hotel—its flashy neighbors are hard to ignore. On the other hand, if you're in the mood to try your luck at the slot machines, the Embassy Suites Resort is the best (and most tasteful) option in the nearby area.

The Bavarian-motif hotel features a series of three soaring nine-story-tall atriums. In the first, water splashes over a paddlewheel and down a flume to a decorative pool surrounded by lush greenery. Umbrella-crowned cafe tables fill the patios of the other atriums, where a buffet breakfast and complimentary afternoon cocktails and hors d'oeuvres are served. A glass elevator lifts you to attractive two-room suites, the kind Embassy Suites is known for, set high above the city.

LAKELAND VILLAGE BEACH   ❥
AND SKI RESORT, South Lake Tahoe
3535 Highway 50
(916) 544-1685
Moderate to Unbelievably Expensive
Wedding facilities are available for a maximum of 300 people.

On the beach off Highway 50, near the base of Ski Run Boulevard, one mile from Stateline, Nevada.

Recommending individually owned and decorated condominiums is tricky business because of their random design and care. Lakeland Village's rental units are no exception: they run the gamut from shabby to luxurious, depending on your luck (and how much you're willing to pay). This sizable condominium complex is sandwiched between a busy highway and a sandy beach, so the closer your accommodations are to the water, the better. Most of Lakeland's units are unimpressive, though we can't resist mentioning the gorgeous lakeside condominiums, appointed with modern furnishings and enclosed in glass, showcasing views of tranquil Lake Tahoe. The price is steep, but the view is worth every penny.

TAHOE SEASONS RESORT, South Lake Tahoe   ❥ ❥ ❦
Saddle Road, at Keller Road
(916) 541-6700
Moderate to Very Expensive
Wedding facilities are available for a maximum of 300 people.

From Highway 50, turn toward the mountains onto Ski Run Boulevard, then left onto Needle Peak, right onto Wildwood, and left onto Saddle Road.

This modern resort, sheltered by woods and situated across the street from Heavenly Ski Resort, has a knack for pleasing everybody: casinos are nowhere in sight but only minutes away. Sumptuous mini-suites are sleek in design and feature beautifully appointed living rooms and bedrooms separated by shoji screens that enclose oversized whirlpools. A gas fire flickers in the hearth of nearly every room, while microwaves and refrigerators make inventive midnight snacks a romantic possibility. Request one of the newly renovated rooms when making your reservation; they are pleasantly decorated with contemporary furnishings accented by teal and mauve fabrics and wall coverings.

TAMARACK VACATION RENTALS, South Lake Tahoe
(916) 541-2595, (800) 232-2123
Inexpensive to Unbelievably Expensive

Call for reservations.

Country chalets, waterfront cabins, pioneer homes, mountainside condominiums . . . take your pick—Tamarack Rentals really has them all. So don't be shy when making your reservation—be sure to specify your desired location, type of accommodation, and price range. If you're willing to get specific, Tamarack is sure to set you up with just what you're looking for.

Restaurant Kissing

CAFE FIORE, South Lake Tahoe
1169 Ski Run Boulevard #5
(916) 541-2908
Moderate to Expensive
Wedding facilities are available for a maximum of 25 people.

Heading east on Highway 50, turn right onto Ski Run Boulevard.

You don't have to worry about distractions at Cafe Fiore—there are only seven tables here! It doesn't get more intimate than this. Candles glimmer at each of the windowside tables arranged in the cozy wood-paneled dining room. Be adventurous: the Italian menu features items such as blackened alligator fillet served with drawn garlic butter, among other unusual selections. Desserts are out-of-this-world, especially the homemade white chocolate ice cream, so deliciously thick it's hard to swallow. We were tempted to spend an extra day in South Lake Tahoe just to come back here.

◆ **Romantic Alternative:** Because Cafe Fiore has so few tables, reservations are hard to come by. Luckily, **NEPHELES**, 1169 Ski Run Boulevard, (916) 544-8130, (Moderate), is located next door and, though not as intimate as Fiore's (what is?), it has a romantic appeal of its own. A large stained-glass window depicting a smiling sun sets the mood for tasty, creative California cuisine and adds a rustic touch to the otherwise almost-too-cutesy Victorian-style dining rooms.

CHRISTIANA INN RESTAURANT, South Lake Tahoe ◆◆◆
3819 Saddle Road, at the Christiana Inn
(916) 544-7337, (800) 4-CAL-SKI
Very Inexpensive to Expensive
Wedding facilities are available for a maximum of 40 people.

From Highway 50, turn toward the mountains onto Ski Run Boulevard, then left onto Needle Peak, right onto Wildwood, and left onto Saddle Road.

As a fire flickers in the brick hearth framed by boulders and antique skis, couples warm themselves in the sunken sitting area of the lounge in this old alpine-style inn. Low-slung couches invite you to relax with a warm drink and chase away the cool of the evening. Lace curtains, beams decorated with tiny white lights, and intimate booths set the scene for heartwarming dishes such as lobster Napoleon—tender medallions of Maine lobster baked with a basil-and-lobster mousse, served between two layers of pastry with a chardonnay sauce—or grilled beef tenderloin served with a roasted shallot demiglace and a fresh artichoke sour cream. You'll have no trouble finding the right wine to go with your meal—the wine list offers more than 200 choices. For a romantic finale, share a dessert for two—bananas flambé, cherries jubilee, or baked Alaska, all flamed tableside.

◆ **Romantic Warning:** Rumor has it that the food isn't always as delectable as it was the night we were here. We recommend that you go and decide for yourselves.

EVAN'S AMERICAN GOURMET CAFE,
South Lake Tahoe
536 Emerald Bay Road
(916) 542-1990
Moderate to Expensive
Wedding facilities are available for a maximum of 45 people.

From South Lake Tahoe take Highway 50 west to the intersection of Highway 50 and Highway 89. Turn right onto Highway 89 (Emerald Bay Road) and drive one mile to the restaurant, located on the left-hand side of the road.

The food at Evan's was so divine, it's hard for me to remember anything but the flavor of my grilled sea scallops tossed with sautéed spinach, fresh grated tomatoes, capers, and Greek olives, swimming in parsley brown butter. Normally I am eager to share my entrées with my partner, but not this time—I wanted to savor every last bite of this impeccably delicious meal. Not that the surroundings weren't lovely—they were. Floral window coverings, lovely watercolors, and fresh flowers at every table infuse the crisp cafe with color. But the food . . . simply unforgettable.

TOP OF THE TRAM RESTAURANT, South Lake Tahoe
Heavenly Valley Ski Resort, halfway up the California side
(702) 586-7000, extension 6347
Moderate (restaurant)
$10.50 per adult round-trip on the tram

To reach the ski resort from Highway 50, turn toward the mountains onto Ski Run Boulevard, then left onto Needle Peak, right onto Wildwood, and left onto Saddle Road. Catch the tram at the base lodge.

It's no surprise that Mark Twain called this view "the fairest picture the whole earth affords." Witness the splendor with your own eyes in a large tram that climbs to a soaring 2,000 feet above Lake Tahoe. Once on top, forgo the cafeteria, which is perfect for heavy-booted skiers, and head to the Top of the Tram Restaurant, which is a bit too posh for skiers anyway. Linen cloths and wood paneling add a touch of elegance to the basic American fare, but the real draw is the wall of windows framing a heavenly view of crystal blue Lake Tahoe enfolded by jagged, often snowcapped, mountain peaks. If you come for dinner in the summer, be sure to arrive before sunset.

◆ **Romantic Note:** Though food prices are reasonable here, keep in mind that the tram *alone* is $10.50. The Top of the Tram Restaurant serves lunch, dinner, and Sunday brunch in summer, lunch only in winter. The tram runs daily, from 10 A.M. to 10 P.M. June through September, and 9 A.M. to 4 P.M. November through May.

Outdoor Kissing

BORGES CARRIAGE & SLEIGH RIDES,
South Lake Tahoe   ◗ ◗ ◖
In the meadow across from Caesar's
(916) 541-2953
$15 per couple; $30 for two-person cutter sleigh

Call ahead for reservations and directions.

"Dashing through the snow, in a one-horse open sleigh," is more than the familiar words of a Christmas song to the Borges family. They offer rides in a selection of sleighs, ranging from six- to 20-passenger rigs pulled by two Belgian draft horses to two-person, one-horse cutters. It's wonderful to skim through a snowy meadow overlooking the sapphire lake. Plus, an intriguing history lesson gives you a new perspective on glitzy South Lake Tahoe.

Stateline, Nevada

Restaurant Kissing

THE SUMMIT RESTAURANT, Stateline, Nevada
16th and 17th floors of Harrah's Hotel and Casino
(702) 588-6606, (800) 648-3773
Very Expensive

Heading east on Highway 50, Harrah's Hotel and Casino is located on the right side of the road, several blocks from the California-Nevada state border.

A romantic restaurant in Harrah's? Are we kidding? (I thought the joke was on *me* when somebody first recommended the Summit for this book.) Luckily, this is not a joke. In fact, you would never guess this restaurant is situated on the upper floor of one of Nevada's best-known casinos. (The lofty setting actually once served as Harrah's Star Suite, the secluded aerie reserved for visiting royalty and Hollywood VIPs.)

A fire blazes in the hearth and candles flicker in a candelabra on the ebony piano where a tuxedo-clad virtuoso plays. Each dining area is intimate and romantically lit, whether you sit by the fire or climb the stairs to the mezzanine with its smoked glass balustrade. Windowside tables look out at the city lights and the velvet expanse of Lake Tahoe far below.

The cuisine is as heavenly as the ambience. Feast on appetizers like pumpkin fettuccine with Gorgonzola cream or smoked salmon cheesecake with lemon aioli, salads so beautiful they could double as centerpieces, and live Maine lobster Thermidor or salmon with basil, ricotta cheese, and sun-dried tomatoes in phyllo. The Summit is a touch of heaven—possibly the only touch this side of the state border.

West Shore

Homewood

Of the three developed shores of Lake Tahoe, the west shore remains the most pristine. You won't find big hotels, flashy casinos, or shopping centers in tiny Homewood. What you will find are a few fine establishments set amidst towering pines.

Hotel/Bed and Breakfast Kissing

ROCKWOOD LODGE, Homewood ◆ ◆ ◆
5295 West Lake Boulevard
(916) 525-5273, (800) 538-2463
Moderate to Expensive
Wedding facilities are available for a maximum of 500 people outside or 10 people inside.

On West Lake Boulevard (Highway 89), about six miles south of Tahoe City.

You will immediately feel comfortable upon entering this stone "Old Tahoe"-style home, so take off your shoes (required) and relax a while. Honey-colored knotty pine walls, hand-hewn open-beam ceilings, and soft cream carpeting work together to create warm, soothing surroundings. If this atmosphere alone doesn't shake the chill off snow-kissed cheeks, then a snuggle by the roaring fire in the living room and some kisses from your honey instead of the snow should do the trick.

The knotty pine throughout the house might suggest a rustic look, but instead the five guest rooms, decorated with antiques and country linens, are stylishly simple. Each one has a cozy down comforter, fluffy feather bed, fresh flowers, and warm bathrobes. Both the Secret Harbor and the Rubicon Bay rooms have excellent views of the lake, and tile tubs with dual shower heads. The Zephyr Cove Room, with a view of the forest, is like your own private loft, but until renovations are done this coming year, it shares a detached bath.

An ample full breakfast is served in the backyard beneath tall pines or on the front patio in front of the outdoor stone fireplace, when the weather permits. Otherwise it is served at a large table in the dining room.

◆ **Romantic Suggestion:** For spectacular views of the glistening lake while rushing down the slopes, try the nearby **HOMEWOOD SKI AREA**, (916) 525-7256.

Restaurant Kissing

SWISS LAKEWOOD RESTAURANT, Homewood   ◗◖
5055 West Lake Boulevard
(916) 525-5211
Moderate to Expensive
Wedding facilities are available for a maximum of 150 people.

Six miles south of Tahoe City, on the west side of West Lake Boulevard (Highway 89).

Old Swiss photographs, cow bells, and other memorabilia fill the walls and corners of Swiss Lakewood's dining room, and the most prominent color throughout is red. Sound a little garish? We thought so at first, but after we were greeted by a charming international staff and had a scrumptious meal, we decided this place was "tastefully cluttered." Authentic Swiss cuisine graces the menu year-round, but fondue—cheese or beef—is the specialty during winter. Feeding this tasty treat to each other is a fun way to warm hungry stomachs and playful hearts.

Outdoor Kissing

D.L. BLISS PARK, West Shore
Highway 89

From Highway 89 south, follow signs to the park on your right, between Emerald Bay and Meeks Bay.

Bliss is a fitting name for this park hugging the shore of emerald Lake Tahoe, where the sand is visible through transparent water and snow-capped Sierra peaks ascend in the distance. The best place to kiss in *all* of Tahoe is located here at **RUBICON POINT,** a quarter-mile hike from the last accessible parking lot. Views of the lake grow more magnificent at every turn as you traverse a well-worn path that weaves along the shore and winds higher and higher into the rock cliffs above. Though Rubicon Point is not well marked, you'll know when you've arrived—the already gorgeous view becomes almost spellbinding. Pine trees give way to a panoramic view of the lake, mountains, and neighboring inlet. Waves lap gently at the rocky shore below, and the sound of chattering birds and wind rustling in the trees provides background music for a long kiss.

North Shore

Incline Village, Nevada

The affluent residential neighborhood of Incline Village sits on the Nevada side of Lake Tahoe. On this side of the state line, most hotels put their energy into providing captivating casinos rather than romantic rooms, so lodging options are limited. One advantage of staying here is that the area is self-contained: skiing, shopping, swimming, and boating are all nearby.

Hotel/Bed and Breakfast Kissing

HYATT LAKE TAHOE RESORT HOTEL,
Incline Village Country Club Drive and Lakeshore Boulevard
(702) 831-1111, (800) 233-1234
Very Expensive
Wedding facilities are available for large groups; call for details.

On the corner of Lakeshore Boulevard and Country Club Drive, in Incline Village.

Unlike the more developed shores of South Lake Tahoe, the north shore has retained its natural forested setting. You'll actually enjoy a moonlit stroll along the curved paths that lead from this modern high-rise through the woods, past earth-toned cottages, to the lakeshore. The Hyatt typically caters to an executive clientele, but a unit in one of the 24 lakeside cottages could inspire a lot more than a business meeting. Wood furnishings, richly colored decor, stone fireplaces, and private decks with up-close views of the sparkling lake create an alpine lodge look and an amorous mood.

Guest rooms in the 12-story main building are a cross between a charming inn and a standard hotel, with blond pine furnishings, rich floral spreads, plenty of playful throw pillows, and views of the lake or mountains. On the Regency floors, complimentary afternoon wine, liqueurs, and hors d'oeuvres and an expanded continental breakfast are served in the private common room to stoke romantic hearts.

Restaurant Kissing

HUGO'S, Incline Village
111 Country Club Drive
(702) 831-1111
Moderate to Expensive
Wedding facilities are available; call for details.

At the corner of Country Club Drive and Lakeshore Boulevard, the restaurant is near the water, on the Hyatt's property.

Although Hugo's is owned by the Hyatt, it is removed from the high-rise hotel and nestled in the woods on the lakeshore. Windows wrap around two sides of the restaurant, and diners risk becoming mesmerized by the shimmering facets of Lake Tahoe, as dazzling as sapphires on a necklace. Above, a simple wood-paneled ceiling stretches to a crowned point. In the center of the room, flames flicker in a free-standing hearth, gladdening the hearts of those not close to a window.

Duck is a specialty here, served with your choice of Oriental, orange, lingonberry, or green pepper sauce. The extensive menu has something for everyone, including chicken, seafood, beef, and veal dishes. There is also a complimentary creative salad and delectable dessert buffet.

MARIE FRANCE RESTAURANT, Incline Village
Tahoe Boulevard (Route 28)
(702) 832-3007
Moderate to Expensive

On Tahoe Boulevard (Route 28), across from Raley's.

Like lovers, some restaurants shouldn't be judged by their outside appearance. This unassuming bistro is on a busy street in a strip mall, but once inside you'll feel as if you're in a cafe in France. A cheerful pianist playing cabaret tunes at an upright greeted us as we walked into this room with less than a dozen tables. Because the restaurant was full, as it usually is, we settled down on the overstuffed love seat by the blazing fire. On the coffee table lay albums with photos of Marie and friends in her restaurant, along with a Paris picture book.

This is truly a family-run operation. Marie's husband or daughter may wait on you, and, as they banter back and forth in melodic French, Marie is sure to come by and talk of food or her home country in her heavily accented English. The sauces are cooked *after* you order this French country cuisine, so be prepared for a leisurely dining experience. It's worth the wait for such scrumptious dishes as rabbit in prune sauce or scallops in lobster sauce served in a pastry crust. *Ooh la la!*

Outdoor Kissing

DIAMOND PEAK CROSS COUNTRY, Incline Village
Off Highway 431
(702) 831-3249
$11 for an adult day-pass or all-day ski rental

From Incline Village, take Highway 431 toward Reno. Near the crest of the mountain, park along the street. The entrance to Cross Country Trails is on your right.

If a kiss gives you that top-of-the-world feeling, just wait until you kiss at Diamond Peak. High on a mountaintop, groomed cross-country ski trails lead through pristine forest to spectacular eagle-eye views of crystalline Lake Tahoe and its ring of snowcapped peaks. Even beginners will find rentals, lessons, and one easy trail here; try the rolling intermediate trails if you can laugh together at your snow-softened falls. Along the intermediate Vista View loop, climb up the aptly named "Knock Your Socks Off Rock" and you'll know what kissing on top of the world is all about. Tables are provided at the base of the rock for chilly but heartwarming picnics.

◆ **Romantic Alternative:** Down by the lake, on its western shore, in the Taylor Creek Forest Service Area, (916) 573-2600, off Highway 89, just north of Camp Richardson, about a 15-minute drive from South Lake Tahoe, are several marked cross-country ski trails varying in difficulty. Our favorite is the one that leads past the eagle wintering area to the lakeshore. Follow the lakeshore, then circle back through the rustic but grand historic estates built in the 1920s. You'd never guess that casinos are just a short drive away from this forested shoreline. Be sure to buy a $3 Sno-Park permit in South Lake Tahoe for parking at Taylor Creek.

Crystal Bay

Restaurant Kissing

SOULE DOMAINE RESTAURANT, Crystal Bay   ❖ ❖ ❖
993 Cove Street
(916) 546-7529
Expensive
Wedding facilities are available for a maximum of 50 people.

On Cove Street, across from the Tahoe Biltmore.

Curiosity drew us to this tiny log cabin set in its own Lilliputian pine grove in a neighborhood of hulking 1950s-style casinos. At first I was skeptical, but we ducked inside to discover not only a precious artifact of old Tahoe, but one of the lake's best and most romantic restaurants. The warmth of the fire in the stone hearth casts a cozy glow on the intimate setting, with its walls of rotund pine logs caulked with rope. Chef and owner Charles Edward Soule's motto is "Every dish is a specialty of the house." The eclectic menu may include prosciutto and artichoke hearts sautéed with garlic, olives, and tomatoes and tossed with angel-hair pasta, or filet mignon sautéed with shiitake mushrooms, Gorgonzola, brandy, and burgundy butter. Even the soups here were scrumptious. If ever a meal will leave you feeling more in love for having shared it together, this one will.

Outdoor Kissing

MOUNTAIN HIGH BALLOONS
(916) 587-6922, (800) 231-6922

Call for directions and reservations.

If you're thinking that a hot-air balloon ride sounds like a frivolous, expensive, childish sort of excursion, you're right. If you also think it sounds like an unforgettable experience, you're right again. Both the enormous mass of billowing material overhead and the loud, blistering dragon fire that heats the air filling the balloon are astonishing. Once aloft, the wind guides your craft high above treetops and shimmering water, and the world seems more peaceful than you ever thought possible. From this perspective, Lake Tahoe glitters like a diamond and the shore appears to have brilliant emeralds scattered along the water's edge. This is a thoroughly heavenly experience, meant to be shared with someone you love.

◆ **Romantic Warning:** Be forewarned that the burner that keeps the balloon full of hot air is terribly loud and hot on the top of your head. Don't let this hold you back though: the flame doesn't run constantly. It can just be startling if you aren't expecting it.

◆ **Romantic Note:** Some balloon companies serve champagne and a light picnic brunch after the flight.

Tahoe Vista

Tahoe Vista doesn't offer much more than a busy street of wall-to-wall businesses. Most likely you'll quickly travel through here and won't feel inspired to linger, unless you want to do some shopping.

Restaurant Kissing

LA PETIT PIER, Tahoe Vista   ◆ ◀
7252 North Lake Boulevard
(916) 546-4464
Expensive to Unbelievably Expensive
Wedding facilities are available for a maximum of 20 people.

On the water side of North Lake Boulevard (Highway 28) in Tahoe Vista.

Development along the lake is so dense in Tahoe Vista that you could easily miss this gem of a French restaurant literally perched at the water's edge. Inside, the incredible view and the aromatic smells from the kitchen are a welcome invasion of the senses. A lantern glows at each table and the decor is contemporary. Generous prix fixe meals are offered; one day diners could feast on Oregon smoked salmon, soup, spinach and dried apricot salad with balsamic vinegar dressing, pheasant Souvaroff for two, and a delectable dessert. Individual entrées and single dishes prepared for two are also available.

Tahoe City

Like Tahoe Vista, Tahoe City is a bustling community filled with businesses, but fortunately they are a little more spread out. You can go to the center of town for provisions and a great dinner, then head to the outskirts for tranquil lodgings.

Hotel/Bed and Breakfast Kissing

THE COTTAGE INN, Tahoe City
1690 West Lake Boulevard
(916) 581-4073
Moderate to Expensive

On West Lake Boulevard (Highway 89), about two miles south of the town center.

You'll feel like pioneers in this little roadside village of rustic cabins by the lakeshore. Far from the glitz of the casinos and the sterility of high-rise hotels, the Cottage Inn embraces nature rather than trying to overwhelm it. The five cabins, each with a private entrance, sit in a circle. Two are newly remodeled in a rustic alpine theme, with fuzzy white sheepskin throw-rugs, and the others are simply yet nicely decorated. Nothing too fancy here, but outdoor types will find it refreshing. Some of the two-room suites are warmed by wood stoves, one by a fireplace. You can also warm yourself by the fire in the 1938 Pomin House, where wine and home-baked cookies are laid out in the evening and a full breakfast is served in the morning. After a day of hiking, indulge in an evening sauna or stroll to the private beach where you can dig your toes into the cool sand and kiss to the lullaby of Lake Tahoe's quiet, lapping waters.

♦ **Romantic Note:** Additional renovations include an intimate honeymoon suite with a similar alpine feel, Jacuzzi tub, and a private entrance facing away from the circle of other cabins.

SUNNYSIDE LODGE, Tahoe City
1850 West Lake Boulevard
(916) 583-7200, (800) 822-2SKI (California only)
Inexpensive to Expensive
Wedding facilities (outside) are available for a maximum of 300 people .

On West Lake Boulevard (Highway 89), about two miles south of the town center.

A true mountain lodge of wood and gables, Sunnyside takes full advantage of its perch on Lake Tahoe's forested western shore. In the warmer months, put a blush in your cheeks on its expansive, sun-soaked wooden deck. Boaters can pull up to the dock or, if the water is too low, use the restaurant's buoy shuttle. In winter, a blazing fire crackles in the large river rock fireplace in the lounge. Boat enthusiasts and skiers will appreciate the mixture of nautical and ski memorabilia throughout the lodge and restaurant (see "Restaurant Kissing"). Guest rooms are sleek and airy, with high ceilings, modest wall coverings, chests for coffee tables, and boating or skiing prints decorating the walls. All the rooms are oriented to the sparkling lake view. Some have fireplaces and balconies where you can stand together in the twilight, kiss, and imagine you're on the prow of your private yacht.

Restaurant Kissing

CHRISTY HILL RESTAURANT, Tahoe City
115 Grove Street
(916) 583-8551
Expensive

Heading east on North Lake Boulevard, turn right onto Grove Street. The restaurant is behind the Village Store.

Make your reservation before the sun goes down—you don't want to miss a sunset here, even though Christy Hill's dining room is romantic at any time of day. Picture windows allow views of the lake; watercolor paintings accentuate the cushioned booths and tables covered in pink tablecloths. The menu here is the safest bet around. The mixed organic greens with fresh peach, crispy pecans, and Gorgonzola cheese with champagne vinaigrette, and the fresh Canadian halibut baked with garlic breadcrumbs, served over a sauce of golden tomato, garlic, ginger, sesame, soy, scallion, and fresh basil were two of our favorites. Dinner is served every night except Monday.

SUNNYSIDE RESTAURANT, Tahoe City
1850 West Lake Boulevard
(916) 583-7200
Moderate

On West Lake Boulevard (Highway 89), about two miles south of the town center, in the Sunnyside Lodge.

The nautically inspired Chris Craft dining room, paneled in mahogany, is so close to the lake that you'd think it was floating. You can enjoy a piping hot bowl of clam chowder with a seafood dish or grilled entrée here, as well as a remarkable view of the glistening lake.

WOLFDALE'S RESTAURANT, Tahoe City
640 North Lake Boulevard
(916) 583-5700
Moderate to Expensive
Wedding facilities are available for a maximum of 100 people.

Head east on North Lake Boulevard; the restaurant will be on your right.

California-Japanese food has never tasted so good—or taken so long (service was ultra-slow the night we were here). No lake views, though the two dining rooms separated by shoji screens are pleasant, punctuated with a collection of provocative modern art. We were partial to the first dining room with its hardwood floors, white tablecloths, and potted flowers at each table. The Monterey salmon with a spicy crust and the grilled Columbia River sturgeon with baked black-eyed peas and a juniper berry vinaigrette are both delicious. Save room for peach kuchen with a lemon-blackberry mousse and berry coulis or an autumn apple mascarpone tart served with fresh cream and ginger-plum sauce.

Squaw Valley

From Highway 80, take Highway 89 south to Squaw Valley Road. Turn left and drive two miles to a fork; veer left and then take the first right.

Nestled at the base of jagged peaks, Squaw Valley is one of the High Sierras' most picturesque settings. It is some distance from the sapphire sparkle of Lake Tahoe, but its soaring mountains rival the Swiss Alps in their rugged beauty. A village of hotels, condominiums, and restaurants is tucked away in the valley, along with stables, golf courses, and other recreational facilities. Although this first-class ski resort first gained renown for hosting the 1960 Winter Olympics, sports buffs convene here year-round.

Hotel/Bed and Breakfast Kissing

SQUAW VALLEY INN, Squaw Valley
1920 Squaw Valley Road
(916) 583-1576
Moderate to Very Expensive
Wedding facilities are available for a maximum of 500 people.

Located at the base of Squaw Valley Ski Resort.

Originally built for Olympic contestants in 1960, this two-story wood-shingled lodge is strategically situated at the base of the mountain, next to the gondola and the resort's parking lot. In other words, this is Grand Central Station. Still, if you can ignore the crowds, it's an amiable and very convenient place to stay. Each of the 60 guest rooms has two queen beds, attractive blond wood furnishings, and rich color schemes; some even have beautiful large kitchens. An outdoor heated pool and hot tubs are nice amenities, but, not surprisingly, often too crowded for comfort . . . or romance.

SQUAW VALLEY LODGE, Squaw Valley
201 Squaw Peak Road
(916) 583-5500, (800) 922-9970
Moderate to Unbelievably Expensive
Wedding facilities are available for a maximum of 75 people.

Located at the base of Squaw Valley Ski Resort.

I think it was the whirlpool tubs that won me over—three of them, just off the exercise room, with a fireplace in the corner and a view of the snowy peaks outside. Or maybe it was the spacious, contemporary Southwest-style guest rooms equipped with full kitchens that make possible a late-night cup of cocoa or a no-hassle bathrobe breakfast. Then again, the setting, adjacent to some of the best skiing and hiking in the Tahoe area, is a definite plus. If your toes get cold while you're outside, you can simply ski off the mountain, straight to your room.

As if skiing weren't enough exercise already, you can tone up on Nautilus equipment and Lifecycles in the gym, indulge in a sauna, dive into the outdoor heated pool, or melt in the hands of a masseuse. If you have any energy left, celebrate your health together in your room over-looking the mountains.

◆ **Romantic Alternative: THE RESORT AT SQUAW CREEK,** 400 Squaw Creek Road, Squaw Valley, (916) 583-6300, (800) 327-3353, (Expensive to Unbelievably Expensive), is the newest and grandest addition to Squaw Valley's expanding village. The dramatic lobby alone is worth a peek, with its wall of cathedral-high windows framing the mountain face. Outside, the resort's own waterfall tumbles down past its skating rink to three whirlpools. A shopping arcade, spa and health center, restaurants, water slide, and plunge pool—every amenity of a modern resort is here. Surprisingly, the guest rooms are merely standard, with a comfortable but comparatively unimaginative hotel feel.

Outdoor Kissing

OLYMPIC ICE PAVILION, Squaw Valley   ◆ ◆ ◆ ◆
On top of the world (or close to it)
(916) 583-6985
$11 for the cable car, $7 for skating with skate rental,
$9 for the cable car, skating, and skate rental after 4 P.M.

Look for the cable car building at the base of Squaw Valley Ski Resort. Take the aerial tramway to the top of the mountain.

Having frequented Tahoe for many years, I thought I had seen the most magnificent views the area could afford—that is, until we rode the cable car to the Olympic Ice Pavilion. Riding the aerial tramway is an adventure in itself, as you soar above the eagles, over one pinnacle, then high to the zenith of the mountaintop. A building is perched on the edge of the summit, almost like a gateway to heaven, especially in the rosy light of sunset. The outdoor skating rink is perched on the mountainside, overlooking the vast expanse of the valley far below. In the distance, Lake Tahoe winks on the horizon. After a kiss here you'll never be the same.

◆ **Romantic Note: THE TERRACE RESTAURANT,** (916) 583-6985, literally on top of a mountain peak, next to the Olympic Ice Pavilion, shares the same extraordinary panorama. Despite this magnificent setting and the pleasant ambience of the restaurant, lunch features basic American hamburgers, chili, and sandwiches served cafeteria-style at very reasonable prices. This may be the only cafeteria in the world that inspires kissing. Nearby, **ALEXANDER'S POOLSIDE CAFE AND BAR** looks out over a swimming pool (you can't be shy if you plan to swim here) and the peaks and valleys beyond.

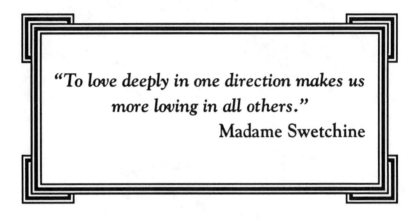

"To love deeply in one direction makes us more loving in all others."

Madame Swetchine

GOLD COUNTRY

Highway 49 travels directly through most of the Gold Country towns. From San Francisco, take Interstate 80 east toward Sacramento. From Sacramento, continue on Interstate 80 to intersect with Highway 49 in Auburn, or take Interstate 50 to Highway 49 in Placerville.

When news spread in 1848 that gold had been discovered in the Sierra foothills, people from all walks of life rushed toward the promised land of California. This sudden flood of settlers who had crossed the treacherous Sierra Nevada range, determined to find riches, made the Gold Country a ruthless, gun-toting region. Finding the mother lode was a prime objective, and the end, for many, often justified the means. Although many travelers still think of California as a desirable destination for the pursuit of fame and riches, gold fever is a thing of the past. However, the Sierras' Western heritage still reigns, and serious romancing can be your main objective today.

At the height of the Gold Rush, little Nevada City at the northern tip of Gold Country was as big as Sacramento, and towns like Auburn, Coloma, Sutter Creek, Jackson, and Jamestown, tucked amidst rolling golden hills and valleys, bustled with activity. As the gold supply began to dwindle, though, settlers deserted the area just as quickly as they had rushed in. Many of the original buildings remain, creating a ghost-town feeling in some of these now-quiet small towns. History buffs will want to stop and read the countless historical markers that dot the highway, and who knows, you might even strike it rich . . . in the memories you bring home together.

◆ **Romantic Warning:** Highway 49, which runs directly through most of the Gold Country towns, is a surprisingly busy two-lane road. Expect driving to be a hassle on weekends, especially in the summer. Also, unless the place you stay has soundproof windows or is far from the highway, it is hard to escape traffic noise.

Sacramento

The capital of the "Golden State" exudes an amiable, small-town charm despite the fact that it is a four-county metropolis and one of the ten fastest-growing regions in the United States. Year-round sunshine graces Sacramento's wide streets, which are lined with tall shade trees and renovated turn-of-the-century homes. Coffeehouses, antique stores, stylish restaurants, and a handful of elegant Victorian bed and breakfasts enrich Sacramento's friendly allure. But although Sacramento may feel like a small town, keep in mind that it is not. Traffic noise goes without saying, but you probably won't even notice—you'll be too busy kissing.

Hotel/Bed and Breakfast Kissing

AMBER HOUSE, Sacramento
1315 22nd Street
(916) 444-8085, (800) 755-6526
Very Inexpensive to Very Expensive

Turn off eastbound Interstate 80 onto northbound Interstate 5. Take the J Street exit, go to 22nd Street, and turn right. The inn is on the corner of N and 22nd streets.

Poets and artists inspired the decor at the Amber House, and now it's your turn to be inspired. This bed and breakfast has nine rooms, housed in two early-20th-century homes: the Poet's Refuge and the Artist's Retreat. The Poet's parlor, with its massive exposed beams, dark brick hearth, and hardwood floor, is the perfect counterpoint to the parlor in the newer Artist's Retreat, which boasts rose walls, a white hearth, and overstuffed floral sofa. The Poet's rooms are engaging, especially the double Jacuzzi in the Lord Byron Room and the antique tub beneath the skylight in the Longfellow Room. Still, our penchant for impressionists made us partial to the Artist's accommodations. The Van Gogh is a stunning, bright yellow bedroom that opens to a solarium bathroom. If not for the trees, even the immodest would blush, because the double Jacuzzi and shower are encased entirely in glass. The Degas and Renoir rooms invite you to soak in a double whirlpool surrounded by pink and gray marble.

AUNT ABIGAIL'S, Sacramento
2120 G Street
(916) 441-5007
Very Inexpensive to Moderate

From the Business 80 Loop, take the H Street exit. Cross H Street and turn left onto G Street. The inn is near the corner of G and 22nd streets.

Book your reservations early—Aunt Abigail's is one of Sacramento's most sought-after inns, and we know why. The grand foyer of this 1912 Colonial Revival mansion embraces guests with old-world elegance. A fire crackles in the antique-filled parlor; the hardwood floors are accented with Oriental rugs. You may want to spend the evening tucked away in your room sipping herb tea and nibbling on scrumptious home-baked cookies or, better yet, soaking in the whirlpool set in the backyard garden. Staying in the Solarium, appointed with windows on three sides, is like sleeping in a treehouse; a private door leads to a private deck. Margaret's Room is lovely, with soft tones, an immense vanity with a hand-painted sink, and a claw-foot tub. Uncle Albert's Room is decidedly more stalwart, with maroon and gray paisleys and stripes. In the morning, guests join together for a hearty breakfast that may include warm applesauce, vegetable and cheese strata, fresh fruit, cinnamon muffins, and an assortment of teas and coffee.

HARTLEY HOUSE INN, Sacramento ◆
700 22nd Street
(916) 447-7829, (800) 831-5806
Inexpensive to Moderate

From Interstate 80 east, take the H Street exit. Cross H Street and turn left onto 30th Street. Go one block, and turn left onto G Street. The inn is on the corner of G and 22nd streets.

A certain straightforward simplicity dominates this smaller turn-of-the-century Italianate Victorian. Hartley House's dark-stained woodwork, hardwood floors, distinctive Oriental carpets, leaded and stained glass windows, and the stately ticktocking of its old clocks will appeal to many guests as a fresh alternative to the frilly accoutrements of other bed and breakfasts. Although Hartley House caters to executives during the week, weekends are prime for romantic getaways. The four guest rooms are handsomely outfitted with brass beds, antique wardrobes, converted gas fixtures, and dusky paisley bedcoverings. Brighton is the brightest room in the inn: daylight streams in through a dozen lace-trimmed windows in this former sun porch. In the morning, a full breakfast of stuffed French toast or blueberry-raspberry pancakes is served in the dining room.

STERLING HOTEL, Sacramento
1300 H Street
(916) 448-1300
Moderate to Expensive

From Interstate 80 east, go to Interstate 5 north. Get off at the J Street exit. Turn left onto 13th Street. The hotel is on the corner of 13th and H streets.

Don't let the word "hotel" mislead you. This baronial Victorian set in the heart of downtown Sacramento has the intimacy of a bed and break-fast—without the breakfast. (Actually, breakfast in bed *is* available via room service; it's just not included with your stay.) Because of its location and amenities, business executives flock here on weekdays, but weekends at the Sterling cater primarily to couples and relaxation. The common area's contemporary decor is simple yet sophisticated, with black marble fireplaces, Oriental carpets, and a recently added refreshment bar. Each of the handsome, though sparsely appointed, guest rooms has a marble-tiled Jacuzzi (several of which are spectacular), intriguing artwork, and a four-poster or canopy bed with floral linens.

◆ **Romantic Note:** The restaurant here, **CHANTARELLE**, is an amorous place to dine (see "Restaurant Kissing").

VIZCAYA, Sacramento
2019 21st Street
(916) 455-5243
Inexpensive to Very Expensive

From Business 80 east, take the 15th Street exit. At the foot of the ramp, con-tinue on X Street, parallel to the freeway, to 21st Street. Turn left onto 21st Street. The inn is about four blocks up on the right.

One of the capital's more formal inns, this stately 1899 Colonial Revival crowns a grassy knoll in the heart of downtown. The spacious parlor is furnished with turn-of-the-century antiques and nearly dwarfs the grand piano (only a concert pianist would dare to tickle the ivories). Those who want to skip the formalities and go straight to kissing will not be disappointed at Vizcaya. Four of the nine guest rooms have marble-tiled fireplaces; five have Jacuzzi tubs. An unusual touch is the Penthouse Suite, reached by a narrow spiral stairway. Its modernistic black tables and pink sofas, separate bedroom done up in black and pink, and black tile double whirlpool make it a unique departure from Victorian lace and frills. The Carriage House in back is preferable because it is farthest from the adjacent busy street and provides cozy, countrified rooms with marble fireplaces or corner wood stoves.

Restaurant Kissing

BUGATTI'S, Sacramento   ❤ ❦
1209 L Street, at the Hyatt Regency Sacramento
(916) 443-1234
Moderate to Expensive

From Interstate 80 east, take Interstate 5 north and turn off at the J Street exit. Drive to 12th Street and turn right. Parking for the hotel is on the left side of 12th Street.

Marble lions stand guard at the entrance to the Hyatt's modern rendition of an Italian restaurant. Laughter and the clinking of glasses spill from an open bar, mingling with melodies offered by a pianist playing a glossy black grand piano. Fortunately, cathedral ceilings and floor-to-ceiling windows absorb some of the commotion, allowing quiet, tender moments. Enjoy grilled seafood indoors or on the outside garden terrace, where the hum of nearby traffic is nearly engulfed by the sound of a burbling fountain. All this makes a nice prelude to an evening stroll through the capitol grounds across the street.

◆ **Romantic Alternative: BIBA**, 2801 Capitol Avenue, Sacramento, (916) 455-BIBA, (Moderate to Expensive), is another romantic dining possibility in downtown Sacramento. Reservations are a must at this art-deco Italian eatery highlighted by square white pillars, arched windows, surrounding mirrors, and modern artwork. Fresh flowers add a dash of color to cozy tables draped in white. Among the pasta specialties are spinach lasagne, filled with meat, tomatoes, and bechamel sauce, and penne with smoked salmon and red onion in a light cream sauce. Service is pleasant, but due to the restaurant's popularity can be a little too slow.

ATAVOLA, Sacramento
2627 Town Country Plaza
(916) 973-1800
Moderate
Wedding facilities are available for a maximum of 150 people.

Head east on 16th Avenue, which turns into Highway 160 and then becomes Interstate 80. Take the Marconi exit and turn right onto Marconi Avenue. Drive to Fulton Avenue and turn left, then take an immediate right into the Town Country Shopping Plaza.

As you drive into the Town Country Shopping Plaza looking for this restaurant, you'll wonder if we gave you the wrong directions. It's hard to imagine that anything remotely romantic exists around here. But your skepticism will instantly dissolve the moment you set foot inside. Cathedral ceilings, open natural-wood beams, and lovely murals create an authentic provincial Italian ambience, enhanced by terra-cotta floors and simple table settings. In the open kitchen, pumpkin ravioli in a white wine-mushroom sauce and spinach-potato gnocchi with lobster and lemon thyme in cream sauce simmer to blissful perfection.

CHANTARELLE, Sacramento
1300 H Street, at the Sterling Hotel
(916) 448-1300, (800) 365-7660
Moderate to Expensive

From Interstate 5 north, take the J Street exit. Turn left onto 13th Street. The hotel is on the corner of 13th and H streets.

Sunlight sifts through leaded glass windows and streams into three separate dining rooms adorned with provocative modern paintings at this daylight-basement restaurant. A single long candle flickers at every white-clothed table, infusing the otherwise subdued atmosphere with warmth. The smoked salmon Caesar topped with goat cheese croutons or the seafood lasagne with shrimp, scallops, and lobster is sure to satisfy. Go out in style with a slice of chocolate decadence cake resting on a bed of raspberry sauce.

FRANK FAT'S, Sacramento
806 L Street, between Eight and Ninth streets
(916) 442-7092
Moderate

From Interstate 5 north, take the J Street exit. Turn right onto Ninth Street and then right again onto L Street. The restaurant is on the left side of the street.

This venerable Chinese restaurant has been a Sacramento landmark for 50 years. Although it may be a stomping ground for government types at lunch, in the evening the cozy tables, high-backed booths, and blend of modern and traditional Asian decor create a romantic ambience that isn't often found in Chinese restaurants. The menu lists all the traditional favorites, plus a selection of Mandarin, Cantonese, and Szechuan delicacies. A perfect place to share the spices of life together.

Outdoor Kissing

ADVENTURE LIMOUSINE SERVICE, Auburn
(916) 878-8212
From $325 per day

Call for information about pickup and drop-off details.

Although I'm not one to splurge capriciously, I would be remiss if I didn't tell you how much fun it can be to tour the Gold-Country wineries in the backseat of your own private limo. Your driver will take you almost anywhere your heart, or your sweetheart, desires. Your itinerary could begin with a continental breakfast en route to a stop at the **SOBON** and **SHENANDOAH WINERIES** to check out their tours, tastings, and on-site museums. Next would be a choice of lunch in Sutter Creek or a picnic at **MONTEVINA WINERY**. Return home via antique stores, photo shops, or more wineries, and share one last chauffeur-driven kiss.

◆ **Romantic Note:** Adventure Limousine also will arrange tours of the Napa wineries, including lunch for two at one of the valley's fine restaurants.

Old Sacramento

Take the Old Sacramento exit off Interstate 80 and follow the signs to the area.

The restored Western-style facades lining Old Sacramento's narrow streets are just authentic enough to make you feel as though you've stepped into a John Wayne movie. Unfortunately, this is as nostalgic as it gets (and if you're not a John Wayne fan you might be more annoyed than nostalgic). The drone of neighboring highways bombards the sleepy stillness of this little village, and the horse-drawn buggies seem sadly out of place. Nevertheless, you can browse in quaint boutiques, stroll along the placid Sacramento River, indulge in old-fashioned chocolate fudge, or investigate the **WELLS FARGO MUSEUM** in the B.F. Hastings Building at Second and Jay streets, where you can sit across the room from each other and telegraph endearments to your partner.

THE DELTA KING, Sacramento   ❖
1000 Front Street, Old Sacramento Waterfront
(916) 444-KING, (800) 825-KING
Moderate to Expensive

From Interstate 80 east, take Interstate 5 north. Take the J Street exit to Fifth Street and turn left. Drive to I Street and turn left. Follow signs to Old Sacramento, take Second Street to K Street, and turn right. The dock is at the end of the dead end.

The night was quiet and the river still as we boarded this grand old riverboat for an after-dinner cocktail. We glided up a broad staircase to the fine saloon, aglow with rubbed mahogany and teak, and gazed out windows overlooking the water on one side and the vintage Western-style facades of Old Sacramento on the other. This stern-wheel paddleboat, the kind so often connected with the Mississippi, plied the river between Sacramento and San Francisco from 1927 to 1940. It was a floating pleasure palace for flappers when Prohibition outlawed drinking in landlocked lounges. Today, the restored vessel is a dockside voyage into the past. Its restaurant rates high on romantic ambience; unfortunately, the cuisine is, only passable.

THE FIREHOUSE, Old Sacramento
1112 Second Street
(916) 442-4772
Moderate to Expensive

From Interstate 80, take Interstate 5 north. Take the J Street exit, drive to Fifth Street, and turn left. At I Street turn left, and follow signs to Old Sacramento. Turn left onto Second Street, then right onto L Street. Parking is in the alley.

As we ventured into the Firehouse, we felt like gold miners who had finally struck it rich. This unexpected find is well hidden among the storefronts of Old Sacramento. In spite of its name, the Firehouse revels in its Gold Rush history both subtly and graciously. Unusually high cathedral ceilings offset by beautiful red brick walls and a wrought-iron spiral staircase winding down through the lobby are the only visible traces of the restaurant's past as an actual firehouse. Chandeliers illuminate a handful of tables, and oversized impressionist paintings adorn the walls, lending a European air to the intimate dining room. An appetizer of lobster and foie gras ravioli with white truffle and chervil provides the luscious beginning of an exquisite dining experience, culminating in a selection of ambrosial desserts. Savor every bite—it's not every day you strike gold.

Grass Valley

Grass Valley was the most heavily mined area in the northern section of Gold Country, but, like most Gold Rush communities, when the gold ran out so did the locals. Today it retains some of that rundown, almost ghost-town feel, but there are some charming little shops and a few good restaurants, and the folks who do live here will make you feel welcome and comfortable.

Hotel/Bed and Breakfast Kissing

MURPHY'S INN, Grass Valley
318 Neal Street
(916) 273-6873
Inexpensive to Expensive

From Highway 49, take the Colfax/Highway 174 exit and turn left at the first stop sign. Turn left at the second light, onto Neal Street. The inn is three blocks up, on the right, at the corner of Neal and School streets.

Manicured ivy and lovely gardens trim this opulent estate built by one of Gold Country's most successful mine owners as a wedding present for his wife. The six guest rooms in the main house are richly decorated with Victorian elegance, all have private baths (some with dual shower heads), and two have fireplaces. If you can't get a room with a fireplace, the two sitting rooms on the main floor each have one you could snuggle by, although on warm days you might prefer to cuddle outside in the big hammock or soak up some sun on the spacious deck surrounded by gardens and fountains. Wherever you decide to relax, there are enough common areas that you won't feel crowded by other guests. A full breakfast is served at one large dining table in the breakfast room.

◆ **Romantic Note:** A separate house across the street has two rooms, both with a king-size bed, fireplace, and a private bath. Families with children are encouraged to stay here, so unless you have to bring the kids on your romantic getaway, ask for a room in the main house.

Restaurant Kissing

HOLBROOKE HOTEL
RESTAURANT, Grass Valley
212 West Main Street
(916) 273-1353, (800) 933-7077
Moderate

From Highway 49, take the Colfax/Highway 174 exit and turn left at Main Street. The hotel is on the right side of the street between South Church and Mill streets.

Step off the dusty trail and into the refined elegance of this wonderful restaurant. A globe chandelier hangs from the high ceiling, antique wall fixtures subtly light each of the tables, and brick walls and archways make cozy alcoves for intimate dining. Seasonal menu offerings might showcase sea bass baked with an herbed sun-dried tomato bread crust in a lime-cilantro jus, or grilled filet mignon with stir-fried vegetables and sherry-soy sauce. The fine food is sure to delight, but try to save room for the "Grand Dessert." We suggest you share this one, because you don't just get a dollop of a few of the scrumptious desserts, you get what looks like a full serving of each. Awesome!

◆ **Romantic Note:** The historic **HOLBROOKE HOTEL**, 212 West Main Street, Grass Valley, (916) 273-1353, (800) 933-7077, (Inexpensive to Expensive), also has a variety of rooms upstairs. A few are spacious and others are pretty small, but all have antique furnishings and private baths (with a claw-foot tub in every room except number 15), and many have private balconies and comfortable sitting areas. The decor ranges from dark paisley and brass to pink florals and wood. The brochure boasts that legendary individuals such as Mark Twain and Ulysses S. Grant stayed here, but if their rooms were anywhere near the noisy saloon on the main floor they surely didn't sleep well.

Nevada City

With a name like this, one might expect a town full of flashing lights, nondescript motels, and oversized hotels, but instead Nevada City is one of the most picturesque towns in Gold Country, and quality accommodations abound. It has been compared to a rural New England community, and on crisp fall afternoons, after the leaves have turned myriad shades of red, orange, gold, and purple (yes, purple!), you'll see why. Many of Nevada City's earliest settlers were from the New England area, and some brought along their favorite trees as they journeyed west more than a hundred years ago.

◆ **Romantic Suggestion:** Give yourselves at least a day to behold the grand display of fall colors, then visit the shops and restaurants of the downtown streets. The annual blaze of autumn glory usually begins early in October and lasts about six weeks. For more information and a walking map of the town, contact the **NEVADA CITY CHAMBER OF COMMERCE**, (916) 265-2692, or (800) 655-NJOY.

Hotel/Bed and Breakfast Kissing

DEER CREEK INN, Nevada City
116 Nevada Street
(916) 265-0363
Inexpensive to Moderate
Wedding facilities are available; call for details.

From Broad Street (the main street in town), head east. At the first stop sign turn left onto Nevada Street. The inn is immediately after the bridge on the right side of the road.

Luckily this prime kissing locale, right on Deer Creek, opened just in time to be included in our book. We realized upon entering the sunny, refined parlor that much time and energy had been spent restoring this grand Queen Anne Victorian. The Honeymoon Suite, with its own entrance, has a wrought-iron canopied bed, down comforter, striking black and white bathroom, and a private garden area that faces the grassy lawn and the rushing creek. This might be the most secluded unit, but the four other rooms, with features like private verandas, claw-foot tubs, marble baths, and four-poster or canopied king- or queen-size beds, are also noteworthy. Each one is decorated differently, but nothing is overdone.

A delicious full breakfast is served on the deck overlooking the creek, or in the formal dining room on cooler days.

GRANDMERE'S, Nevada City
449 Broad Street
(916) 265-4660
Moderate to Expensive

Heading north on Highway 49, take the Broad Street exit and head west on Broad Street. The inn is on the left side of the road at the top of the hill.

Grandmere's has been called the "grand dame" of local bed and breakfasts, and rightly so. This stately white Colonial holds seven commodious guest rooms, each with a private bath (one has a claw-foot tub and two others have oversized tubs). The handsome Master Suite is huge, with hardwood floors, a four-poster king-size bed, and a spacious sitting area with an overstuffed couch and chairs around an antique gas fireplace. Quilts, baskets, and pine antiques create a slightly country feel, but in this elegant home nothing looks rustic.

A full country breakfast is served in the dining room, but we suggest that you take your trays to a secluded spot in the Victorian garden—a wonderful place to set an affectionate mood for the rest of the day.

◆ **Romantic Note:** There is a two-night minimum on weekends and holidays April through December.

RED CASTLE INN, Nevada City   ❦ ❦
109 Prospect Street
(916) 265-5135
Moderate to Expensive
Wedding facilities are available; call for details.

Heading north on Highway 49, take the Sacramento Street exit. Follow Sacramento Street just past the Chevron station and turn right onto Adams Street, then take the first left onto Prospect Street. The inn will be on your left.

Tucked into a forested hillside, this imposing four-story mansion with wraparound verandas and intricate white trim seems oddly out of place. Maybe that's because it is one of only two genuine Gothic Revival brick houses on the West Coast and we hadn't seen anything like it before. As you enter through the tall front door of the estate, lace curtains, rich colors, and elegant chandeliers set the mood. Of the eight rooms, the more spacious ones on the entry level and first floor are recommended. Each room has a queen-size bed, private bath, and features like high ceilings, chandeliers, French doors, and four-poster canopied or antique beds. The top and middle-level rooms are less amorous, not only because you have to carry your luggage up extra flights of stairs, but because features like shared or detached baths, double beds, and a low seven-foot ceiling on the middle level don't contribute to romance.

A generous full breakfast is served buffet-style on the main floor, but you are welcome to savor it privately in your room or on the veranda, or to find a secluded spot near a fountain. There is a half acre of lovely terraced gardens here, so an intimate site won't be hard to find.

◆ **Romantic Suggestion:** On this hillside, you're far enough away to escape the rush of busy little Nevada City, but if you're in the mood to shop or simply want to enjoy an afternoon stroll together, a winding pathway leads from the gardens to the town below.

◆ **Romantic Alternative:** The **DOWNEY HOUSE**, 517 West Broad Street, Nevada City, (916) 265-2815, (800) 258-2815, (Very Inexpensive to Moderate), is worth mentioning simply because of its unique charm. The contemporary pastels and Southwest accents throughout this historic home seem out of place at first, but each of the six soundproofed rooms has a queen-size bed with down comforter, a private bath, and a small bedside aquarium. A little different, but it is a refreshing change of pace from the Victorian decor you'll find everywhere else.

Restaurant Kissing

POTAGER AT SELAYAS, Nevada City
320 Broad Street
(916) 265-5697
Moderate to Expensive

Heading north on Highway 49, take the Broad Street exit. Turn left onto Broad Street; the restaurant is two blocks down, across from City Hall.

Formerly Peter Selaya's Restaurant, this dining room is trying to hold on to the great reputation the former owner had earned and his many faithful customers relied on. Hopefully, people will give them a chance. The new chef trained with the past one, so creative California cuisine and scrumptious dishes like freshly made ravioli, and scallops Rockefeller served over spinach with Pernod, hollandaise, and Gruyere cheese, still grace the menu.

The country-style decor accents the white table linens, lace curtains, and chandeliers in the front section, but you and your partner should venture deeper into the restaurant for the most romantic tables in the back, called the Diggin's because it resembles a mine shaft with open wood and is lit only by candlelight. Table number 9 is set away from the others and is especially romantic. Reservations are recommended.

◆ **Romantic Alternative:** If you're looking for a similar, slightly more casual atmosphere and want good French food, try **THE COUN-TRY ROSE CAFE**, 300 Commercial Street, Nevada City, (916) 265-

6248, (Moderate to Expensive). The dinner menu changes nightly, but the seasonal fresh fish and seafood dishes are consistently delicious.

Lodi

Have you ever heard the song "Stuck in Lodi Again"? Unfortunately, it fits all too well. Lodi is a lackluster suburb of Sacramento, and that's putting it mildly. There isn't any romantic reason to come here, unless, of course, you're headed to Wine and Roses Country Inn. In that case, all is forgiven and almost forgotten.

Hotel/Bed and Breakfast Kissing

WINE AND ROSES COUNTRY INN, Lodi
2505 West Turner Road
(209) 334-6988
Inexpensive to Moderate (inn)
Moderate to Expensive (restaurant)
Wedding facilities are available, call for details.

From Interstate 5, take the Turner Road exit. Head east five miles to the inn, which is on the left.

Well suited to its name, this five-acre country estate is replete with flowers of every imaginable color and kind: azaleas, impatiens, violets, daisies, and, of course, roses. Flowers are not the only thing blossoming here. Diamond engagement rings are frequently presented alongside filet mignon or lamb chops in rosemary in the intimate pink dining room warmed by a fireplace. Proposals are a specialty at Wine and Roses Country Inn, as are the garden weddings that follow.

The Victorian farmhouse inn has been beautifully renovated and radiates a fresh country charm. "Moonlight and Roses" is one of the more romantic guest rooms, with a white brass bed, sitting area surrounded by windows, and claw-foot tub. "White Lace and Promises" is a lovely two-room honeymoon attic suite exulting in garden views from its own private terrace. The televisions in each room, a necessity for the midweek business clientele, can be removed on request so as not to distract you from more important matters of the heart.

◆ **Romantic Warning:** West Turner Road runs adjacent to the inn and is heavily trafficked. Particularly at rush hour, the whiz of cars pervades the otherwise tranquil country setting.

◆ **Romantic Note:** The dining room is open for lunch Tuesday through Friday, for dinner Wednesday through Saturday, and for Sunday brunch.

Plymouth

Plymouth is best known for the Shenandoah Valley: wine country paradise. Acres upon acres of well-tended vineyards grace the sloping Sierra Nevada foothills, creating a wondrous setting for bed and breakfasts, award-winning wineries, and kissing.

Hotel/Bed and Breakfast Kissing

AMADOR HARVEST INN, Plymouth   ◆ ◆ ◖
12455 Steiner Road
(209) 245-5512
Inexpensive to Moderate
Wedding facilities are available; call for details.

From Highway 49 north in Plymouth, turn right onto Shenandoah Road, then left onto Steiner Road. The Amador Harvest Inn is on the left; watch for signs.

Set in the heart of the Shenandoah Valley, this picturesque gray and white farmhouse is a breath of fresh air, surrounded by manicured grounds and a lush green lawn. A shady back porch commands a view of two scintillating lakes (where you can fish for bass), and rolling vineyards rise in succession in the distance. The bed and breakfast's common areas are warmed by a wood stove and feature modern but homey furnishings. Not surprisingly, the four upstairs guest rooms are tributes to wines: Zinfandel, Cabernet, Chardonnay, and Mission. Each of these rooms has oak and brass furnishings and enjoys views of the nearby lakes, vineyards, and orchards. Samples are available at the tasting area next door, so you can bring home a bottle of your favorite room.

INDIAN CREEK BED AND BREAKFAST, Plymouth
21950 Highway 49
(209) 245-4648, (800) 24-CREEK
Inexpensive to Moderate

From Plymouth, follow Highway 49 north for three miles. Turn right at the sign for the bed and breakfast.

In Gold Country things start to look alike. After you've passed through several small Gold Rush towns sporting historic Western-style facades and Victorian inns, it becomes difficult to distinguish one place from the next. The Indian Creek Bed and Breakfast is a welcome change. Built in 1932 by a Hollywood producer, this refined two-story log house is sequestered on the edge of ten acres of woodland. The home's interior has been masterfully crafted with pine walls and Douglas fir floors, endowing it with a unique bucolic elegance. A floor-to-ceiling fireplace made of quartz warms the large living room, where Hollywood's select were entertained in the '30s and '40s.

A wood staircase climbs to a manzanita-wood balcony overlooking the living room, leading to the upstairs guest rooms. We were partial to the Joan Elaine Room, finished in cream and white and appointed with a draped ceiling, wicker furniture, fireplace, private bath, and a large private deck. All of the four guest rooms have private baths and lovely antiques, though some of the color schemes leave much to be desired. Guests can lounge in the outdoor pool and Jacuzzi or walk alongside the seasonal creek that purls through the property (nine months out of the year) through serene meadows to the goldfish pond.

Outdoor Kissing

SHENANDOAH VALLEY

For a closer look at the beautiful Shenandoah Valley, take a day or two and tour the host of wineries here, set in the gently sloping Sierra hillsides. Many of the wineries here offer sublime views of the countryside in addition to tastes of the superb and award-winning local wines. Although most of the wineries are worth stopping at, the list below reflects our particular favorites.

AMADOR FOOTHILL WINERY, 12500 Steiner Road, Plymouth, (209) 245-6307; open noon to 5 P.M. weekends and holidays. Perched high on a hillside, the Amador Foothill Winery offers exquisite views of the orchards, vineyards, and shimmering lakes in the valley below, encircled by the Sierras, which are snowcapped in the winter. Sit at one of the umbrella-shaded picnic tables here, where you can survey the pastoral scenery and sample an award-winning zinfandel or fume blanc.

SHENANDOAH VINEYARDS, 12300 Steiner Road, Plymouth, (209) 245-4455; open 10 A.M. to 5 P.M. daily. An enormous Saint Bernard greets guests (don't worry, he's friendly!) at this small family estate nestled among vineyards. Partake of classic vintages while you browse in the contemporary art and ceramics gallery or admire views of the vineyards at a cozy picnic table outside.

KARLY, 11076 Bell Road, Plymouth, (209) 245-3922; open noon to 4 P.M. daily. A long, winding, and dusty drive past sprawling oaks and rows of grape arbors brings you to Karly's beautifully landscaped winery. Views of the surrounding country are almost as delicious as Karly's wines.

STORY WINERY, 10525 Bell Road, Plymouth, (209) 245-6208; open 11 A.M. to 5 P.M. weekends and by appointment. The Story Winery is more like a fairy tale. Far off the beaten path, this family-operated winery takes pride in its 50-year-old vineyards that still produce extraordinary vintages. Sip wine to your heart's content as you bask in the visual splendor of the gorgeous Cosumnes River Canyon.

Amador City

Restaurant Kissing

BALLADS, Amador City
14220 Highway 49
(209) 267-5403
Moderate to Expensive

Head north on Highway 49; Ballads is located just after the curve about two miles north of Sutter Creek.

If the ambience were as wonderful as the food, this would be a real kissing plus in this neck of the woods. Unfortunately, Ballads' renowned cuisine far outshines its atmosphere. The highlight of the stark, albeit unpretentious, gray wood-paneled dining room is a fire that crackles and glows in the large stone hearth. Still, the menu here is comparable to many of San Francisco's finest. The pork tenderloin with tomatillos, jica-ma, and poblana peppers was the perfect coupling of sweet and spicy. Everything on the menu was appealing, from the smoked duck tortellini with pesto sauce appetizer to the beef tenderloin with shiitake mush-rooms, artichokes, and thyme.

IMPERIAL HOTEL RESTAURANT, Amador City
14202 Highway 49, at the Imperial Hotel
(209) 267-9172
Moderate

Follow Highway 49 north, about two miles north of Sutter Creek. The hotel is on the right.

Though you can't elude the past anywhere in Gold Country, the Imperial Hotel is one of the few places that encourages you to feel right at home in the present. The brick interior of this Gold Rush-era mercan-tile-turned-hotel lends a warm elegance to the airy dining room, enhanced by high ceilings and elaborate but tasteful art. Tables covered in white linens are embellished with fresh flowers, and sunflowers adorn the hanging lamps. Dine outside under Japanese lanterns on a secluded patio made of native stone, surrounded by plants, more flowers, and a murmuring fountain. Ambience isn't the only thing the Imperial does right—the food here is heavenly. Request the grilled prawns with sweet ginger sauce, peaches, and acorn squash (utter bliss) or the chicken mar-bella baked with prunes, green and black olives, apricots, and oregano in a light wine sauce.

◆ **Romantic Note:** The Imperial Hotel's dining room has more to offer than its upstairs guest rooms simply because the hotel sits adjacent to Highway 49 and traffic noise can be invasive. What a shame. The rooms have been beautifully restored with brick interiors, hardwood floors, Oriental carpets, and colorful art pieces.

Sutter Creek

Set in the brown velvet folds of the surrounding hills, the former Gold Rush town of Sutter Creek has retained its whitewashed overhanging balconies, balustrades, and Western-style storefronts. Boardwalks hemmed with antique shops, gift boutiques, and casual cafes invite a relaxing stroll together.

Hotel/Bed and Breakfast Kissing

THE FOXES, Sutter Creek
77 Main Street
(209) 267-5882
Moderate to Expensive

In the center of town, along Highway 49.

This beautifully restored 1857 Victorian is one of the better finds in Gold Country. The Victorian furnishings throughout the inn are elegant but not at all pretentious. Polished silver tea services gleam in the large country kitchen, hinting at the indulgent gourmet breakfasts delivered to your room in the morning.

Walk through a garden to the private entrance of the spacious Honeymoon Suite, which features an antique claw-foot tub and a half-tester bed warmed by a wood-burning fireplace. (A fire also crackles in the hearths of two other rooms, including the cozy private library in the Foxes Den guest suite.) Sleep like royalty in the Victorian Suite's bed, graced with a magnificent nine-foot-tall carved wood headboard. Here, a fragrant bowl of potpourri, a shelf with a motif of carved lovebirds, and a cascade of sheer fabric above your bed blend to create the perfect retreat for kissing.

GOLD QUARTZ INN, Sutter Creek
15 Bryson Drive
(209) 267-9155, (800) 752-8738
Inexpensive to Moderate
Wedding facilities are available; call for details.

On the crest of the hill to the south of town. Bryson Drive is off Highway 49, just north of its intersection with Highway 88.

If you're weary of staying in century-old homes but love the style of the Victorian era, check into the Gold Quartz Inn. This brand-new, white-gabled hotel boasts a Queen Anne motif, but brings you up-to-date with the deluxe appointments of today. The spacious parlor and several sitting areas are filled with graceful wing chairs and plush sofas, accented with floral needlepoint pillows. Past the lobby, a sunny break-fast room overlooks the inn's lawns and gardens. Throughout these rooms, lace-curtained French doors open onto the wraparound veranda. Guest rooms are spacious and feature soft blue and pink color schemes, echoed in the sunsets you can watch from your porch.

THE HANFORD HOUSE, Sutter Creek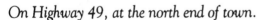
61 Hanford Street
(209) 267-0747
Inexpensive to Moderate

On Highway 49, at the north end of town.

The owners here deny responsibility for the 200-plus decorative teddy bears that peer from every corner of the inn's living room. Nearly every one of these too-adorable bears is a former guest's token of appreciation, which gives you some idea of the kind of service you can expect here. Don't worry if teddy bears aren't your cup of tea. The furry theme is much more subdued in the nine guest suites, which feature early pine furnishings, white-washed walls, and high ceilings that lend an air of clean spaciousness to each area. One oversized room even has a corner fireplace and an elaborate white brass bed with a white eyelet comforter.

You'll find plenty of space for outdoor kissing on the sunny redwood deck above Sutter Creek's pleasant jumble of rooftops or on the sun-dappled patio on the west side of the inn. A continental breakfast buffet is served in the cheerful breakfast room, where guests have left their names and appreciative comments on every inch of the walls and ceiling. (Definitely different, but better a written comment than another teddy bear.)

Restaurant Kissing

PELARGONIUM, Sutter Creek
51 Hanford Street, at Highway 49
(209) 267-5008
Moderate

Heading south on Highway 49 in Sutter Creek, the restaurant is on your left at Hanford Street.

Looking somewhat out of place perched on the edge of Highway 49, this blue and white country farmhouse really belongs out in the country amidst trees and lush foliage. Surprisingly, the traffic hasn't affected the Pelargonium's reputation in the slightest, and once you've eaten here you'll know why. The house's original living areas serve as intimate dining rooms, where candles flicker atop cozy tables covered with pink lace tablecloths and set with crystal stemware and silver tableware. Dinner selections change regularly and can include appetizers of baked Brie or Greek spanakopita and entrées of delectable stuffed sole Monterey or crab cakes with black bean sauce.

SUTTER CREEK WINE
AND CHEESE BISTRO, Sutter Creek
#15 Eureka Street
(209) 267-0945
Inexpensive to Moderate

From Highway 49 in Sutter Creek, turn left onto Eureka Street. The Courtyard and the restaurant are on the left.

Just follow your nose into this aromatic bistro and you'll understand why the sign on the door reads: "THE NOSE KNOWS." You can trust your senses here. Casual yet charming, this bistro is nestled in the back of the lively Eureka Street outdoor courtyard, adjoining several other sandwich and gift shops. Enjoy the open air at one of a handful of picnic tables or, if you prefer more privacy, eat inside where the scent of freshly baked goods wafts through the countrified dining room. Consider a wine and cheese board that includes a sampling of wine, cheese, pâtés, and meats, served with an array of vegetables. Come with a hearty appetite—they're more than happy to oblige you here.

Ione

Many of Gold Country's dry and dusty historic towns are little more than tumbledown testaments to days gone by. Sad to say, the town of Ione is no exception. Yet, once you've passed beyond the crumbling storefronts of this small two-block town, you'll be spellbound by the golden beauty of Ione's surrounding countryside.

Hotel/Bed and Breakfast Kissing

THE HEIRLOOM, Ione
214 Shakeley Lane
(209) 274-4468
Very Inexpensive to Inexpensive
Wedding facilities are available for a maximum of 150 people.

From Highway 88, take the Ione exit (Route 124). Turn left onto Main Street, then right onto Preston, then left onto Shakeley Lane. Look for two stone pillars at the entrance to a long dirt drive.

Built by a transplanted Virginian in 1863, this bed and breakfast is a world apart from anything else in Gold Country, or in California for that matter. Set back from the road and encircled by lawns bordered with thickly leafed trees, the brick two-story inn feels completely secluded, a sanctuary for romance. Many of the extraordinary antiques that crowd the spacious parlor are family heirlooms, including the massive 450-year-old carved wood table from Italy and the elaborate fans, now framed, that cooled the cheeks of the host's great-great-grandmother from France. The square rosewood piano once belonged to the famous Gold

Rush-era entertainer Lola Montez. You get the picture. You could settle by the wood-burning fireplace in this old manor home and spend an entire evening nibbling on appetizers and admiring antiques.

As you might expect, more antiques fill the six cozy guest rooms upstairs. "Springtime" opens onto a small balcony that drips with wisteria in its namesake season. "Winter," warmed by a fire, holds a four-poster Colonial bed with flouncy drapes above the headboard. Away from the main house, an authentic rammed-earth adobe harbors our two favorite, graciously rustic rooms, warmed by a blend of cedar, redwood, and pine paneling and wood stoves.

Outdoor Kissing

GREENSTONE WINERY, Ione
Highway 88, across from Jackson Valley Road
(209) 274-2238
Wedding facilities are available for a maximum of 150 people.

The setting of this majestic winery is as beguiling as its award-winning vintages. A long drive rambles over vineyard-laden hills, past a duck pond, to a stately stone structure akin to a French country manor. In the modern tasting room, sunlight pours through multipaned windows set high near the cathedral ceiling, casting a golden glow over the wood paneling. Outside, picnic tables set in the natural greenstone outcroppings and shaded by old oaks overlook Eden-like fields and Bacchus Pond, and beyond them a stretch of Miwok Indian land. Be sure to bring a picnic lunch with you to enjoy with a bottle of Greenstone's finest to complete this dreamy vision.

SUTTER CREEK-IONE ROAD

From Ione's Main Street, turn right onto Preston, then right again onto Highway 24. Look for signs to Sutter Creek-Ione Road.

Those interested in exploring Ione's enchanting countryside can veer off the highway and take the road less traveled. This backcountry road winds for ten miles through velvety rolling hills and valleys speckled with venerable oaks and grazing cattle. Every season imparts a beauty of its own: autumn leaves heighten the already bronzed landscape; winter brings rain (when there isn't a drought) and turns the hillsides a delicious green; and wildflowers dabble color everywhere in the spring and summer.

Jackson

As the Amador County seat, in the center of Gold Country, Jackson is home to most of the businesses in the area. I wouldn't call it a prime romantic destination; rather, it is a place where folks from surrounding towns come to do their shopping. Great for provisions, but definitely not for maximizing moments together.

Hotel/Bed and Breakfast Kissing

THE COURT STREET INN, Jackson   💋
215 Court Street
(209) 223-0416
Moderate to Expensive
Wedding facilities are available for a maximum of 20 people.

Heading north on Highway 49, turn right onto Historic Main Street, follow it two blocks to Court Street, and turn left up the hill, with a slight jog to the left around the court house. The inn is three houses behind the court house.

Attitude may not be everything, but it is what makes the Court Street Inn special. The innkeepers understand affectionate couples, and have installed a working traffic light outside the enclosed Jacuzzi tub in the backyard. What better place to stargaze, and what better way to ensure (and promote) intimacy?

This pale yellow Victorian is set right in downtown Jackson, which is not a heart-throbbing location by any means. The five cozy rooms in the main house are decorated with floral wallpapers and linens, and filled with antiques. Violets and ivy trim the sunny Blair Suite, which has a wood stove and a whirlpool tub for two. The rustic Indian House guest cottage behind the main house is a bit more private, and features a wood-burning fireplace and claw-foot tub. Some will find this bed and breakfast cozy, but believers in the "less is more" theory of decorating will feel cramped by the overflowing abundance of antiques.

A hearty full breakfast is served at large tables amidst many antique cash registers and, you guessed it, more antiques.

WEDGEWOOD INN, Jackson
11941 Narcissus Road
(209) 296-4300, (800) WEDGEWD
Inexpensive to Expensive

Take Highway 88 east from Jackson to the 2,000-feet elevation marker and turn right onto Irishtown-Clinton Road (do not make an earlier turn onto West Clinton Road). Veer right onto Clinton Road, follow it to Narcissus Road, and turn left. The inn is one-third mile up.

"Country" is the perfect word to describe every aspect of this Victorian replica far away from drab downtown Jackson. Family heirlooms abound in each of the six spacious rooms. The walking paths that cover the carefully landscaped grounds lead through a rose arbor to a Victorian gazebo, a perfect place for moonlit kisses.

Murphys

From north Highway 49, turn east onto Highway 4 and drive ten miles to Murphys.

"Above the fog and below the snow," as the locals say, sits the quaint little town of Murphys, at an elevation of 2,200 feet. As you ascend, the surroundings become more forested with pine trees and the air is a tiny bit cooler. Walk along the main street of town on raised wooden boardwalks, past buildings with Western-style facades that now house boutiques, an intriguing mineral and fossil store, a historic saloon, and an ice cream shop. You'll feel like you've stepped back in time.

◆ **Romantic Warning:** Events are scheduled almost every weekend during summer, which overloads this tiny community. On a busy weekend you might feel more like getting out of town.

Hotel/Bed and Breakfast Kissing

DUNBAR HOUSE, 1880, Murphys
271 Jones Street
(209) 728-2897, (800) 225-3764, extension 321
Moderate to Expensive

From Highway 49, exit at Route 4 east, then take the Murphys exit. The inn is on the left, set back from Main Street, across from the Milliaire Winery tasting room.

If there is a crown jewel in any of the Gold Country's towns, this 1880 Italianate Victorian is it. From the moment you cross the threshold, you will be indulged with old-fashioned hospitality and romance. Chocolate macadamia nut cookies, along with coffee, tea, and cocoa, are served in the dining room every afternoon. A full country breakfast is also served here beside the wood stove (or in your room, or in the lovely garden with its brick patio and white porch swing).

There are wood stoves in each of the four guest suites, so you can warm yourselves as you toast each other with the complimentary bottle of wine affectionately provided by the innkeepers. All the guest rooms have queen-size beds, down comforters, and are furnished with antiques. In the Sequoia Room, settle into a bubble bath in the claw-foot tub, with its hand-painted flowers, set next to the wood stove. In the spacious Cedar Suite, commonly reserved by couples looking for a special romantic getaway, guests are given a complimentary bottle of champagne. In this room you can cuddle on the white brass bed before the warm wood stove, relax on your private sun porch in the late afternoon, or pamper yourselves in the two-person whirlpool bathtub. No matter which room you choose, get ready to feel more than comfortable.

◆ **Romantic Note:** There is a two-night minimum when a Saturday-night stay is involved.

Outdoor Kissing

STEVENOT WINERY, Murphys
2690 San Domingo Road
(209) 728-3436

From the center of Murphys, follow signs for Mercer Caverns. Just before the road dead-ends at the caverns, turn right and follow a narrow, winding road down into the valley. Look for the Stevenot sign on the left at the bottom of a hill.

You'll feel like an adventurer when you go wine touring in Gold Country, especially as you search for this winery. Although this is one of the oldest wine-grape growing regions in California, wineries here are ensconced in secluded rural areas, unlike the domino set-up in Napa Valley. Stevenot is one to discover together. In the rustic, sod-roofed tasting room, you can sample wines, specialty mustards, scrumptious chocolate sauce, and delectable kiwi jam, then choose one of each, add Brie and bread, and enjoy your repast at one of the picnic tables beneath the arbor. Besides the winery buildings themselves, all you'll see around you are acres of idyllic vineyards and forested rolling hills.

◆ **Romantic Alternative: INDIAN ROCK VINEYARD,** Pennsylvania Gulch Road, off Highway 4, Murphys, (209) 728-2266, is located on a country road lined with small horse ranches. The tasting room is little more than a shack, but a few picnic tables are set by a small pond with horses grazing next door and old wagons set picturesquely in the grass.

Columbia

As you walk along the narrow street hemmed with Old West storefronts and overhanging balconies, you venture away from the cares of today and into the nostalgia of yesterday. **COLUMBIA STATE HISTORIC PARK,** the best restored and most unusual of Gold Country's portals to the past, includes about a block of shops with only the Wells Fargo stage and assorted ponies (absolutely no automobiles) to share the street with as you and yours stroll hand-in-hand. Shopkeepers and waitpersons in period costume greet visitors to antique stores and old-fashioned restaurants. Fiddlers and banjo players enliven the street with foot-stomping tunes, and children clamber onto the stagecoach and pan for gold in seeded wooden troughs. Tourist attractions might not be very intimate, but this one certainly is entertaining.

◆ **Romantic Option:** The **CITY HOTEL DINING ROOM**, Main Street, Columbia, (209) 532-1479, (Expensive), with its high-backed leather chairs, burgundy velvet draperies, brass chandeliers with etched tulip glass, classical music, and elegant cuisine, is a relatively refined departure from rough-and-ready Columbia. Established in 1856, this is where the wealthy celebrated their fortunes, away from the dusty trails. Today it is a training kitchen for hotel management students from nearby Columbia College. Eager beginning chefs create such unusual entrées as rack of lamb with curry crust, minted carrot jus, and potato-eggplant croquettes, or grilled tenderloins with sun-dried tomato and black olive butter and roasted garlic-potato gratin. It isn't always perfect, but it is consistently interesting. Wedding facilities are available for a maximum of 20 people.

◆ **Romantic Warning:** Both the **CITY HOTEL**, Main Street, Columbia, (209) 532-1479, (Very Inexpensive to Inexpensive), and the **FALLON HOTEL**, Main Street, (209) 532-1470, (Very Inexpensive to Inexpensive), rent rooms to overnight visitors, but they feel too much like public museums, as tourists come up to explore the vintage settings during the day. Also, the shared shower situation doesn't lend itself to privacy or romance.

Sonora

Sonora is a shock to the senses if you've spent time in the rest of Gold Country because it is significantly larger and more populated than most of the other Gold Rush towns. Sonora, too, flaunts its history with vintage old-fashioned storefronts and inns, though the development here is a glaring reminder of what century you're really in. Sonora's primary advantage is its size: your kissing options are increased significantly.

Hotel/Bed and Breakfast Kissing

BARRETTA GARDENS INN, Sonora
700 South Barretta Street
(209) 532-6039
Inexpensive to Moderate
Wedding facilities are available for a maximum of 25 people.

Follow Highway 49 into Sonora. At the stoplight in the center of town, turn right onto Washington Street. Take Washington to Barretta Street and turn left. The inn is high on a hillside on the left.

"Gardens" is an appropriate middle name for this recently refurbished turn-of-the-century inn perched on a hillside above the sprawling town of Sonora. A wraparound veranda overlooks compact terraced gardens, while a back balcony faces western sunsets over rolling hills. The owners here strive to give their guests as much kissing room as possible and have designed the inn with ample common space. Wander through the gardens or seek out the bright sun porch filled with lush greenery and wicker and rattan furnishings. A wood-burning fireplace glows in the comfortable parlor, though the television here is a rude convenience.

The common areas aren't the only reason to come here. The five guest rooms are also lip-worthy, highlighted with details such as the original crystal chandelier, ornate floor-to-ceiling gilded mirror, and silver vanity set in the Periwinkle Room. While antiques set the mood, sparkling new baths (including a whirlpool in the Dragonfly Room) ensure modern comfort.

LA CASA INGLESA, Sonora   ◆ ◆ ❬
18047 Lime Kiln Road
(209) 532-5822
Moderate

Follow Highway 49 south through the town of Sonora, where it becomes Washington Street. Follow Washington Street until it intersects Highway 108. Cross the intersection and head straight on Lime Kiln Road for one and a half miles. The inn is on your left.

The rural country road that winds to La Casa Inglesa looks so uninhabited it's hard to believe you haven't lost your way. Have faith and keep driving—you'll discover one of Sonora's best-kept secrets. This English wood-and-stone Tudor, enveloped by flower gardens and nine and a half acres of dry but wooded country, was built near the site of an early gold mine. The mine shaft itself lies on the property, deep in the center of a one-acre pond teeming with fish.

The historical setting, though interesting, is not the focus here. In fact, it's easy to forget you're in Gold Rush country at this modern-day bed and breakfast. A comfortable living room is the place to enjoy complimentary iced tea, fruit, and freshly baked cookies, and a redwood patio shelters a hot tub. Five guest rooms have simple but attractive country decor and private baths, some with beautiful antique claw-foot tubs. The room that was our particular favorite has unusual pointed and arched angles accented with green pin-striped wallpaper, highlighted by a prism of colors as sunlight filters through the stained glass windows. Luxuriate in this room's private Jacuzzi and be sure to notice the detailed floral tiles in the bathroom shower.

RYAN HOUSE, 1855, Sonora
153 South Shepherd Street
(209) 533-3445, (800) 831-4897
Inexpensive

Follow Highway 49 into downtown Sonora. Turn left onto Washington Street to continue on Highway 49. After one short block, turn right onto Theall Street. Drive two blocks to the inn, on the corner of Theall and South Shepherd.

If you stop to smell the roses at the Ryan House, your senses will be more than satiated by the time you reach the front door. A long garden walkway lined with blooming bushes summons you into this small 1850s Victorian. The interior, though dim, is pretty in its simplicity. The decor is clean and uncluttered, with soft lavenders or blues accented in patchwork quilts and dried flower wreaths. The upstairs suite, endowed with a spacious private parlor warmed by a pellet stove and with a large two-person soaking tub, offers the most privacy and is really the reason to stay here. The inn's emphasis is on old-fashioned comfort, from ultra-cozy beds to the warm aromas of baking—cookies for your afternoon sherry break or fresh scones for your breakfast. In the evening you can share a favorite book on the love seat by the wood stove in the library downstairs or venture out for a stroll beneath the branches of the hawthorn tree.

♦ **Romantic Alternative:** If you want to make beautiful music together, **LULU BELLE'S**, 85 Gold Street, Sonora, (209) 533-3455, (Inexpensive), is the perfect venue. Innkeeper Chris Miller is a musician, and a symphony of instruments, including a piano, organ, guitars, and clarinet, are provided for your use in the music room. Recent renovations have resulted in a sunny solarium in which to enjoy your full breakfast. Guest rooms are spacious but a bit too homespun, although each has a private bath and entrance.

SERENITY, Sonora
15305 Bear Cub Drive
(209) 533-1441, (800) 426-1441
Moderate
Wedding facilities are available for a maximum of 25 people.

From Highway 49 north take Business Highway 108 east to Phoenix Lake Road and turn left. Drive three miles to Bear Cub Drive and turn right. Follow the drive to the end.

An American flag ripples in the wind on the wraparound porch of this brand-new white Colonial-style home, setting the stage for a Gold Country retreat with East Coast flair. Aptly named, the inn is sheltered on six acres of woodland and exudes quiet country elegance at every turn. Unwind with a glass of fresh local apple cider on the breezy veranda or in front of the wood-burning stove in the parlor. The four upstairs guest rooms are modestly pleasant and feature private baths, lace-trimmed linens, modern-looking antique furnishings, and bright color schemes (sometimes a little too bright). Peruse the floor-to-ceiling bookshelves lining the walls of the library, where sunlight spills through a tall arched window. Breakfast is the clincher. As you relish carved pineapple boats or eggs florentine, remember to save room for dessert: strawberry shortcake, apple cake, or, if you're lucky, warm gingerbread with homemade whipped cream.

Restaurant Kissing

GOOD HEAVENS RESTAURANT, Sonora   ◆
49 North Washington Street (Route 49)
(209) 532-FOOD
Inexpensive
Wedding facilities are available for a maximum of 30 people.

Follow Highway 49 into downtown Sonora and turn left onto Washington Street to get to the restaurant.

This unpretentious eatery is a favorite with the locals. Exposed brick lines one wall, and windows peek out to Sonora's small-town main street along another. In between, a cluster of cafe tables topped with country-style blue-and-pink floral cloths and linen napkins fanned in wine goblets invites diners to enjoy hearty brunch specials, quiches, and sandwiches. No frozen waffles here. The crêpes Normandie are filled with sautéed apples, onions, garlic, capers with a hint of ginger, and country sausage; topped with rum raisin sauce; and served with mixed veggies in a Parmesan flan. With this, you have your choice of four homemade salads and soups. Rumor has it that their famous orange crunch cake was sought after by *Bon Appetit*, but the recipe remains secret.

◆ **Romantic Note:** Good Heavens is open only for lunch and Sunday brunch.

HEMINGWAY'S CAFE RESTAURANT, Sonora   ♥
362 South Stewart Street
(209) 532-4900
Moderate to Expensive

Take Highway 49 north into Sonora. At the stoplight adjacent to the Bank of America Building, turn right onto Stockton, left onto Gold Street, and right again onto Stewart Street.

The unusual combination of dinner and live entertainment found at this contemporary bistro can be a lot of fun, but you have to be in the mood for it. The chef plays piano while your food cooks, and the waitresses sing Broadway tunes between taking orders. White construction paper tops the few tables, and crayons are provided if you wish to write love notes by candlelight. The only problem was that we felt like we had to pay attention to the tableside performance instead of each other, and we wondered if the bouillabaisse served over lemon pepper linguine tasted a bit overdone because a song lasted longer than our meal should have been simmering.

◆ **Romantic Note:** Generally, musical performances only occur on weekends and holidays.

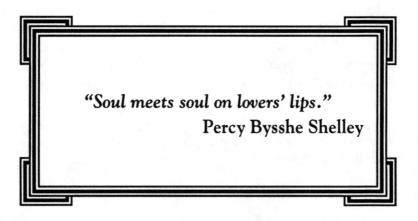

"Soul meets soul on lovers' lips."
Percy Bysshe Shelley

YOSEMITE NATIONAL PARK AND ENVIRONS

Oakhurst

If you've ever been to Oakhurst you might wonder why we would bother to include this nondescript town as a romantic destination. Most people pass through Oakhurst without blinking an eye (or wanting to stop) on their way to Yosemite National Park. Well, no longer. Chateau du Sureau and Erna's Elderberry House have become nationwide attractions, making Oakhurst a four-lip location.

Hotel/Bed and Breakfast Kissing

CHATEAU DU SUREAU, Oakhurst   ❖ ❖ ❖ ❖
48688 Victoria Lane, at Highway 41
(209) 683-6860
Unbelievably Expensive
Wedding facilities are available; call for details.

From Oakhurst, follow Highway 41 west. Signs to the chateau will be on your right. The chateau is located 20 minutes south of Yosemite National Park on Highway 41.

A four-lip rating system fails us when we run across properties like Chateau du Sureau, which warrants at least ten lips (if not more). In fact, we were tempted to demote all of the other four-lip places in our book to three lips, because nothing we've seen compares to the luxurious grandeur of this authentic French provincial country estate. There aren't enough words (or lips) to describe what makes this place so extraordinary—you have to see it for yourselves to believe it.

Wrought-iron gates swing open to reveal a luminous white stucco castle with a stone turret and red tiled roof, ensconced on seven acres of wooded hillside. Stone walkways meander past a murmuring fountain, a stream-fed swimming pool, and lovely gardens.

Inside the manor walls you are greeted like royalty and ushered past common areas brimming with luxurious appointments to the palatial comfort of your room. Soon after, a plate of delicious appetizers arrives at your door, the first of many pampering touches. Chandeliers hang from the ceilings in each of the nine guest rooms; other amenities include fine European antiques, richly colored linens, large stone fireplaces, and French doors that open onto private balconies or patios. The rooms' spacious bathrooms are nearly like bedrooms themselves, with beautiful hand-painted tiles and, best of all, two-person soaking tubs.

In the morning, poached apples with cinnamon, vegetarian quiche with pesto sauce, homemade chicken sausage, gourmet cheeses, and homemade bread, among other gourmet delicacies, await guests in the sunny terra-cotta-tiled breakfast room.

Once you've played king and queen of the castle for a day or two, you'll find that returning to reality is almost more than any mortal can bear.

◆ **Romantic Alternative:** If Chateau du Sureau is booked for the evening, you're not without options. **THE HOMESTEAD,** 41110 Road 600, Ahwahnee, (209) 683-0495, (Moderate), is located ten minutes away and offers sophisticated adobe, stone, and cedar cottages set on 160 acres of wooded foothills and ranch country (you can even bring your horse). The cabins appeal primarily to naturalists who are looking to escape the city, but guests can still enjoy the modern comforts of spacious baths with pedestal sinks, fully equipped kitchens, queen-size beds, and a blend of contemporary and antique furnishings.

Restaurant Kissing

ERNA'S ELDERBERRY HOUSE, Oakhurst
48688 Victoria Lane, at Chateau du Sureau
(209) 683-6800
Unbelievably Expensive
Wedding facilities are available; call for details.

From Oakhurst, follow Highway 41 west. Signs to the chateau will be on your right.

People drive for hours just to have dinner at Erna's Elderberry House. You're apt to wonder why a restaurant in such an obscure location merits so many hours in a car. Once you've spent a blissful evening dining at this luxurious French restaurant nestled among elderberry trees, you'll undoubtedly be willing to drive for hours too. Chandeliers softly illuminate two country dining rooms filled with antiques, fine art, French fabrics, and cozy tables adorned with pink linens and flickering candles. Erna's exquisitely presented six-course, prix-fixe dinners change daily. We savored an aperitif of champagne and elderberry nectar, followed by sautéed scallops with red pepper timbale, polenta, and spicy pepper sauce; minted pea soup; compote and sorbet of pears and plums; broiled medallions of beef fillet; assorted garden lettuces with fruit vinaigrette; and mocha cloud torte or fresh raspberry tart. Utter perfection.

Bass Lake

Located just 14 miles from Yosemite National Park, Bass Lake is a sizable freshwater lake surrounded by evergreens and Sierra mountain peaks. Although much of the lakeshore has been inundated by residences and lodges, one side remains free from development, adding to its romantic allure and beauty.

Hotel/Bed and Breakfast Kissing

THE PINES RESORT, Bass Lake
54432 Road 432
(209) 642-3121
Moderate to Very Expensive
Wedding facilities are available; call for details.

From Highway 41, take the Bass Lake turnoff (Road 222) north of Oakhurst. Proceed four miles to Bass Lake and go left where the road divides. Continue two and a half miles to the Pine Village sign; turn right onto Road 434 and right again onto Road 432.

Reminiscent of a ski lodge, the Pines features 20 distinctive lakefront suites and custom two-story chalets. Though the decor is fairly standard, newer furnishings, private balconies, lake views, and two-person Jacuzzi tubs in some of the rooms are sure to assuage weary skiers. Those who aren't so weary can take advantage of the Pines' tennis courts, sauna and hot tub, outdoor swimming pool, and lake recreation (boating, waterskiing, fishing, and swimming), not to mention Yosemite National Park— only 14 miles away.

Restaurant Kissing

DUCY'S ON THE LAKE, Bass Lake   ◆
54432 Road 432, at the Pines Resort
(209) 642-3131
Moderate to Very Expensive
Wedding facilities are available, call for details.

From Highway 41, take the Bass Lake turnoff (Road 222) north of Oakhurst. Proceed four miles to Bass Lake and go left where the road divides. Continue two and a half miles to the Pine Village sign; turn right onto Road 434 and right again onto Road 432.

Knotty-pine walls adorned with antique skis and snowshoes lend rusticity to this dining room overlooking a marina on Bass Lake. Bare wood tables and cozy booths create a casual but comfortable atmosphere for enjoying sandwiches, burgers, or seafood. Ducy's is a perfect stopover on your way to or from Yosemite.

Fish Camp

Hotel/Bed and Breakfast Kissing

TENAYA LODGE, Fish Camp   ◆ ◆
1122 Highway 41
(209) 683-6555
Moderate to Expensive
Wedding facilities are available for a maximum of 1,000 people.

Follow Highway 41 north toward the southern entrance to Yosemite National Park. The lodge is on the right.

The mere fact that awe-inspiring Yosemite National Park is minutes from Tenaya Lodge might be incentive enough to trek here, though the lodge has earned its reputation on its own merits. Set just off the highway, Tenaya commands views of a luscious valley hemmed by trees rising in succession to the horizon. This panorama would be heavenly if it weren't for the parking lot that surrounds the hotel. Still, the advantages of staying here are tenfold. You might not have uninterrupted views of Yosemite's splendor, but at least you get what you pay for in terms of accommodations, service, and amenities—which is more than we can say for the other hotels found farther inside the park.

Chandeliers trimmed with candles hang from cathedral ceilings in the lobby, where a fire crackles in an immense stone fireplace. Relaxed Southwestern themes in all of the 242 guest rooms are executed tastefully and add a colorful flair to the otherwise conservative decor. Some rooms even have hand-carved wood four-poster beds. An indoor pool, fitness center, sauna, Jacuzzi, and rental bicycles are available for guests who still have energy after breathtaking tours of Yosemite.

Yosemite National Park

To say that Yosemite National Park is paradise on earth is not an exaggeration. I could use every adjective in my thesaurus and still not begin to describe Yosemite in its full glory. No matter which entrance you take to get into the park, your first stunning view of Yosemite is sure to literally take your breath away. Myriad waterfalls cascade over towering granite rock formations that rise thousands of feet above lush valleys and meadows, surrounding you with sublime splendor.

A visit to this extraordinary park could easily change your life, giving you a newfound respect for the awesomeness of nature. Although 89 percent of Yosemite's 1,170 square miles is designated wilderness, millions of yearly tourists are taking their toll on park resources. The Park Service is striving to preserve Yosemite's renowned beauty and hopes to eventually eliminate private vehicles in the park altogether. In the meantime, visitors are asked to tread lightly and disturb the land and the wildlife as little as possible.

◆ **Romantic Note:** For hiking information, contact the **WILDER-NESS OFFICE** at P.O. Box 577, Yosemite, CA 95389; for campground information contact the **CAMPGROUND OFFICE** at (209) 372-0200.

Hotel/Bed and Breakfast Kissing

AHWAHNEE HOTEL, Yosemite Village   ◆ ◆
(209) 252-4848
Very Expensive
Wedding facilities are available for a maximum of 100 people.

Follow signs to Yosemite Village and the Ahwahnee Hotel.

Even if you've never been to Yosemite you're probably familiar with pictures of the legendary Ahwahnee Hotel. Built in 1927, this landmark six-story hotel is made of native granite and concrete stained to look like redwood—an architectural masterpiece set beneath Yosemite's majestic Royal Arches. Walk-in fireplaces warm a colossal lounge where wrought-iron chandeliers plunge from cathedral ceilings and floor-to-ceiling windows capture wondrous views of Yosemite's sheer rock walls. Native American mosaics, rugs, and artwork adorn the lodge and embellish the notable, though somewhat standard, guest rooms.

◆ **Romantic Warning:** The Ahwahnee attracts an overabundance of tourists year-round. Reservations are hard to get, and when you do get them, the hotel staff is often overtired and sometimes downright rude. At these prices you should receive first-class service, but unfortunately you're a captive audience and the Ahwahnee takes full advantage of this fact.

◆ **Romantic Suggestion:** Even if an overnight stay at the Ahwahnee isn't in your romantic budget, do at least visit the magnificent lobby. Even though the lodge can get very busy, and even though the lobby is huge, the two of you can find a cozy and serene spot where you can relax by the fire and quietly visit.

YOSEMITE LODGE, Yosemite Village   ◆
(209) 252-4848
Very Inexpensive

Follow signs to Yosemite Village and the Yosemite Lodge.

This isn't the lap of luxury by any stretch of the imagination, but at least the price is right. Located near the base of Yosemite Falls, Yosemite Lodge has 495 rooms that range from better-than-standard to less-than-standard, in addition to rustic cabins both with and without private baths. (I know it sounds like faint praise, but you don't have much choice.) This is roughing it compared to the Ahwahnee, but it is a much less costly way to enjoy Yosemite Valley.

Restaurant Kissing

AHWAHNEE DINING ROOM, Yosemite Village   ❖ ❖
Ahwahnee Hotel
(209) 252-4848
Very Expensive

Follow signs to Yosemite Village and the Ahwahnee Hotel.

Given the poor service found at the Ahwahnee Hotel (see "Hotel/ Bed and Breakfast Kissing"), it's not surprising that our dinner there was straight out of a Laurel and Hardy movie. (If we hadn't been so hungry we might have found it humorous.) The mismanaged wait staff tripped and stumbled over themselves as they forgot our drinks, forgot to refill our drinks, and took an eternity to take our orders and bring our food. When our food finally did arrive, it was disappointingly mediocre, not to mention cold.

After all that, why did we bother to mention this place at all? Because the ambience is unquestionably romantic and its gorgeous surroundings nearly compensate for the appalling service. Grand sugar-pine trestles and granite pillars endow the enormous room with rustic elegance. During the day, full-length windows let in ample sunshine, as well as views of Glacier Point and Yosemite Falls. In the evening, chandeliers hanging from the high cathedral ceiling and slim candles in wrought-iron holders provide soft light for the cozy tables. To thoroughly enjoy this setting, consider limiting yourselves to drinks—it will be easier on your patience, as well as your stomachs.

◆ **Romantic Alternative:** The **MOUNTAIN ROOM BROILER,** Yosemite Lodge, (209) 372-1281, (Moderate), is really the only other dinner option in Yosemite Valley. The dining room, surrounded by murals depicting Yosemite scenes, is attractive, though somewhat dated. The menu is limited, but the food is quite good (how can you go wrong with pasta or chicken burgers?), prices are more than reasonable, and the service is attentive (imagine that!).

Outdoor Kissing

GLACIER POINT, Yosemite National Park

From Yosemite Valley follow signs to Glacier Point Road, which leads to Glacier Point.

No matter where you go, Yosemite abounds with spectacular views, but Glacier Point beats them all. The one-hour drive there (closed in winter) winds through fertile meadows and dense forest and sets the mood for the visual ecstasy that awaits you. Perched 3,200 feet above Yosemite Valley, Glacier Point commands mesmerizing panoramic views of the valley below, as well as Nevada and Vernal falls, the Merced River, and the Sierras rising in the distance. Yosemite's near-constant tourist traffic deters much of the wildlife from wandering here, but red-tailed hawks are often seen soaring effortlessly in the sky, and coyotes or deer sometimes emerge from the forest to forage for food.

◆ **Romantic Note:** An abundance of hiking trails originate from Glacier Point. Follow signs to these trails or get more information at the **VISITORS CENTER**, (209) 372-0200, located in Yosemite Valley.

MARIPOSA GROVE, Yosemite National Park

From the park's south entrance, follow signs to the Mariposa Grove on your immediate right.

This awesome grove of giant sequoia trees is right out of a storybook—you almost expect the trees to talk. What better place to pucker up than under the shade of the Grizzly Giant? (It takes 27 fifth-graders to reach around the trunk of this monstrous tree.) Cars are not allowed here (except for shuttle buses), so wander on foot through the hushed forest to your hearts' content.

TIOGA ROAD, Yosemite National Park

From Yosemite Valley, follow Big Oak Flat Road to Tioga Road and turn right.

Thirty-nine miles of scenic roadway might sound like a lot of driving, but Tioga Road boasts a multitude of wondrous turnouts, vistas, and natural attractions to keep you occupied. This long and winding road climbs high into the Sierras past forested hillsides, luxuriant meadows, and steep granite rocks. Be sure to stop at **TENAYA LAKE**, where mammoth granite mountains plummet right into a clear blue lake fringed by evergreens and granite rubble. Farther on you'll discover **TOULUMNE MEADOWS**, a peaceful roadside glen framed by mountains. If you continue to the eastern side of the Sierra Nevada, you'll find **MONO LAKE,** one of the oldest and most beautiful lakes in North America. Because of its high concentrations of salt and alkali, this crystal blue lake is outlined by white salt deposits that have been sculpted over time to resemble artistic sand castles.

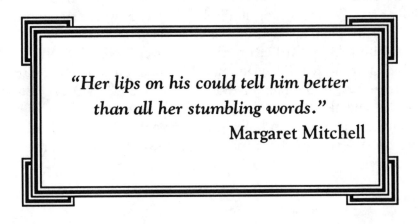

"Her lips on his could tell him better than all her stumbling words."

Margaret Mitchell

SOUTH COAST

Traveling the coastline of California is visual entertainment *par excellence*. The fury of the coast and the majestic scenery are nothing less than scintillating for literally hundreds of miles. Despite this seemingly unending spectacle, there are distinct differences between the coastal areas south and north of San Francisco.

Chic, urbane communities are scattered along the South Coast. Carmel, Monterey, and Pebble Beach are far more upscale than any of the little coastal towns found up north, or, for that matter, in many other regions of Northern California. If you and your beloved relish the chance to shop in stylish boutiques, eat in great restaurants, and relax in quality lodgings, the South Coast villages will more than live up to your dreams. And so will the area's incredible, dramatic views of the mighty Pacific.

Moss Beach

Hotel/Bed and Breakfast Kissing

SEAL COVE INN, Moss Beach
221 Cypress Avenue
(415) 728-7325
Expensive to Very Expensive

From Highway 1, turn west onto Cypress Avenue in Moss Beach. The inn is located on the right.

All the nuances for an enamored escape from city life are here, only 25 minutes away from San Francisco. Seal Cove Inn's adobe-colored stucco exterior with green trim is very distinctive. Inside, everything is first-class and immaculate. All of the ten spacious rooms feature a wood-burning fireplace with a nearby sitting area, private deck or terrace, complimentary wine, and a TV with VCR tastefully tucked away in an armoire; the upstairs rooms have vaulted ceilings and the two suites have Jacuzzi tubs.

The decor is simple yet comfortable, accented by linens that are either plaid, paisley, or floral. Full breakfast in the morning may include cinnamon French toast and fresh pastries. With all this comfort surrounding you, you won't be disappointed with your stay at this beautiful getaway.

◆ **Romantic Note:** My only hesitation in recommending Seal Cove Inn is that the rooms are a bit austere and there is a conference room next to the dining room. The "corporate retreat" feel here is great for executives, but for the purposes of this book a little cozier would be nice. On the other hand, the lack of lacy pillows and fuzzy teddy bears found at so many other bed and breakfasts might be a welcome change of pace. Especially if anything even slightly frilly isn't your idea of romantic.

◆ **Romantic Suggestion:** Unlike nearby Half Moon Bay, Moss Beach is in a small neighborhood setting, minus the development. Just around the corner from the inn, explore the fascinating natural tide pools at FITZGERALD MARINE RESERVE. And diminutive MOSS BEACH is the perfect place to observe the sun's nightly glissade into the ocean.

Princeton-by-the-Sea

Hotel/Bed and Breakfast Kissing

PILLAR POINT INN, Princeton-by-the-Sea   ◆ ◆
380 Capistrano Road
(415) 728-7377, (800) 400-8281 in California
Expensive

From San Francisco, head south on Highway 1. In about 25 miles, turn right at the traffic light for Capistrano at Princeton-by-the-Sea. The inn is on the right.

Immerse yourselves in quiet, carefree time together at this comfortably modern seaside inn that looks like it was transplanted from a New England village. From any of the 11 rooms, you can sit back and take in the profile of the harbor and ocean, leisurely viewing the movement around you. Boats anchored close to shore rock in rhythm with the waves, and fishing boats come and go, increasing your expectations of a fresh fish dinner. Accompanying this tableau are a tiled fireplace, downy

European feather bed, and the usual hotel-like amenities such as a telephone, refrigerator, and concealed television; one room has a walk-in steam bath. New England was never this warm (or this conveniently close to San Francisco). Until now, that is.

Breakfast in the morning is a delicious combination of homemade granola, fresh muffins, coffee cake, waffles, and egg dishes. A fireplace glows in the breakfast room, making your morning meal even more satisfying.

◆ **Romantic Note:** For a momentary change of pace from the solitude of Pillar Point Inn, be sure to stop across the street at **THE SHORE BIRD RESTAURANT**, 390 Capistrano Road, Princeton-by-the-Sea, (415) 728-5541, (Moderate). The building resembles a Cape Cod-style cottage and is bordered by a quaint flower garden. Inside, the rustic furnishings and low ceilings create a friendly, easygoing environment in which to enjoy locally caught fresh fish. Outdoor dining in the garden, with the ocean as backdrop, is also an option. Romancing may not be the primary reason to visit the Shore Bird, but the food and relaxed pace certainly are something you can get accustomed to.

Half Moon Bay

When the rest of the world is heading north of San Francisco to Stinson Beach and other points along the exquisite Marin County and Mendocino County coastlines, you can be winding your way south to Half Moon Bay. This quintessentially quaint little hamlet by the water feels literally a hundred miles away from big-city life (although it's only about 25 miles from San Francisco).

Half Moon Bay lovingly hugs the seaside along the rocky Pacific Coast Highway. With all that epic scenery, it is difficult to find a place that isn't suitable for hugging and kissing. The area is replete with miles of sandy beaches, equestrian trails, and bicycle paths; adventurers can arrange fishing charters, sailing sessions, and whale expeditions. Local wineries, charming little lunch spots, and plenty of parks will help round out your day. At night, visit one of the restaurants serving up an eclectic assortment of cuisines, or a club featuring classical and jazz music. Both can keep you busy well into the wee hours of morning, unless, of course, you can find something better to do.

Hotel/Bed and Breakfast Kissing

CYPRESS INN, Half Moon Bay
407 Mirada Road
(415) 726-6002, (800) 83-BEACH (in California)
Expensive to Very Expensive
Wedding facilities are available for a maximum of 50 people; call for
details.

*The Cypress Inn is off Highway 1, between Princeton Harbor and Half Moon
Bay. Take Medio Road toward the ocean; the inn is on the corner of Medio and
Mirada roads.*

Imagine that you could capture the vast ocean for one night and keep
it only for yourselves. At the Cypress Inn, you can. Elegance in nature is
the theme here, and your first clue is the inn's winding, wooden porch,
which has been built around a lone cypress tree to accommodate its
growth. The inn's exterior is covered with stained, not painted, wood to
give it the look of a grand beach house, but the true romantic extravaganza begins when you step inside. Your eyes will be dazzled by the celebra-
tion of Native folk art and fresh Santa Fe-style decor. Warm tones of
salmon, deep green, and unstained natural wood surround you as you venture up the stairs to your own distinctive room.

The eight rooms, each one named after an element in nature, feature
exceptional gas fireplaces, tile floors, spacious bathrooms with all the
amenities (the penthouse has a two-person Jacuzzi tub), and private balconies inviting you to cuddle close and gaze out at what feels like your
own private ocean. Climb under your cozy down comforter, listen to the
raging Pacific conducting a symphony right outside, and leave the shutters on the expansive windows open; the night sky might hypnotize you
with amorous dreams. When you wake, enjoy some morning kisses during
a bountiful breakfast. Choose from peaches-and-cream French toast,
salmon roulade, or blue cheese waffles with mushrooms and bacon. The
Cypress Inn is filled with natural wonder, and the feeling you'll leave with
will stay with you for the rest of your travels.

◆ **Romantic Note:** This inn was recently purchased by the owners of
the celestial **INN AT DEPOT HILL** in Capitola (see Capitola,

"Hotel/Bed and Breakfast Kissing"). Renovations, including the addition of four suites in an adjacent building, are planned. If the same loving care and special touches are devoted to the Cypress Inn, this place will ascend from merely sublime to absolutely phenomenal!

MILL ROSE INN, Half Moon Bay
615 Mill Street
(415) 726-9794
Expensive to Very Expensive
Wedding facilities are available for a maximum of 125 people.

Two blocks west of Main Street, at the corner of Mill and Church streets.

Framed by a classic white picket fence, a lush garden bursting with beaming colors welcomes you to the Mill Rose Inn. From the manicured rose garden in the courtyard to the luscious chocolates and liqueurs in every room, attention to detail hasn't been spared. This English country inn is obviously well taken care of, and as guests, you will be too. Leave your frazzled city nerves behind and get ready for pampered luxury and quiet intimacy.

Each of the six suites has its own private entrance through the garden, a European feather bed, garden view, and fresh flowers, and all but one have a glowing fireplace. Decor in each is subtly different, but two of my favorites are the Briar Rose and the Bordeaux Rose. The snug, homey Briar Rose has a hand-painted tile fireplace, a bay window large enough for two, and an ample whirlpool tub (also large enough for two). The Bordeaux Rose is intimate and inviting: shades of peach and ivory accent a lace-covered canopied bed framed by a hand-sculpted stained glass window. If you get tired of your room, which hardly seems possible, step downstairs for afternoon wine and cheese or a decadent dessert in the evening. If you don't stay in the suite with the in-room tub for two, you can visit the flower-shielded gazebo that encloses a Jacuzzi spa enhanced by lush greenery, more flowers, and a bubbling fountain. Don't worry about finding a crowd in the spa—you can reserve time here for a private, hot steamy soak of your own. After a good night's sleep, enjoy a champagne breakfast in the dining room or, better yet, have it delivered to your room or to a table in the peaceful rose garden.

Mill Rose Inn prides itself on offering special, affectionate services, such as preparing snacks and towels for a picnic on the beach or helping arrange a candlelit dinner in your room. Also, romantic board games are in each suite for you to playfully get to know each other even better than you already do.

OLD THYME INN, Half Moon Bay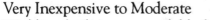
779 Main Street
(415) 726-1616
Very Inexpensive to Moderate
Wedding facilities are available for a maximum of 20 people.

Four blocks east of Highway 1 in Half Moon Bay.

Sometimes "cute" can spark even the most skeptical among us to expose our amorous, snuggly side; at other times it can do just the opposite. The Old Thyme Inn is careful to make sure its cute touches are only warmhearted, not trite or corny. The stuffed bears in every room, which can sometimes be too much, literally captured my heart. This handsomely renovated home, built in 1899, is packed with a sense of history, but feels warm and affable. The seven rooms are simple, but each is outfitted with something distinctive that makes it welcoming and delightful: a fireplace, a four-poster bed, a private bathroom with a whirlpool tub built for two, or a stained glass window, for example. The Garden Suite is by far the most romantic room. It has a private entrance, a double Jacuzzi tub under a large skylight, vaulted ceilings, and breakfast brought to your room at your leisure.

In the evening, wine and sherry are served around a wood-burning stove in the parlor. Breakfast in the morning is always a plentiful offering of fresh scones, fruit and nut breads, quiches, and fresh fruits. Garnishes are provided by the inn's own overproductive herb garden, which contains more than 80 aromatic varieties, all available for tasting by inquisitive guests. This may not be the most luxurious place you'll ever stay, but it could be one of the more interesting.

◆ **Romantic Alternative:** The **ZABALLA HOUSE**, 324 Main Street, Half Moon Bay, (415) 726-9123, (Inexpensive to Moderate), is a great bet for some nonformal rest and relaxation. This country-style bed and breakfast has nine fresh and bright rooms, each decorated in the same ordinary and somewhat out-of-date fashion. Most of the rooms have queen-size beds, but be sure to specify whether you desire a whirlpool tub or a fireplace, because you can't have both (as nice as the whirlpool tubs and fireplaces sound, the rooms are still just standard.) A full breakfast is served in the parlor at one long table, adding to the feeling of friendship that glows throughout the house.

Restaurant Kissing

SAN BENITO HOUSE, Half Moon Bay   ◗ ◗ ◖
356 Main Street
(415) 726-3425
Inexpensive to Moderate
Wedding facilities are available for a maximum of 150 people.

Three blocks south of Highway 92, at the corner of Main and Mill streets.

The aroma of freshly baked bread caught my attention as I happened past the San Benito House Restaurant one extremely lazy, sun-drenched summer afternoon. Unfortunately, it was not open for lunch that day. I continued on, but found nothing else particularly interesting. As the day progressed, that tempting fragrance lingered in my memory and I couldn't resist the idea of returning for dinner. We called for reservations and went that same evening.

This French country dining room is adorned with a fanciful blend of dried and fresh flowers, wicker baskets, and original oil paintings. The impression is one of charming sophistication. Guests who know the restaurant call first to see what the chef has prepared for dinner. The prix fixe meal consists of several courses and a choice of three entrées. Almost always, the menu incorporates fresh fish brought in by local fishermen and fresh produce from local farmers. Our dinner that evening was delicious, the service professional and helpful, and the homemade bread tasted even better than it had smelled.

◆ **Romantic Note:** Dinner is served Thursday through Sunday only; a lavish buffet brunch is offered on Sunday.

◆ **Romantic Warning:** The hotel attached to San Benito House is not as expensive as some of the other places to stay in Half Moon Bay, but be forewarned: it is not anywhere near as nice, either.

Santa Cruz

The 1989 earthquake hit this area pretty hard. Five years later, it looks like it hasn't recovered. Granted we were recently there during the off-season, but Santa Cruz felt eerie and empty. The boardwalk and downtown areas were devoid of life, houses looked empty, and everything seemed rundown. In the summer it's a completely different story (except things are still rundown). Huge crowds stroll the boardwalk, cotton candy and tickets for the roller coaster and other amusement-park rides in hand. There is more to Santa Cruz than the bustling boardwalk area (like the University of California at Santa Cruz), but this is what the town is most known for, and a large stretch of beach is beside it.

Hotel/Bed and Breakfast Kissing

BABBLING BROOK INN, Santa Cruz
1025 Laurel Street
(408) 427-2437, (800) 866-1131
Moderate
Wedding facilities are available for a maximum of 40 people.

From Highway 1 (Mission Street), turn south toward the water at Laurel. The inn is a block and a half down, on the right.

An acre of redwoods, pines, flower gardens, tumbling waterfalls, a graceful babbling brook with a massive waterwheel, and covered footbridges highlights this delightful bed and breakfast. The landscaping is impeccable from every perspective. Inside, a French country atmosphere is evident throughout the guest rooms and cottages. There are 12 units here, some with private entrances, private decks, fireplaces, two-person whirlpool tubs, and sturdy canopied beds. Nibble on homemade cookies before strolling down to the beaches and the sparkling Pacific Ocean. In the early evening, after a long day of building sand castles, you will find wine and cheese waiting for you. In the morning, a generous country breakfast gives your day a good start.

♦ **Romantic Note:** If you could transport the Babbling Brook Inn to a quiet neighborhood or a wide stretch of beach, it would be sublime.

Unfortunately, it is located on a busy, rather noisy street. Nevertheless, the setting and the churning waterwheel will help you ignore the traffic.

◆ **Romantic Alternative:** Attached to a noteworthy restaurant (see "Restaurant Kissing") is the **CASA BLANCA INN,** 101 Main Street, Santa Cruz, (408) 423-1570, (Inexpensive to Expensive). The 27 rooms here are spacious and attractive. Most have spectacular views of the water and boardwalk, many have their own private deck, and some have a fireplace. Rooms 18, 19, and 22 have more privacy than the others (meaning no view of the boardwalk), and are cozier and more romantic. The other rooms are also quite nice, but if you look past the boardwalk and focus your attention on the Pacific Ocean in all its endless blue glory, your stay will be more mellow and intimate.

Restaurant Kissing

CASABLANCA RESTAURANT, Santa Cruz
101 Main Street
(408) 426-9063
Moderate
Wedding facilities are available for a maximum of 45 people.

Take Highway 1 to Bay Street, proceed to West Cliff Street, and turn left. Drive half a block to Beach Street. The inn is at the corner of Main and Beach in the heart of Santa Cruz, a half block east of the Santa Cruz Wharf.

If you're looking for a restaurant with a view, you need look no further. This renovated 1918 mansion is directly across the street from the beach, and the dining room's tall, stately windows overlook this wonderful sight past the boardwalk. You'll glimpse boats rocking on the ocean and the surf rolling onto the shore. Just beyond, the wooden pier seems to change moods as the sun sets and street lamps begin to brighten the scene. The Casa Blanca's interior feels like a small country inn, and the menu offers classic continental steak and seafood dishes. A wonderful brunch is served on Sundays, and dinner is served nightly. After an enjoyable meal, don't be surprised if the one you're with reaches for your hand and attempts a Bogart impression, saying something like, "I think this is the beginning of a beautiful friendship."

◆ **Romantic Note:** The **CASA BLANCA INN** (see Romantic Alternative to Babbling Brook Inn in "Hotel/Bed and Breakfast Kissing"), attached to the restaurant, offers nice rooms if you don't mind being this close to the boardwalk.

Outdoor Kissing

NATURAL BRIDGES STATE PARK, Santa Cruz
West Cliff Drive
(408) 423-4609
$6 per day per car

From the Santa Cruz boardwalk, follow West Cliff Drive north along the shore to the park entrance.

Once upon a time, a beautiful orange-and-black monarch butterfly came to court its mate in a wooded canyon near the seashore. Before long, other wooing butterflies discovered this lover's lure. Today, hundreds of thousands of monarchs return to this spot each winter, creating a kaleido-scope of color among the sweet-scented eucalyptus. The two of you can stroll hand-in-hand into this storybook setting along a wooden walkway that leads down into the woods to a platform nested in the monarchs' winter home. Or you can simply lie on the platform and watch them flutter above you like colorful stars touched with life. The beach and tide pools nearby invite additional kissing as you wander toward the ocean.

◆ **Romantic Note:** The best time to visit is midday, late November to early February. Migration times vary, but you can always call ahead to make sure the colorful creatures are around.

Aptos, Soquel, and Capitola

Capitola has been described as "what Carmel was like 30 years ago." This quaint seaside hamlet has just enough handicraft stores and clothing boutiques to make it interesting, but not enough to steal an entire after-noon away from kissing by the melodic Pacific surf. Though farther north than its affluent seaside neighbor, Carmel, Capitola has a decidedly Southern California feel. Brightly clad surfers skim through the waves, students from the nearby college play beach games, and couples picnic on the sand. A promenade stretches along the shore, and the view stretches even farther north and south along the coastline. Benches face out over the ocean, so you can sit, embrace, and daydream.

Nearby and inland, Aptos and Soquel have a certain amount of charm. Although they don't share the ocean drama you'll find at Capitola, they still provide seclusion and country appeal. After all, the beach is only a short drive from here and the prices are not nearly as intimidating as seaside accommodations.

Hotel/Bed and Breakfast Kissing

BLUE SPRUCE INN, Soquel
2815 South Main Street
(408) 464-1137
Inexpensive to Moderate

From Highway 1, take the Capitola/Soquel exit, go east to the first stop sign, and turn right onto South Main Street.

With the nearby Pacific as inspiration, it's no wonder that the Blue Spruce Inn indulges its guests with unpretentious elegance. This renovated 120-year-old home is as fresh as a sea breeze. The colorful Amish quilts that warm the beds are the focal point of each guest room's decor. The innkeepers commissioned local artists to echo the hues and motifs of the quilts in paintings that adorn the walls. Fun and romantic luxuries include a Jacuzzi built for two, a four-jetted massage shower, or a shower that couples can't resist getting wet in together—in addition to the hot tub in the garden. A private entrance opens to Seascape, with its ocean blues and greens, wicker chairs, feather bed, gas stove, and bow-shaped double Jacuzzi. Two Hearts is a cozy hideaway with a deep red heart-patterned quilt, touches of white eyelet, dormer ceilings, and a full-body shower. In the Carriage House, skylights just above the headboard of the raised bed invite kissing beneath the stars.

INN AT DEPOT HILL, Capitola   ◆ ◆ ◆ ◆
250 Monterey Avenue
(408) 462-3376, (800) 57B-AND-B
Expensive to Unbelievably Expensive
Wedding facilities are available for a maximum of 75 people.

From Highway 1, take the Park Avenue exit turning toward the ocean. Continue on Park for one mile and turn left onto Monterey Avenue. The driveway is immediately on the left.

If ever an inn deserves to enter the annals of romance, this one does. I wish I could extend my kiss rating, because it would surely rate ten lips. Opulently decorated rooms evoke the world's most romantic destinations. Imagine kissing your love in a Parisian pied-a-terre, a Mediterranean retreat on the Cote d'Azur, an English cottage in Stratford-on-Avon, or an Italian coastal villa in Portofino: the guest rooms truly do reflect the essence of these locales.

All of the spacious rooms have unbelievably luxurious furnishings, private marble baths, wood-burning fireplaces, stereo systems, televisions with VCRs (concealed unobtrusively in cabinets), coffee makers, hair dryers, fabric steamers, and fresh flowers to match the decor. Five have private Jacuzzis. Cuddle with your love before the blue-and-white Dutch tile hearth in the Delft Room, or embrace beneath the full, white linen-and-lace canopy on the billowing feather bed, or daydream on the window seat while gazing upon your private garden, or indulge in a private whirlpool surrounded by tulips, or splash together in a double-headed shower—and this is just one room! Each room description could fill a book, and we haven't even told you about the private red-brick patios with their own gazebos. Full breakfasts, afternoon wine with appetizers, and evening desserts ensure energy for continuous kissing, because if you can't kiss here, you can't kiss anywhere.

◆ **Romantic Suggestion:** We guarantee that you won't want to leave your room at the Inn at Depot Hill, but be reasonable, you've got to eat! If one of you can talk the other into searching for provisions, try **GAYLE'S BAKERY AND ROSTICCERIA**, 504 Bay Avenue, Capitola, (408) 462-1200, (Inexpensive to Moderate). Outstanding spit-roasted chicken, gourmet salads, and sinful desserts make it worth leaving your sumptuous room just for a minute.

MANGELS HOUSE, Aptos
570 Aptos Creek Road
(408) 688-7982
Moderate

From Highway 1, take the Seacliff Beach exit and turn onto Soquel Avenue. Pass under a bridge, and just before reaching a little shopping center, turn left onto Aptos Creek Road. The inn is a half mile up, on the right.

During the Victorian heyday, the elite vacationed in fabulous country homes, far from the cares of the city but complete with all the luxuries. The Mangels House, built in the 1880s by California's sugar beet king, is one of the most secluded and best restored of these homes. To reach it, you must drive (carefully!) down a one-lane woodland road. Just when you would expect to see a rustic campground, this whitewashed Italianate mansion with a wraparound veranda looms above the forest. Enter the door to a ball-room-size parlor, where the grand piano seems dwarfed. Comfortable contemporary sofas are clustered around the massive stone fireplace.

The five guest rooms preserve the feeling of spaciousness, with delicate color schemes and lush florals reflecting today's luxury in the grand tradition. One room has a fireplace and one has a private porch, but they all have high ceilings, queen-size beds, private baths, and tall windows that look out over a charming English garden with fountain and gazebo. The African Room is decidedly different, with African artifacts, dark walls, shiny white furnishings, and geometric prints. Right outside the door are some of the area's best hiking trails, perfect for an afternoon stroll back to nature.

◆ **Romantic Alternative:** If you're looking for something more old-fashioned than elaborate, spend time at **THE APPLE LANE INN**, 6265 Soquel Drive, Soquel, (408) 475-6868, (Inexpensive to Moderate), a charming 1870s Victorian farmhouse perched on a knoll overlooking orchards. A fire warms the Victorian parlor, the breakfasts will content hearty gourmets, and the five guest rooms are pleasantly decorated with antiques and country flair. The only problem is that some rooms share baths and the dormer ceilings might cramp the style of taller kissers.

Restaurant Kissing

CAFFE LIDO, Capitola
110 Monterey Avenue
(408) 475-6544
Moderate

From Highway 1 take the Capitola/Soquel exit to Bay Avenue and drive toward the ocean. Bay Avenue becomes Monterey Avenue. The restaurant is the last building on your left before the beach.

Somebody had actually left a kiss mark on the window near our table at the Caffe Lido. This contemporary Italian cafe is *perfetto* for fun romance and good food topped off with special liqueur-laced coffees. Classic Italian music, including opera, sets the mood. In the afternoon, as the sun pours in, you can gaze out over the beach and watch couples strolling by, monarch butterflies flitting on the bushes, and surfers searching for the endless summer (it's right here!). Pasta with seafood, grilled Mediterranean chicken dishes, and hearty coppa or prosciutto sandwiches with cheese will delight the palate (although we've had reports saying that the kitchen has been inconsistent). Lunch and dinner are served daily.

◆ **Romantic Warning:** The service at the Caffe Lido leaves much to be desired. Try to focus on the sand and sunny surf outside rather than on how long it takes for your food to come.

CHEZ RENEE, Aptos
9051 Soquel Drive
(408) 688-5566
Expensive
Wedding facilities are available for a maximum of 40 people.

From southbound Highway 1, take the Rio del Mar exit and turn left. Go over the freeway and turn left again onto Soquel Drive. The restaurant is one-third mile down, on the right.

Chez Renee, situated off a small business area, is synonymous with exquisite dining in the Santa Cruz area. This comfortable, unpretentious little restaurant, with its white tablecloths, glowing fireplace, and cozy bar, serves traditional and not so traditional French cuisine. The award-winning dining you will find here is a very serious affair for your palate, but never let it be said that French chefs don't have a sense of humor. The night we were there, we had the "Maui Wowee" entrée: pan-grilled fresh Hawaiian ono served with pineapple salsa and macadamia nuts. It was excellent.

COUNTRY COURT TEA ROOM, Capitola   ◆ ◆ ◖
911-B Capitola Avenue
(408) 462-2498
Inexpensive
Wedding facilities are available for a maximum of 75 people.

On Capitola Avenue, just off Soquel Drive.

A restaurant that specializes in fireside breakfasts and authentic English-style high teas may seem out of place on a busy suburban street, but here it is and it is charming. The interior is simple, with ivy painted on the walls and adorable knickknacks tucked in every corner. The room holds only a handful of small and intimate tables; the ones near the fireplace are the most desirable. The food is excellent, and due to pressure from loyal fans, the chef offers a Friday-night dinner with a choice of two main courses. When we were there the ambrosial entrées were lamb stuffed with feta and pesto and salmon perfectly broiled in lemon butter. I don't think the English ever had it this good.

◆ **Romantic Alternative:** As you enter the **BALZAC BISTRO**, 112 Capitola Avenue, Capitola, (408) 476-5035, (Inexpensive), with its funky, ultra-casual atmosphere, you may wonder why we chose to include it. Keep going. The special spot may take some work to get to (up the stairs, past the rest rooms, and down the kitchen hall), but the room is a starry treat. The garden room, which we recommended only at night, is walled in by glass, with tiny white lights shining like a sky full of stars for your romantic pleasure.

FIORELLA'S, Capitola
911 Capitola Avenue
(408) 479-9826
Moderate

On Capitola Avenue, just off Soquel Drive, behind the Country Court Tea Room.

The location, next to an apartment complex, is a bit peculiar for a romantic spot; nevertheless, Fiorella's is an enchanting place. Subtle and refined, small and intimate—all the right ingredients combine to create an attractive setting for dinner. And speaking of ingredients, the food is absolutely delicious. The pasta dishes are beautifully presented, and the service is polite but casual. Weather permitting, there is garden seating outside in a pretty courtyard. By the way, as you enter the restaurant, be sure to notice the reproduction of the Sistine Chapel's ceiling on the wall in the bar. It was painted by a local high-school boy and is an amazing facsimile.

SHADOWBROOK, Capitola   ◆ ◆ ❬
1750 Wharf Road
(408) 475-1511
Moderate
Wedding facilities are available during the day on Saturday for a maximum of 200 people.

Four miles south of Santa Cruz on Highway 1, take the 41st Street exit and head west for a half mile. Turn left onto Capitola Road and proceed a half mile to Wharf Road, then turn left. The restaurant is on the right.

Shadowbrook is probably the most often recommended romantic restaurant in the Santa Cruz area. Access to this unique dining room, located on the banks of the Soquel River, is gained via a steep, winding footpath surrounded by greenery, or a little red cable car that creaks over its tracks to drop you at the front door. Covered by dense, lush foliage, this Swiss-style chalet has a totally enchanting storybook appearance. Dinner is served seven nights a week, lunch on Saturday and Sunday only. The traditional California cuisine is usually quite good, especially if you order what's fresh. The cocktail lounge is a particularly romantic destination, and well worth a visit for a quiet after-dinner tête-à-tête.

THE VERANDA, Aptos
8041 Soquel Drive, in the Bayview Hotel
(408) 685-1881

Expensive
Wedding facilities are available for a maximum of 125 people.

From southbound Highway 1: Take the Seacliff Beach exit and turn left over the freeway to the first light (Soquel Drive). Turn right onto Soquel; the restaurant is about a half mile down on the left, in the Bayview Hotel. From northbound Highway 1: Take the Rio del Mar exit and turn right, then turn left onto Soquel Drive; the restaurant is about a half mile down on the right.

You may be surprised to find a grand Victorian hotel in the little town of Aptos. You'll be pleasantly surprised at the elegant restaurant that adorns its first floor. Its series of spacious dining rooms are decorated in delicate peach and accented with dried flower wreaths. Creative American dishes with a gourmet twist are the house specialty. Try the salmon cooked in a mustard-herb crust, or the filet mignon in a Roquefort-pecan crust with a Kentucky bourbon demiglace. Pick a table on the glass-enclosed veranda and hold hands across the table on a sunny afternoon. In the evening, one dining room glows with the warmth of an old Victorian hearth.

◆ **Romantic Note: THE BAYVIEW HOTEL,** 8041 Soquel Drive, Aptos, (408) 688-8654, (Inexpensive to Expensive), offers bed-and-breakfast accommodations upstairs from the Veranda. High ceilings, antiques, rich florals, and fireplaces or huge soaking tubs in some of the rooms add a touch of romance, but the modern-style decor seems out of place and the rooms are on the cozy side, as the hotel was built in 1878. The small parlor downstairs, with velvet-covered furniture and a Victorian gas hearth, is for guests, but shares the same entrance as the restaurant.

◆ **Romantic Alternative:** Across the street from the Bayview Hotel is a small, appealing restaurant called **CAFE SPARROW,** 8042 Soquel Drive, Aptos, (408) 688-6238, (Inexpensive to Moderate), that serves health-oriented but savory French cuisine for lunch and dinner. Food this good is usually found in a more sophisticated setting, but the casual country ambience is more than appropriate. This kind of romantic dining can be cherished without any affectation. Breakfast (weekends only) is also very French and superb. Try the omelet with sautéed chicken livers, served with smoked bacon, apples, and crème fraîche.

Monterey

Monterey was once a part of Mexico, and that heritage is reflected in its venerable adobe homes and the meticulously maintained parks bursting with flowers. Many of the surviving historical landmarks now house museums, and you can almost touch the past as you stroll by them. The main signatures of this well-known romantic destination are the cypress forests, rolling hills, and spectacular rugged coastline. Monterey's position at the edge of the Pacific offers those who stop here some of the same advantages that a small (relatively crowded) waterfront town would supply; almost everything you'll want to see and do is within walking distance. There are intriguing restaurants and hotels that put to good use the almost year-round mild weather, and many are blessed with bewitching views of the clear aqua bay and vivid blue sky. Of course, there are also the concomitant tourist attractions, such as Fisherman's Wharf, Cannery Row, and the Monterey Bay Aquarium, which means Monterey can also be dreadfully crowded. Fortunately, that can easily be dealt with by allowing yourselves to concentrate on the stunning location and architecture.

Speaking of popular destinations, **CANNERY ROW** is a bustling reminder that the more things change, the more they stay the same. This building complex once thrived on the business of catching and canning sardines. Now it is a series of shops and restaurants in the business of catching tourists. Why would you want to kiss here? Well, actually you probably won't want to kiss here. What you could do, though, is browse, laugh, hold hands, stroll, and have a leisurely meal by the sparkling blue bay. Cannery Row is not what you would call romantic, but it can be fun, and that's a good prelude to just about anything—including kissing—any time.

Hotel/Bed and Breakfast Kissing

HOTEL PACIFIC, Monterey   ◆ ◆ ◆ ◖
300 Pacific Street
(408) 373-5700
Expensive to Very Expensive

On Pacific Street, one block south of Del Monte.

With so many bed and breakfasts and charming small inns to choose from on the Monterey Peninsula, it's hard to believe anyone would want to stay at a big hotel. Hard to believe, that is, until you see a handful of the very chic, very lavish hotels that have been developed in this area. Hotel Pacific is one of them, and it seems more like a romantic retreat than a traditional hotel. The approach to this genteel escape reveals a flowing fountain at the entry, ring-necked doves serenading guests in the lobby, courtyards trimmed with weathered wooden furnishings, and dense flowering vines lining the pathways and walls. Terra-cotta tiles and Santa Fe-style print fabrics accent the 103 guest rooms, where a wood-burning fireplace, a thick, cushy feather bed with a down comforter, a separate living area with hardwood floors, and a private patio or balcony facing the nearby bay all feel appropriately luxurious. The top-floor rooms all have high beamed ceilings and curtained, canopied beds made from sand-blasted pine logs. The hotel is located in the heart of town, near all of the things you will want to see in Monterey. But don't be surprised if you find yourselves staying in your suite.

A complimentary continental breakfast is served buffet-style in a small plush lobby filled with overstuffed couches and chairs. There aren't enough seats in this room, and even if there were more seats, it is too cramped to accommodate so many guests. We took our pastries and fruit out to the garden-trimmed courtyard, sat at the fountain's edge, and planned our day in peace and quiet.

◆ **Romantic Alternative:** On a downtown street, the **MONTEREY HOTEL**, 406 Alvarado Street, Monterey, (408) 375-3184, (Moderate to Expensive), is small enough to be charming yet large enough to offer all the amenities of a larger resort. Some of the rooms and suites have views of the harbor and bay. Be sure to ask for a description of the room you are booking; while all of them are handsomely furnished, some are too small for even the most intimate of couples.

OLD MONTEREY INN, Monterey
500 Martin Street
(408) 375-8284
Expensive to Very Expensive

From southbound Highway 1: Take the Soledad/Munras exit. Cross Munras Avenue, then turn right onto Pacific Street. Go a half mile to Martin Street;

the inn is on the left. From northbound Highway 1: Take the Munras Avenue exit. Make an immediate left onto Soledad Drive, then turn right onto Pacific Street. Drive a half mile to Martin Street; the inn is on the left.

This is the kind of place you fall in love with the moment you enter the garden gate. It is Eden with all the extras. The gardens are opulent in a natural way, with pots of flowers hanging like jewels from the gnarled branches of old trees and paths that meander to secluded niches where you can kiss to your heart's content. Inside this 1929 English Tudor, every detail spells romance. Eight of the ten guest rooms have fireplaces. An antique book of poetry placed upon a shawl in each room sets the mood for old-fashioned cuddling. In the Garden Cottage, with its own private entrance, a bridal white linen-and-lace crown canopy is draped above the bed, while a fireplace with tile hearth warms the white wicker-furnished sitting room. Even the Dovecote, despite dormer ceilings, feels bright and spacious, with a skylight overhead and a wood-burning fireplace. Rich florals, antiques, full gourmet breakfasts, billowing floral draperies, rich colors—this is one of Monterey's many pieces of paradise. In the warmer months, breakfast is served on brick patios surrounded by a profusion of pink and white impatiens, roses, wisteria, and boxwood hedges.

◆ **Romantic Alternative: THE JABBERWOCK**, 598 Laine Street, Monterey, (408) 372-4777, (Moderate to Expensive), filled with delightful touches from *Alice in Wonderland*, has heaps of character and a charming lived-in ambience that can feel friendly to some and frumpy to others. Its wraparound sun deck in back looks over a delightful lawn and gardens. Romantic touches like the Toves' cathedralesque, carved wooden bed or the Borogrove's spacious sitting area by a hearth will make you forget this was once a convent.

SPINDRIFT INN, Monterey
652 Cannery Row
(408) 646-8900, (800) 841-1879
Expensive to Unbelievably Expensive

On Cannery Row, between Hoffman and Prescott.

In the midst of Cannery Row, right on the ocean, the Spindrift Inn is an elegant, ultra-chic, architecturally beautiful place to stay. The setting makes it even more attractive. Waves roar up onto the rocks below, and the smell of salt water turns the aesthetic suites into sanctuaries for interpersonal introspection. On the ocean side, window seats in each room allow you to nestle together as the surf's magnetism vibrates in the air. Behind you, a wood-burning fireplace bathes the hardwood floors, Oriental carpet, and sumptuous fabrics in an amber glow. Each room also offers a down comforter on a canopied bed, a goose-down feather bed, and a spacious brass-enhanced bathroom. If it's a warm evening, only one irresistible option could possibly tempt you away from all this new-found comfort: a stroll along the silvery moonlit beach. In the morning, a continental breakfast awaits at your door; in the afternoon, high tea is served in the inn's rooftop garden, where there's a magnificent view of Monterey Bay.

◆ Romantic Alternative: The MONTEREY PLAZA HOTEL, 400 Cannery Row, Monterey, (408) 646-1700, (Expensive to Very Expensive), is located in the heart of Cannery Row, which could be a romantic problem if it weren't for what happens once you step inside the foyer. Your eyes will scan past the polished marble floor, the cozy lounge, and the balcony, to focus on the horizon, most of it filled with ocean. Water is the focal point of the Monterey Plaza Hotel, so unless you can get a room with a water view, we don't recommend staying here. The rooms have a standard hotel-like feel with flimsy bedspreads and undistinguished furnishings. Waves break underneath the building, and the sound of the surf swells through its chambers and corridors. After you've enjoyed the sun's dramatic descent, dinner at the hotel's DUCK CLUB RESTAURANT, (Moderate), will be a pleasurable interlude. From its windows you can admire the shimmering moon dancing across the bay and the sparkle of city lights twinkling in the distance.

Restaurant Kissing

FRESH CREAM, Monterey   ❖ ❖ ❖
99 Pacific Street, in the Heritage Harbor building
(408) 375-9798
Expensive to Very Expensive
Wedding facilities are available for a maximum of 160 people in the whole restaurant, or 20 people in a private room.

Across from Fisherman's Wharf, on the second floor of the Heritage Harbor building.

Fresh Cream is one of the most revered French restaurants in Monterey. The dining room, which looks out toward the nearby harbor, is refreshingly bright, with colorful reproductions of early California art highlighting the simple, modern architecture. The service is refined, and the food, artfully presented yet served in hearty portions, is so delicately scrumptious that you will want to savor every bite. The subtle spices of the veal sausage en croûte were enhanced by Madeira and white wine sauces, the rack of lamb was perfectly roasted, and the chocolate cake Celestine was sinfully delicious. Not surprisingly, this is a popular meeting place for friends as well as lovers, ideal if you're in the mood for light-hearted romance rather than a quiet dinner for two.

SARDINE FACTORY, Monterey   ● ◖
701 Wave Street
(408) 373-3775
Expensive
Wedding facilities are available for a maximum of 100 people.

On the corner of Wave and Prescott streets.

The Sardine Factory has the reputation of being one of the more romantic dining spots in Monterey, and unfortunately that makes it a bit of a tourist attraction. Still, despite the fact that it is almost always packed, romance can be found here. The centerpiece of the lounge where we waited for our table to be ready is a stunning 120-year-old hand-carved bar. Friends had told us to request seating in the Conservatory, one of the restaurant's five dining rooms, and we were grateful for their advice. Covered by a glass dome and surrounded by a garden, this lovely room makes a prime setting for inspirational conversation and loving thoughts. The menu offers a mix of fresh seafood dishes.

◆ **Romantic Warning:** We waited in the lounge about 20 minutes for our table. Often, glowing reputations also mean delays, even when you have reservations.

Outdoor Kissing

ADVENTURES BY THE SEA, Monterey ◆ ◆ ◆ ◆
299 Cannery Row
(408) 372-1807
Kayak rentals are $20 per day

Between Reeside and Drake on Cannery Row; across from the Monterey Plaza Hotel.

Kayaking side by side on the gentle waters of the Monterey Bay is a special experience you'll remember long after you return home. Pelicans skim the water's surface. Seals laze on the rocks. Playful otters loop in and out of the kelp, sometimes even plopping coquettishly on the front of your kayak. Beneath you, myriad colors and textures flow by, punctuated with bright orange and gold starfish. These stable boats are made for laid-back drifting, interspersed with unhurried paddling. Far from the crowds of Cannery Row, you can hold hands and, perhaps, steal an adventurous kiss. You'll even stay nice and dry, with special coveralls that pull over your clothes. If you pack a picnic before heading out, you can pull up onto a beach or share it right on the water.

FISHERMAN'S WHARF, Monterey

At the intersection of Scott and Oliver streets.

Like Cannery Row, this is a location worth visiting for an hour or two on a sunny afternoon. Actually, it's not the facility that makes it worthwhile, it's the oceanfront location. Ambling down the boardwalk, your senses tickled with the smell and taste of the swirling, salty ocean currents, you will pass souvenir shops, stands selling OK-to-mediocre seafood, and lots of restaurants boasting views of the bay. Be sure to stop in at **RAPPA'S**, Fisherman's Wharf #1, Monterey, (408) 372-7562, (Inexpensive), at the end of the pier. The restaurant seems to virtually float on the water. From tables near the window you can watch pelicans and sea gulls skim over the water as they rush to feed on the remains of the cleaned fish piled high by the fishermen returning with their daily catch.

MONTEREY BAY AQUARIUM, Monterey   ❖ ❖ ❖
886 Cannery Row
(408) 648-4888

At the end of Cannery Row is another of the city's tourist attractions, but this one presents a not-to-be-missed opportunity to view the marine life that abounds below the water's surface. This aquarium is one of the world's largest and best, housed in an unbelievably realistic underwater setting.

RENT-A-ROADSTER, Monterey   ❖ ❖ ❖
229 Cannery Row
(408) 647-1929
About $30 per hour

We never knew driving could be so much fun. With a toot of the "ahooga" horn, we were off to tour the coastline in our reproduction of a 1929 Model A roadster. The top was down, the sun was shining in, waves were crashing, and people waved to us as we trundled by. This unusual company offers five Model A's and one two-door deluxe phaeton for rent, all very easy to drive, with modern engines capable of doing 55 miles per hour (but why hurry?). Be sure to allow enough time to stop by the seashore along Lovers Point near Pacific Grove, which is only a few minutes away from Rent-A-Roadster. Or plan on doing the 17-Mile Drive (see Pacific Grove, "Outdoor Kissing") in style. If another couple you know is romantically inclined, they can join the fun in the Model A's rumble seat.

◆ **Romantic Alternative:** Another playful way to tool around Monterey is to rent a pedal surrey or a bicycle built for two at **BAY BIKES**, 640 Wave Street, Monterey, (408) 646-9090. The surreys have two sets of pedals and a brightly striped, fringed roof, but you can pedal them only on Monterey's bike path along Cannery Row: the surreys aren't allowed on streets. Athletic romantics can pedal their bicycle built for two along the 17-Mile Drive or all the way to Carmel (about 14 miles). If you're tuckered out, you can leave the bike at **BAY BIKES II**, on Lincoln between Fifth and Sixth in Carmel.

Pacific Grove

For now the developers have left the oceanfront of Pacific Grove alone, which for them might be a disappointment, but for you is a delightful kissing advantage. Pacific Grove is the most overlooked town on the Monterey Peninsula. While Monterey and Carmel are often crowded to overflowing, you can still find a measure of peace and solitude along the Pacific Grove shoreline and in the town of Pacific Grove. The bed and breakfasts and restaurants here are some of the most wonderful we've encountered.

Hotel/Bed and Breakfast Kissing

THE CENTRELLA, Pacific Grove ◆ ◆
612 Central Avenue
(408) 372-3372, (800) 233-3372
Moderate to Expensive

From southbound Highway 1, take the Pacific Grove/Pebble Beach exit (Highway 68) until it veers left. Once you reach Pacific Grove, the highway becomes Forest Avenue. Follow Forest Avenue to Central Avenue, turn left, and continue to the inn.

Warm hospitality and comfortable ambience are what you'll find at this friendly Victorian bed and breakfast. It holds 26 guest rooms, but the best units are the five garden cottages and the three suites in the main house (some of the other rooms share baths). A brick walkway bordered by camellias and gardenias connects the inn to the separate cottages, which all have private entrances, fireplaces, and attractive sitting areas. The spacious suites have skylights over the beds and are adorned with Laura Ashley prints.

Every afternoon, freshly baked cookies and a carafe of cream sherry sit on an old oak table in the bright parlor, where the sun beams in through a wall of beveled glass windows. Here you can relax after a long, unhurried afternoon of meandering through the streets of Monterey and Pacific Grove. In the morning, we stirred to the scent of freshly brewed coffee and more homemade goodies as the innkeepers set out a fabulous morning buffet.

THE GATEHOUSE INN, Pacific Grove
225 Central Avenue
(408) 649-1881
Moderate to Expensive
Wedding facilities are available for a maximum of 100 people outside, or
10 inside.

On Central Avenue, at Second Street.

Built as a seaside "cottage" in 1884, this imposing but gaily restored
Victorian has all the trappings of an elaborate home enhanced with
amenities that its original builders would envy. Elaborate, custom-
designed, hand-silkscreened wallpapers adorn the walls and ceilings. In
some of the nine rooms, you'll want to lie in bed together just to admire
the intricate Middle East-inspired patterns above you. In the Langford
Suite, a lacy canopy hangs like a billowy cloud above the bed while a gas
fire glows in the white, very feminine cast-iron stove. The Sun Room
feels almost like an indoor garden with its white wrought-iron bed and
view of the nearby ocean. The small Victorian Room is the least expensive but has a partial ocean view and is absolutely the most sexy room.
Wine-colored curtains cast a rosy glow over the room's sumptuous burgundy linens and claw-foot tub.

Fresh home-baked cookies, fresh fruit, and tea and coffee are served all
day, and you can help yourself to the fully stocked refrigerator full of juice,
soda, milk, cheese, and yogurt. We also enjoyed the afternoon wine and
appetizers, including delicious homemade cheeses. In the morning, a full
breakfast buffet of specialties such as pumpkin-cornmeal pancakes or
cheese strata with bacon was the perfect start to a romantic day by the sea.

♦ **Romantic Suggestion:** Somehow, not having to get dressed for breakfast makes a morning together that much more romantic. For $5 per person,
you can have breakfast delivered to your room if you arrange it in advance.

THE GOSBY HOUSE, Pacific Grove
643 Lighthouse
(408) 375-1287
Inexpensive to Moderate
Wedding facilities are available for a maximum of 60 people.

At the corner of Lighthouse and 16th.

All of the charm you need, and then some, can be found at this stunning Victorian bed and breakfast. The 22 adorable guest rooms are sumptuously appointed with down comforters, polished natural wood furnishings, delicate wallpapers, and fresh flowers; some have fireplaces. The rooms in the Carriage House were recently refurbished with fireplaces and whirlpool tubs with separate showers. The Trimmer Hill Room has a private balcony with a porch swing and all-new furnishings. No detail is left unattended. The generous buffet breakfast and late-afternoon high tea will be highlights of your stay. In fact, the only thing that's missing here is an ocean view.

GREEN GABLES INN, Pacific Grove ❖ ❖ ❖
104 Fifth Street
(408) 375-2095
Moderate to Expensive
Wedding facilities are available for a maximum of 80 people.

From Highway 1, take Highway 68 west to Pacific Grove. Follow Forest Avenue to the ocean, turn right onto Ocean View Boulevard, and follow it to Fifth Street. The inn is at the corner of Ocean View and Fifth.

From the street the exterior is striking; from the front gate the surroundings look like a fairy tale come to life; and from the moment you step inside this Queen Anne-style mansion, you'll know you are about to begin an enchanting experience. The inn, as its name suggests, is a multi-gabled structure with leaded glass windows that afford a dreamy view of Monterey Bay. The parlor houses a collection of antiques, where a brightly painted carousel horse sits behind a sofa, stained glass panels frame the fireplace, and freshly cut flowers are arranged about the room. Halfway up the stairs that lead to some of the guest rooms, a pair of teddy bears keep company on a small wicker chair.

Most of the 11 rooms are decorated in paisley and country floral prints. Some have sloped ceilings, others have bay windows, comfortable sitting areas, fireplaces, and scintillating views of the nearby ocean. The five rooms in the adjacent Carriage House are more spacious, but the ocean view isn't as grand. Regardless of which corner is yours, you can at least indulge in this soothing setting while enjoying a full buffet-style breakfast, served beside a fireplace and expansive windows that face the shimmering sea.

◆ **Romantic Warning:** All of the rooms but one in the main house share bathrooms, which in the opinion of the editors is not conducive to uninterrupted kissing. Be sure to request a room with private facilities, unless your ability to partake in uninterrupted smooching is contingent upon lower-priced accommodations.

LIGHTHOUSE LODGE SUITES, Pacific Grove
1249 Lighthouse Avenue
(408) 655-2111, (800) 858-1249
Moderate to Very Expensive

Follow Lighthouse Avenue toward the ocean. Check in at 1150 Lighthouse Avenue, then continue down the street to the lodge, on the left just before the shore.

Even those of us who love Victorian decor sometimes grow weary of intricately patterned wallpapers, antique knickknacks, and, yes, claw-foot tubs. The Lighthouse Lodge is a welcome change of pace, combining privacy with modern comfort. All of the 29 contemporary suites feel like little apartments with private entrances, vaulted ceilings, refrigerators, microwaves, wet bars, large Jacuzzis (in all but two rooms), gas fireplaces, plush robes, color televisions, and bedside dimmer switches to help create an amorous atmosphere. Full breakfasts are served in the spacious common room, which has a fireplace at either end. In the afternoon, a hearty variety of complimentary appetizers and local wines invite quiet conversation after a busy day of touring together. All this is a pebble's toss away from one of the Monterey Peninsula's most beautiful seaside settings.

◆ **Romantic Warning:** Often, when properties are bought by large hotel chains, they lose their individuality and charm. Best Western recently purchased the Lighthouse Lodge along with another close-by hotel, but the lodge suites haven't been changed much. When making your reservations, be absolutely sure that you reserve a Lighthouse Lodge suite rather than a unit in the separate hotel section, otherwise you will end up with a below-standard, dark little room that isn't even remotely romantic.

THE MARTINE INN, Pacific Grove
255 Ocean View Boulevard
(408) 373-3388, (800) 852-5588
Moderate to Very Expensive
Wedding facilities are available for a maximum of 80 people.

On Ocean View Boulevard, between Third and Fourth streets.

This towering, light pink mansion is perched above the rocky Monterey Bay coastline. The exterior is classic Mediterranean in style, the interior entirely Victorian. The 19 rooms here are spacious (some border on huge), furnished with authentic, massive antiques, and enhanced by handsome wood detailing. Some have fireplaces and views of the water, but our favorite was the Edith Head Room, with its formidable four-poster canopied walnut bed and lacy linens. The spacious garden cottages have private entrances, but aren't necessarily the most romantic choice; instead, opt for a room with a close-up view of the bay. In the morning, hearty breakfasts are served in the dining room, where the spectacular scene of water crashing against the rocky shore is featured as the main course.

SEVEN GABLES INN, Pacific Grove
555 Ocean View Boulevard
(408) 372-4341
Moderate to Very Expensive

From Highway 1, take Highway 68 and follow the signs to Pacific Grove. Once in Pacific Grove, stay on Forest Avenue to the ocean. Turn right onto Ocean View, and continue two blocks to Fountain Avenue. The inn is at the corner of Ocean View and Fountain.

There is no other word for this celestial bed and breakfast than "perfection." Every detail, every appointment is sheer luxury. The Seven Gables Inn is a prodigious yellow mansion trimmed in white that sits on a rocky promontory in Pacific Grove. From every plush, stately room you can glory in dramatic views of the glistening ocean and coastal mountains. This grand house, painstakingly renovated, is filled with an extensive collection of fine art and antiques. Tiffany glass windows, Persian carpets,

18th-century oil paintings, marble statues, and crystal chandeliers are just some of the collector's items that adorn the inn. The interior is formal and polished, yet it is a place where you will feel at ease and comfortable.

Each spacious guest room is an extraordinary, ultimately cozy, private retreat. Broad windows draped in lace and balloon valances make the rooms bright and sunny by day. At night, the classic lighting fixtures give each room a soft, warm glow. The bathrooms are simple and modern. It must be the elegance and warmth that draw so many honeymooners to the Seven Gables Inn. On most weekends you will find at least one or two couples spending their wedding night here. And even if it's not your honeymoon, all that romance is sure to rub off!

Breakfast, served family-style, is a grand affair of freshly made muffins, croissants, and special egg dishes. A generous, proper high tea, also served in the exquisite dining room, features tortes, homemade fudge, and a large assortment of pastries, not to mention a stunning view of the water.

Restaurant Kissing

FANDANGO, Pacific Grove   ❤ ❤
223 17th Street
(408) 373-0588
Moderate

On 17th Street, just south of Lighthouse Avenue.

This engaging, casual, Mediterranean-style restaurant provides a potpourri of options. Flowers and sunshine engulf a festive patio where brunch can be a gratifying open-air repast. Indoors, a crackling fire and just a few tables in each of the three front dining rooms provide a more intimate experience. If you step down a curved stone staircase, you'll find a wine cellar set up for special occasions. In the glass-domed terrace, the scent of mesquite from the open grill mingles with the sounds of laughter to create an informal setting.

There is only one thing more difficult than deciding where to eat here, and that is deciding what to eat. Lunch and dinner are served daily, and on Sunday you can bill and coo your way through a reasonably priced, incredibly well-done Sunday brunch. The food is flavorful and the menu is full of creative choices. Once the tough decisions are out of the way, though (all decisions should be this tough), you can sit back and unwind. After all, isn't that an integral part of a romantic evening?

◆ **Romantic Alternative:** Another casual dining option is the **THAI BISTRO**, 159 Central Avenue, Pacific Grove, (408) 372-8700, (Inexpensive). The tables are too close together to feel very intimate, but striped cushions and pillows help create a bright, airy atmosphere. Even though the setting on a downtown street isn't extremely charming, the food is great and patio seating is available on sunny days. This could be a great place for a laid-back lunch.

GERNOT'S, Pacific Grove
649 Lighthouse Avenue
(408) 646-1477
Moderate

On Lighthouse Avenue and 19th Street.

Gernot's is special. The stately Victorian mansion houses a polished, plush dining room where every aspect of your evening will be wonderful. The three separate dining rooms are adorned by Victorian floral wallpaper, lace curtains, hardwood floors, and Oriental rugs; one room has a cozy fireplace. The small menu, with a handful of specials every evening, includes such delicacies as simple broiled salmon with angel-hair pasta, and breast of duck roasted with raspberry brandy sauce. The moderate prices and gracious service add to the pleasure, but regardless, the setting is priceless.

OLD BATH HOUSE, Pacific Grove
620 Ocean View Boulevard
(408) 375-5196
Moderate to Expensive
Wedding facilities are available for a maximum of 75 people.

At the edge of Lovers Point, on Ocean View Boulevard.

The Old Bath House provides a beautiful oceanside dining experience. The fact that it's located at Lovers Point Park makes it even more romantic. Waves seem to roll in right below your table. After the sun ebbs into the sea, only the city lights in the distance compete with the flickering flames of candles alight all over the restaurant. Little can compete with the intimacy this place sparks, except the food, which is a blend of French and northern Italian cuisine. The desserts are created by the kitchen's own pastry chef and worth every sinfully rich calorie.

Outdoor Kissing

PACIFIC GROVE SHORELINE

Take Highway 1 to westbound Highway 68. Highway 68 becomes Forest Avenue; take it all the way to the ocean.

The major activity here is relaxing and savoring the majestic scenery. Take time to saunter arm-in-arm along **OCEAN VIEW BOULEVARD**, where a whisper of salt water gently sprays over you as the waves thunder against the rocks at water's edge. Here you can watch sea otters splashing in kelp beds, pelicans perching in sunny spots, and, if the time of year is right, maybe a whale or two swimming by as they migrate south for winter. If you expect your walk to take you to **LOVERS POINT PARK**, at the southern tip of Monterey Bay, consider packing a picnic to share in the shade of a tree or in the warmth of a gloriously sunny day.

For an even more isolated stroll, be sure to traverse the glorious, windswept sands along **ASILOMAR BEACH**.

17-MILE DRIVE
$6 entry fee

From Highway 1, take Highway 68 west to Sunset Drive, and go west again to the Pacific Grove entrance gate.

This drive is so awesome and resplendent that you will take much longer to travel this unspoiled terrain than its 17-mile length suggests. That's because you will want to stop several times along the way to observe the infinite variations as ocean and land meet along the Monterey Peninsula. White, foamy waves wash up on black rocks, sending a spray of sea into the crisp, clean air; sea gulls cry out as unruffled pelicans perch near the water's surface.

As you round one spiral of road, you'll spy a crescent-shaped sandy cove that provides a calm place to pause. Here, sunlight shimmers on the vast Pacific, and in the distance a sailing vessel slowly makes its way across the horizon. Many other turns in the road will reveal undulating sand dunes, violently frothing sea currents, and abundant marine life sanctuaries. Watch for the stark beauty of a lone cypress clinging to the side of a cliff, swaying in the wind, and be sure to stop at **SEAL AND BIRD ROCK** to witness a multitude of marine beasts and birds basking in the sun and frolicking in the water.

As you continue on your passage up a hill, turning to the east, you will enter a deeply wooded area that shelters palatial homes and estates and the occasional world-class golf course. Unless watching the rich and famous is your idea of an intimate interlude, continue on and in a few more turns the natural beauty of the peninsula will be yours again. If you are hungry or would like to pause, you can visit one of the restaurants at the **INN AT SPANISH BAY** or **THE LODGE AT PEBBLE BEACH** (see Pebble Beach, "Hotel/Bed and Breakfast Kissing"). Some of these restaurants overlook the stunningly profound landscape below, and the food almost equals the view.

Pebble Beach

Elite Pebble Beach, located along 17-Mile Drive, is home to millionaires, deluxe accommodations, a crashing coastline, championship golf courses, and sometimes the U.S. Open. Golf isn't typically a couples sport (yes, we know some couples who are exceptions to this rule and love golfing together), but we recommend staying here because it is situated on one of the most gorgeous stretches of California's coastline, not because of the impressive courses. Do not expect to find reasonably priced accommodations.

Hotel/Bed and Breakfast Kissing

THE INN AT SPANISH BAY, Pebble Beach   ❖ ❖ ❮
2700 17-Mile Drive
(408) 647-7500, (800) 654-9300
Unbelievably Expensive

On 17-Mile Drive.

The exclusive Inn at Spanish Bay looks more like a condominium community than an inn, but if being catered to (and playing golf on world-famous courses) appeals to you, then the slick atmosphere and country-club feel shouldn't hinder the romance potential. Rooms facing the ocean are the most exorbitant, but regardless of view, all 270 have a fireplace, deep soaking tub with separate shower, contemporary decor, spartan but elegant furnishings, and all the amenities you'd expect from a luxury resort.

◆ **Romantic Suggestion:** If you don't want to leave this prime locale to find a place to eat, fear not. The inn has two dining options: **THE DUNES** (Moderate), and **THE BAY CLUB** (Very Expensive). The Dunes offers an ocean view from almost every table and a continental mix of salads, sandwiches, and pasta. The atmosphere is casual, with wicker chairs and lavender table linens. The sleek, formal Bay Club specializes in northern Italian cuisine, and is appointed with high-backed plush chairs, track lighting, and a massive flower arrangement at its center.

THE LODGE AT PEBBLE BEACH, Pebble Beach   ◆ ◆ ◆ ◀
17-Mile Drive
(408) 624-3811, (800) 654-9300
Unbelievably Expensive

On 17-Mile Drive.

You want elegance? You've got elegance. In fact, it's hard to get away from it at the world-renowned Lodge at Pebble Beach. (But who would want to?) However, don't be fooled by the word "Lodge"; you won't find any antlers on the walls here. The breathtaking lobby, with its high ceiling, rich cream and dark wood decor, and entire far wall lined with immense floor-to-ceiling windows, is your first clue that this place is an extraordinary find. The view from the lobby takes in the tailored lawn and, beyond that, nothing but dramatic surf as far as the eye can see. Don't worry about finding an exclusive golf-club atmosphere; the mood here is chic without being at all stuffy.

All 14 of the stately white houses that surround the grounds display a Spanish flair and were built some 80 years ago. Inside, the individual sophistication, personality, and design are more than evident. You can't go wrong with any of the rooms; 48 of them have breathtaking ocean views with nothing standing between you and the sea, and 83 have what they call garden views, which really means they overlook the expansive main lawn and, in the distance, the award-winning 18-hole golf course. Some of the rooms have one-person Jacuzzi tubs and wood-burning fireplaces to cuddle up in front of as the murmur of the Pacific Ocean lulls you to sleep. Although the property itself is too large to be considered intimate, the incredible rooms more than make up for it with posh refinements. One of the more choice buildings is the Sloat, where the rooms are dressed in soft browns and accented with rich maroon and hunter green linens. The antique-style overstuffed couches and chairs invite you to surround yourselves in snuggly comfort. Whatever your taste, from timeless antiques to fresh art deco, or somewhere in between, the Lodge at Pebble Beach will inspire many elegant ocean kisses between the two of you.

♦ **Romantic Suggestion:** CLUB 19 (Moderate to Expensive), at the edge of the lodge's manicured lawn, is a delightful place for a light lunch or, better yet, for a French dinner highlighted by a blazing coral sunset. The glass-enclosed dining room faces the glistening ocean and is filled with glass tables and dark green iron chairs. The other dining option is the **TERRACE LOUNGE**, which would be considered romantic only by die-hard golfers because of all the golf memorabilia lining the walls.

Carmel

After spending a great deal of time looking for kissing places, I take pride in knowing that I've been to (probably) all of the most romantic places in Northern California. From that perspective, when I say that no other place I've seen is quite as quaint or as charming or as crowded as Carmel, I'm saying a lot. Much of that allure I attribute to what Carmel lacks—namely, billboards, neon signs, tall buildings, parking meters, and high heels. (There is actually a law on the books stating that it is illegal to wear high heels on the sidewalks, but don't worry, I assure you that it is not enforced!)

Carmel is home to some of the most colorful boutiques, interesting galleries, adorable inns, and finest restaurants in the state. Since these are clustered in a very small area, discovering all of Carmel is an outstanding way to spend a day or two. A few blocks away from the center of town are enviable seaside homes, and white sandy beaches lie just in front of them, proffering a more restful way to while away the hours. Without question, you will find yourselves captivated by this town's charm and its flawless setting.

◆ **Romantic Note:** Part of Carmel's appeal is its small size; most of the establishments don't even have numbers on their doors. Therefore, most of the entries in this section of the book do not include formal addresses, only street junctions. Once you are in Carmel, these will be more than enough to help you find your destination. Because of Carmel's popularity, be warned that most weekends during the entire year are disturbingly crowded, and the entire summer season goes beyond just being crowded to the point of bursting.

Hotel/Bed and Breakfast Kissing

CARMEL VALLEY RANCH RESORT, Carmel   ◆ ◆ ◆ ◆
One Old Ranch Road
(408) 625-9500, (800) 422-7635
Very Expensive to Unbelievably Expensive
Wedding facilities are available for a maximum of 180 people.

From southbound Highway 1, turn left onto Carmel Valley Road. Drive six miles past ranches and rolling hills to Robinson Canyon on the right. Look for the gated entrance to Carmel Valley Ranch Resort on the left.

Alas, we regret the limits of a four-kiss system, for even the memory of the Carmel Valley Ranch Resort makes us long for an embrace. Once through the gated entrance of this 1,700-acre estate, we were greeted by name, then led to a secluded suite nestled in the branches of old, sculpted oak trees. Although the buildings are contemporary and new, they seem right at home in this stunning natural setting. For one magical evening, this was our private retreat. The sun was setting over the valley below, and a small herd of deer pranced by our window as we settled before the wood-burning fireplace in the living room. A cathedral ceiling soared above, soft floral watercolors set the mood, and a second wood-burning fireplace in the bedroom promised late-night romance. Before dinner, we indulged in a romantic soak beneath the stars in our private hot tub on a wraparound deck set up high in the trees, a true nest for lovebirds.

As if this were not enough, we headed to the resort's restaurant, reserved exclusively for guests, for a meal that was impeccable. The food filled our senses like the kiss of true love, from the home-baked whole wheat hazelnut bread to the shiitake mushrooms with cream in filo to the veal medallions with prosciutto to the chocolate marquise cake. Artfully presented and flawlessly served, this masterpiece was complemented by an award-winning wine list, a warm fire, and the clear tones of a grand piano that we felt was being played just for us.

♦ **Romantic Note:** There are 100 individually decorated rooms here, but the suites with wood-burning fireplaces in the bedroom and private decks are the most romantic; 12 of them have a private spa in the deck.

CARRIAGE HOUSE INN, Carmel
Junipero, between Seventh and Eighth
(408) 625-2585
Expensive to Very Expensive

All that Carmel has to offer is right outside the door of this attractive country inn, but you'll feel worlds away from the bustling village once inside your room. All 13 comfortably appointed rooms have wood-burning fireplaces, king-size beds, and down comforters. The upstairs rooms have open-beam ceilings and sunken or whirlpool bathtubs. In our two-room suite, touches of mauve accented the massive four-poster pine bed, an exposed beam ceiling towered overhead, and a fireplace crackled right by the bed. Another fireplace in the sitting area was supplied with plenty of logs, ideal for fireside kissing to our hearts' content. An assortment of wines and cheeses is served every afternoon in the lobby area. In the morning a generous continental breakfast is delivered to the room for your convenience and privacy.

♦ **Romantic Alternative:** The **SUNDIAL LODGE**, Monte Verde, at Seventh, Carmel, (408) 624-8578, (Moderate to Expensive), is cordial and cozy. The rooms are done in an assortment of French country, wicker, and Victorian styles. The red brick courtyard, surrounded by multicolored flowers, is a nurturing place to spend time outdoors on a sunny afternoon.

COBBLESTONE INN, Carmel
Junipero, between Seventh and Eighth
(408) 625-5222
Moderate to Expensive

The common rooms at the Cobblestone Inn are hardly what anyone would call common: you cross a cobblestone courtyard to enter a living room-like lobby that is also covered in stone (and teddy bears). This is where a lavish breakfast buffet and afternoon hors d'oeuvres are served in front of a massive stone fireplace. (You can also have breakfast served in your room if that is your romantic preference.) All of the 24 guest rooms have the same cozy country feel and a river rock fireplace. This is reputed to be one of Carmel's best-run bed-and-breakfast establishments, and in this part of the world that's saying a lot.

◆ **Romantic Warning:** The largest window in every room looks out toward the charming cobblestone courtyard, which unfortunately also doubles as a parking lot, making your room feel less private.

◆ **Romantic Alternative:** PINE INN, Ocean Avenue, between Monte Verde and Lincoln, Carmel, (408) 624-3851, (800) 228-3851, (Inexpensive to Expensive), has a slow-burning fire in the hearth of the main lobby, and beside it a love seat of rich, red velvet. It would be easy to lose track of time here, were it not for the grandfather clock in the corner striking each hour. Upstairs, some of the 49 guest rooms have fireplaces and ocean views, and all have comfortable antique beds and choice Edwardian-style furnishings. The restaurant at the inn is nice, and the reasonably priced meals are quite good. Be sure to have breakfast or lunch in the restaurant's indoor/outdoor garden—on a sunny day, the domed glass ceiling rolls back to reveal a crystal-clear blue sky. The Pine Inn is located in the heart of Carmel, close to the beach, shopping, and theater.

THE HAPPY LANDING, Carmel
Monte Verde, between Fifth and Sixth
(408) 624-7917
Moderate to Expensive

You may feel like you've entered the land of the Lilliputians in this charming fairy-tale inn. Each guest room is a cozy little cottage with high peaked ceilings that are quaint without being too cutesy. All rooms have a private entrance with a rounded, gabled door that opens to a delightful inner courtyard, a perennial blue-ribbon winner in the Carmel Garden Fair. Romantic touches include Victorian fringed lamps, hand-painted floral sinks, and a decanter of sherry with glasses for two. If you splurge on a suite, which is the same price as many standard hotel rooms in Carmel, you can cuddle up by a fire. If not, warm your toes by the fire in the Victorian common room and nibble on cookies and tea in the afternoon. In the morning, a breakfast of home-baked muffins or scones is delivered to your door. The memory of your time together will live happily ever after at this adorable inn.

◆ **Romantic Note:** The "manly man" may feel a bit out of place here in the land of happy. If your honey doesn't mind "cute," then this is the place to be.

LA PLAYA HOTEL, Carmel ❖ ❖ ❖
Camino Real and Eighth
(408) 624-6476, (800) 582-8900
Moderate to Unbelievably Expensive
Wedding facilities are available for a maximum of 100 people.

At the grand La Playa Hotel, where the Pacific Ocean peers at you through pine and cypress trees, and the sound of the dramatic surf echoes in the distance, the world is a dazzling place. In spite of its "hotel" appellation, this is the place to stay if you long for a graceful setting that also has all the luxury of a larger establishment.

La Playa's lobby is warmed by an enormous fireplace and decorated with hand-loomed area rugs and antiques. The 75 guest rooms are filled with hand-carved Spanish-style furnishings, and some have incredible ocean views and fireplaces. The cottages and suites at La Playa are even better places to find yourselves, but only if you have very deep pockets. These are some of the most expensive units available, but they are also the most enticing. Each has its own full kitchen or wet bar, terrace or garden patio, and most have fireplaces. Surrounding this handsome Mediterranean-style villa are sprawling, neatly manicured lawns awash with colorful flowers. There is even a heated pool encircled by lavender poppies swaying on slender stems. If you believe sheer beauty can conjure up romantic rapport, your time at La Playa will be pure magic.

◆ **Romantic Alternative:** While **THE CYPRESS INN**, Lincoln and Seventh, Carmel, (408) 624-3871, (Moderate), is inspired by the same Spanish influence as the La Playa Hotel, it is a much smaller place. The rooms here are not quite as elaborate, but the simple beauty of the inn and its cobblestone courtyard evokes the appropriate frame of mind for encounters of the heart. Wedding facilities are available for a maximum of 30 people.

◆ **Romantic Suggestion:** The **THUNDERBIRD BOOKSHOP AND CAFE**, 3600 Barnyard, off Highway 1 and Rio Road, Carmel, (408) 624-9414, (Inexpensive), is not your typical romantic location, but I urge you to seek it out. After you've perused the aisles and selected a book together, you can sit by an open fireplace in one of the rooms and lose yourselves in your new literary find. The golden warmth from the fire helps set the mood for spicy reading while you sip a cup of coffee and nibble on one of the Thunderbird's fresh pastries. All this can add up to a perfect expenditure of time. If you want a table with more content, dinner is also served here.

LINCOLN GREEN INN, Carmel   ◆ ◆ ◖
Carmelo, between 15th and 16th
(408) 624-1880
Moderate
Wedding facilities are available for a maximum of 20 people.

Register and pick up room keys at the Vagabond's House Inn, at Dolores and Fourth, near the town center. Directions will be given from there.

I would love to slightly change the name of this picturesque place, because there is nothing resembling an inn here. Lincoln Green Cottages would be a much more appropriate moniker. Set in a quiet neighborhood, far away from Carmel's bustling town center and two blocks from the legendary Carmel shoreline, are four quaint country cottages encircled by immaculate gardens, venerable shade trees, and a white picket fence. Each cottage is painted white with forest green trim and shutters, much like you would expect to find in the English countryside. The only drawback is that the interiors are not as splendid as the exteriors. Even though the cottages are large, have beamed cathedral ceilings, and three have stone fireplaces and a full kitchen, they are more utilitarian than plush or charming. Still, they are a great secluded place to call home while you explore the Monterey Peninsula. And from this vantage point, you may never know that the summer crowds are only a mile down the street.

THE MISSION RANCH, Carmel
26270 Dolores Street
(408) 624-6436, (800) 538-8221
Expensive to Very Expensive

From southbound Highway 1, turn right onto Rio Road. Follow Rio Road one-half mile to Lasuen Drive and turn left. Mission Ranch is at the end of Lasuen Drive and Dolores Street.

A short distance away from the sometimes intense city of Carmel lies a downhome surprise. The Mission Ranch looks as if it were dropped here straight out of the ranchlands of Texas. This friendly place, owned by Clint Eastwood (this distinction may give it more prestige than it deserves), allows you to leave any notion of city life behind. Settle into any one of the 31 comfortable rooms in any one of the six different cottages. White walls, cozy queen- or king-size beds with warm floral or country-style patchwork quilts, and soft cloth curtains surrounding picture windows adorn each room. The two of you can sit to your hearts' content gazing out at the lush green meadows dotted with sea grass. Some rooms, like the Meadow View Rooms and the Hay Loft Bedroom, have gas fireplaces and one-person whirlpool tubs, although you do pay a dear price. The Bunkhouse cottage is equipped with a full kitchen in case you want to cook a lovers' feast and dine in together. The Mission Ranch is complete with everything you'll need for some easygoing country togetherness.

◆ **Romantic Warning:** The bar-and-grill-style Restaurant at Mission Ranch features checked tablecloths and an informal atmosphere. Look elsewhere for romantic and intimate dinning.

SAN ANTONIO HOUSE, Carmel
San Antonio, between Ocean and Seventh
(408) 624-4334
Moderate to Expensive

Four generous suites, each with its own entrance, cozy antique furnishings, and a radiant, wood-burning fireplace, await you at the San

Antonio House. The light and airy Treetops Room is the most private, with a beautiful view of manicured gardens. The gardens, rimmed by stone terraces, help round out this intimate place, and you're just one short block from the sun-clad beach.

In the morning, a generous continental breakfast tray of fresh pastries, egg dishes, and fresh fruit is brought to your room or served on the beautiful garden patio. Such an intimate place is a wonderful find in the Carmel area.

VAGABOND'S HOUSE INN, Carmel   ❖ ❖
Fourth and Dolores
(408) 624-7738, (800) 262-1262
Inexpensive to Moderate
Wedding facilities are available for a maximum of 20 people.

This handsome English Tudor home is engulfed by oak trees that softly shade this inviting property. Each of the 11 rooms is generous and comfortable. Special amenities include kitchenettes, recently remodeled bathrooms, a decanter of sherry beside the bed, and a view of the inner courtyard overflowing with camellias, rhododendrons, ferns, and colorful flowers. Some rooms even have wood-burning fireplaces. One particularly romantic room has a view of a massive oak tree adorned with tiny white lights that could easily be mistaken for twinkling stars against the midnight sky. The Vagabond's House Inn is a great place to call home for a few days of relaxing time together.

Restaurant Kissing

ANTON AND MICHEL, Carmel   ❖ ❖ ❖
Mission, between Ocean and Seventh
(408) 624-2406
Expensive
Wedding facilities are available for a maximum of 28 people in a semi-private room, or other arrangements can be made. Call for details.

As we walked by Anton and Michel one evening, we could see that there was something extraordinary about this restaurant. Impressive oil paintings were hung on pastel walls; long, slender white columns separated one part of the dining room from another; and one entire wall of windows framed a patio that had a cascading water fountain at its center. Quickly we made reservations for the next night. The setting seemed to inspire intimate conversation and long loving looks at each other—that is, until the food arrived. We tried the house specialty, rack of lamb, and would recommend it to anyone. It's cooked to perfection and carved at your table. A little later, after turning our attention back to each other, we ordered a chocolate mousse that was sinfully rich and beautifully served. The focus of the menu is fresh meats carved at your table, but the fresh fish is equally good. This is a place where you can share a truly memorable evening. In fact, lunch here is also wonderful, and a romantic bargain. The restaurant is open daily for both lunch and dinner.

◆ **Romantic Alternative:** It's not easy to find **KENNY'S FLYING FISH GRILL**, Mission, between Ocean and Seventh, Carmel, (408) 625-1962, (Moderate), where traditional Japanese table cooking is the specialty of the house. Nevertheless, the warm, casual atmosphere, glowing wood interior, excellent food, and uncommon setting combine to make this an international find.

CASANOVA, Carmel   ◆ ◆ ◆
Fifth, between San Carlos and Mission
(408) 625-0501
Expensive
Wedding facilities are available for a maximum of 50 people.

When we asked a friend who grew up on the Monterey Peninsula for Carmel's most romantic restaurant, she immediately answered, "Casanova." This charming restaurant, located in an old home once owned by Charlie Chaplin's cook, is tucked away on one of Carmel's quiet side streets. Behind the unassuming entrance is a surprising visit to old Europe. Inside, a series of cozy dining rooms invites intimacy. An inner courtyard offers dining beneath the stars, with the splash of a marble fountain and heaters that will keep you warm even in winter. One can hardly help but hold hands across the table and imagine a faraway honeymoon. Dinners, with entrées like linguine alla scapesce (pasta with lobster) and filet mignon béarnaise, come complete with three courses, including antipasto and homemade soup.

LA BOHEME, Carmel
Dolores and Seventh
(408) 624-7500
Moderate

La Boheme is a small cafe with a festive European rural theme. The walls of the cottage-like interior are covered with murals, and the ceiling is decorated with a hand-painted pastel blue sky accented with white fluffy clouds. The tables are adorned by floral tablecloths and fresh flowers. Living up to this amiable interior, the creative chef serves a very French three-course prix fixe meal that changes every night. The homemade desserts are delicious and worth lingering over, accompanied by the one you love and two spoons. By the way, the diminutive size of the restaurant is such that you won't have to worry about sharing this place with too many other hungry diners. La Boheme is open for dinner only.

PATISSERIE BOISSIERE, Carmel
Mission, between Ocean and Seventh
(408) 624-5008
Inexpensive to Moderate

As you enter this polished, choice French restaurant, a glass case full of sinfully sweet selections greets you (and reminds you to save room for dessert). With offerings that range from lamb chops to extravagant fish dishes, the eclectic menu is sure to please. The European country-style interior is distinguished by sapphire blue table linens, regal window treatments, and a sparkling chandelier. A tiled fireplace warms the casually elegant, intimate dining room. In a separate dining area, white iron chairs and tables are set on green astroturf, creating a totally different, sunny, lunch-on-the-lawn feeling.

◆ **Romantic Note:** By the way, if you don't want a full meal, a cappuccino and one of their wickedly rich pastries would be wonderful too.

SANS SOUCI, Carmel
Lincoln, between Fifth and Sixth
(408) 624-6220
Expensive
Wedding facilities are available for a maximum of 80 people.

Locals have been renewing romance at Sans Souci for more than 30 years. Perhaps it's the crystal chandeliers or the warmth of the fire, but this elegant restaurant feels more like a country French dining room than a commercial enterprise. The menu is classically French, with innovative treatments of local seasonal produce and seafood. If you fancy the flamboyant, tuxedo-clad waiters will prepare several dishes at your table, including chateaubriand and rack of lamb. Desserts made only for two are the perfect finale: we recommend the cherries jubilee or crêpes with ice cream and fresh fruit, both flamed tableside.

Outdoor Kissing

CARMEL BEACH

From Highway 1, turn west onto Ocean and follow it until it dead-ends at the beach.

Carmel Beach is an awesome stretch of surf and sand. Those lucky souls who have houses that border this mile-long parcel of heaven are in an enviable position. The landscape is an inspiring combination of surging waves, rolling hills, and endless ocean. A sandy stroll in the morning (before the populace wakes up) or at sunset, when the sky is burnished with fire (and it doesn't matter who else is there), can renew the soul. All kinds of sparks can be kindled from this vantage point. Don't miss it.

POINT LOBOS STATE RESERVE, Carmel
(408) 624-4909
$6 per car day-use fee

Located on the ocean side of Highway 1, four miles south of Carmel.

It's been called "the greatest meeting of land and water in the world." Where better to share a lasting kiss with your love? Point Lobos is one of my favorite spots in the Monterey area. I visit it often, but each time I'm struck by that sense of experiencing something new and vibrant, like love itself. At the Sea Lion Point parking lot, the first sound you'll hear are the sharp barks of these robust creatures. Follow the short trail along a hillside blanketed with ice plants to the promontory, and you'll see them crowded on the water-washed rocks. Nearby, you can explore the tide pools together, searching out battling crabs and purple sea urchins. Or follow one of the less traveled trails that hug the cliffs of this rugged coastline. Seclusion and spectacular scenery are yours to share.

ROBINSON JEFFERS' TOR HOUSE, Carmel
26304 Ocean View Avenue
(408) 624-1813
$5 for adults

From Highway 1, turn onto Ocean Avenue toward downtown Carmel. Turn left onto Scenic, left onto Stewart, and then left onto Ocean View. Look for Tor House and its stone Hawk Tower on the left.

A poet's home needn't be extraordinary to be considered a rendezvous with romance. This one is, but not in its size or architectural significance. The aura of love and romance is so strong here that even those who have never heard of Robinson Jeffers will be inspired. Tor House ("tor" is an old Irish word for a craggy knoll) is a simple Tudor cottage, built in 1918, where Jeffers wrote all his major works and most of his poetry. More important, this is where he lived in splendid happiness with his wife, Una, and their twin sons. Throughout the home, loving epigrams are carved into the timbers. Jeffers built the Hawk Tower by hand, making "stone love stone," as a treasured retreat for Una and a magical playground for the children. In Una's room, at the very top of the tower, an epigram carved in the wooden mantel of the fireplace reads, "THEY MAKE THEIR DREAMS FOR THEMSELVES," truly reflecting Jeffers' lifestyle, and perhaps enhancing the affections of others who come here.

◆ **Romantic Warning:** Tor House is open by guided tour only on Friday and Saturday, from 10 A.M. to 3 P.M. Reservations are advised.

Carmel Valley

Hotel/Bed and Breakfast Kissing

STONEPINE, Carmel Valley
150 East Carmel Valley Road
(408) 659-2245

Very Expensive to Unbelievably Expensive
Wedding facilities are available for a maximum of 250 people.

From Highway 1, take Carmel Valley Road east about 15 miles and watch for the sign on the right side of the road.

We drove up a mile-long access road lined with gnarled oaks, crossed a wooden bridge over a swiftly running creek, and passed energetic corralled horses to get to Stonepine. When we finally reached the wrought-iron reception gate, we had the feeling that something unforgettable was waiting for us within its grounds. As we gazed at this formidable Mediterranean-style villa, our jaws dropped wide open and "Wow" was all we could utter. Stonepine offers a fashion of living that is hard to surpass, and hard to imagine.

The spacious foyer and living room of the main house, Chateau Noel, fill with morning light that flows in through a gallery of windows, enhancing the subtle elegance of the damask sofas and love seats. A handwoven Chinese rug, threaded with rose tones, stretches across the hardwood floor, and golden flames gently caress each other in an oversize stone hearth. In the evening, this room is often graced by the sounds of a string ensemble.

There are eight elegant suites in Chateau Noel, some with Jacuzzi tubs and fireplaces. Four other suites in the separate ranch-style Paddock House all have Jacuzzi tubs and use of a complete country kitchen. The single unit in the two-bedroom Briar Rose Cottage is extremely secluded, with a rustic stone fireplace and its own porch overlooking a fragrant rose garden. No matter where you stay, each room has lavish appointments, and every exquisite detail has been attended to. We were thoroughly delighted at everything we saw and experienced. Even the restaurant (reserved for guests only) was a cornucopia of superb food and courtly service. Our first kiss at Stonepine was only the beginning of a truly magnificent weekend.

◆ **Romantic Suggestion:** Stonepine also runs an equestrian center, where you can saddle up two horses and explore some of the 330 prodigious acres of forest, meadow, and bridle trails. The center is not exclusively for guest use.

Restaurant Kissing

THE COVEY RESTAURANT, Carmel Valley
8205 Valley Greens Drive, at the Quail Lodge
(408) 624-1581
Moderate

From Carmel, take Highway 1 south. Turn left onto Carmel Valley Road. The restaurant is three and a half miles down, on the right.

Need a cure for the ordinary dining experience? Your prescription is the Covey Restaurant. The first view as you enter the dining room is of the awesome far window, and through the glass the scene is exceptional, with a quaint little pond, a sparkling fountain, and a footbridge pulled straight from a storybook. The surrounding walls are paneled with rich, dark wood that seems to literally radiate warmth. Above, an open ceiling features exposed, heavy beams and soft lighting that illuminates the entire place with soft romance, which would be perfect if the dining area wasn't so big. Deep-colored paintings of ducks and other waterfowl emphasize the theme. There are two levels to the restaurant, with the larger tables on the upper level. A few steps below, and closer to the grand windows, is the more intimate seating. The tables are a bit too close together, but beautifully adorned with soft white linens and fresh flowers. Bask in the glow of your own personal candlelight as you feed each other bites of the refined European cuisine. Jackets and reservations are required, and seating for dinner begins at 6:30 P.M. on weeknights and 6 P.M. on weekends. Be sure to make time before or after your meal for a drink in the separate, but equally romantic, bar. You can enjoy the same view from here, and together with the fireplace and the grand piano, it will be virtually impossible to keep your lips away from your sweetheart's.

♦ **Romantic Note:** Don't look for romance at the Quail Lodge Resort & Golf Club. The restaurant is the only romantic part of the property.

♦ **Romantic Alternative:** The **RIDGE RESTAURANT** at Robles Del Rio, 200 Punta Del Monde, Carmel Valley, (408) 659-0170, (Moderate), is set high above the Carmel Valley. One dining room has a stone fireplace and a grand piano, but ask for a table on the glass-enclosed terrace overlooking the pastoral valley and nearby village; the view below is stunning. Little lanterns at each table, wood accents, and warm tones of peach and maroon create a cozy atmosphere. Service is gracious, and the small menu offers excellent French cuisine.

Carmel Highlands

Hotel/Bed and Breakfast Kissing

HIGHLANDS INN, Carmel Highlands   ◆ ◆ ◆ ◀
Highway 1
(408) 624-3801
Very Expensive to Unbelievably Expensive
Wedding facilities are available for a maximum of 120 people.

Just south of Carmel, on the east side of Highway 1. Look for a small sign on the left indicating where to turn in to the inn.

When discussing the encapsulated world of the Monterey Peninsula, the subject of elite, posh places to stay (and the area has several) just may come up. Less opulent than some, the Highland Inn comprises a captivating series of rooms and restaurants with a fairly captivating accompanying price tag. Money aside, you really need to see this location to appreciate what a rare romantic treat you are in for.

The Highland Inn sits above an incredibly breathtaking expanse of coastline. From this prominence, windswept trees, white surf breaking over outcroppings of rocks, and an occasional pod of spouting whales are all showcased. The glass-enclosed view from the formal **PACIFIC'S EDGE** restaurant alone is worth the price of Sunday brunch ($25) or dinner (Expensive). Even if you opt for drinks alone, the fireside lobby is just as formidable a place to watch sunset, when the sky explodes in a riot of intoxicating, evocative colors.

All of the contemporary-style rooms here share this explosive view, and all have fireplaces and lanais. The one- and two-bedroom suites (including townhouse-style apartments) have spa baths, fireplaces, and fully equipped kitchens. Everything here is very first-class, very California, and very wonderful.

TICKLE PINK INN, Carmel Highlands
155 Highland Drive
(408) 624-1244, (800) 635-4774
Expensive to Very Expensive
Wedding facilities are available for a maximum of 25 people.

Four miles south of Carmel, along Highway 1.

Perched atop coastline cliffs, the Tickle Pink Inn overlooks endless miles of the Pacific Ocean. All but one of the 35 rooms share this colossal view. The Senator's Cottage, a totally separate stone cottage that is lower on the hillside, might be the most secluded lodging option, but we preferred the 17 newly renovated rooms and suites. All of these rooms are adorned with blond wood furnishings, new floral bedspreads, partially canopied beds, private decks, tiled baths, Botticelli prints or similar artwork, and river rock fireplaces.

Complimentary fruit, wines, breads, and cheeses are served every evening in the glass-enclosed wood patio overlooking the crashing waves of the Pacific. This is also where a continental breakfast is served unless you ask for it to be delivered to your room.

Big Sur

Hotel/Bed and Breakfast Kissing

VENTANA, Big Sur   ◆ ◆ ◆
Highway 1
(408) 667-2331
Expensive to Unbelievably Expensive

Located on Highway 1, about 28 miles south of Carmel.

The unspoiled Santa Lucia Mountains seem to tumble directly into the sea; these rocky slopes and jagged outcroppings abut Big Sur's astonishing coastline. Ventana, set on a forested mountainside, has a ringside view of all this, and its amenities will satisfy every other need you might have for a sultry weekend away from the world at large, far removed from anything vaguely resembling civilization. Stimulate or soothe your senses in two heated pools, Japanese hot baths, a sauna, and a Jacuzzi, then retreat to your room for more of the same. All of the 62 guest rooms have roaring fireplaces, plus private patios or balconies that face the towering mountains or the endless ocean in the nearby distance below. Everything is designed to direct your interests to romantic interactions.

A short stroll from the inn, Ventana's restaurant (Expensive) offers another dramatic view of Big Sur and the surrounding mountain majesty. Lunch and dinner are served daily here, but during the summer the outside terrace is by far the most beguiling place. Outside and inside, blazing fireplaces provide solace and warmth. A stay here is a departure from the burdens and pressures of everyday living. The feelings that will fill your souls during your stay may surpass every expectation.

◆ **Romantic Note:** Bathing suits are considered optional attire in the hot-tub baths, and the sun deck is clothing-optional.

Restaurant Kissing

NEPENTHE, Big Sur   ◆ ◀
Highway 1
(408) 667-2345
Expensive

Take Highway 1 south till you reach Big Sur; signs will point you toward the restaurant.

Nepenthe is hardly a secret—you may even call it a tourist attraction of sorts. The expansive landscaped grounds are covered with interesting Zen-inspired sculptures. This famous restaurant, designed by a student of Frank Lloyd Wright, was the honeymoon cottage of Rita Hayworth and Orson Welles. It is also one of the few dining establishments to be found anywhere in Big Sur. The food is casual and good, but not great. What makes it a kissing location? How about its perch on a cliff 800 feet above the Big Sur shoreline. This feature alone is enough to make eating here a rapturous adventure.

Sunset is perhaps the best time to visit Nepenthe for a snack or drink. As the sun begins to settle into the ocean, its light penetrates the drifting clouds with a pale lavender-blue haze. Suddenly, these soft dusky colors shift into an intense golden amber, culminating in a deep red that sets the sky afire. As night makes its definitive entrance, the clouds fade to steel blue and the sky turns from cobalt to indigo. "Awesome" is the only applicable word for this scenery. Incredible outdoor seating is perfectly arranged to take advantage of the view. Weather permitting, this floor show is performed nightly along the Big Sur coast, and Nepenthe (which means a potion for easing or obliterating grief and pain) has some of the best seats in the house.

◆ **Romantic Note:** If outside dining appeals to you, **CAFE KEVAH** (Inexpensive), at Nepenthe, serves lunch on a spacious patio, and also overlooks the Big Sur coast.

◆ **Romantic Alternative:** The **GLEN OAKS RESTAURANT**, Route 1, Big Sur, (408) 667-2623, (Moderate), doesn't have the view or the star-studded past of Nepenthe, but what it lacks in glamour it makes up for in charisma. Gourmet cuisine, a charming log cabin exterior, and an intimate candlelit interior with gold walls and a corner fireplace make Glen Oaks a ripe kissing location along Big Sur.

Outdoor Kissing

BIG SUR COASTLINE

Located on Highway 1, about 150 miles south of San Francisco.

The drive from Carmel to Big Sur provides unsurpassed scenery in which to lose yourselves in an afternoon together. The road along this rugged, arduous coastline offers some of the most glorious, breathtaking views you may ever see in your life. We almost guarantee that once you've passed through Big Sur, its potent impact will be felt in your lives for years to come—it is that compelling. Take it slow through here—an experience of this magnitude needs to be approached with patient appreciation and reverent awe. Besides, there is no real destination to head for or to end up at, because there isn't an actual town of Big Sur to be found. According to the signs, though, Big Sur stretches for about six miles along Highway 1 and then continues south for more of the same impeccable scenery.

What makes all this such a heartthrob? The road follows a precariously severe landscape, literally snaking its way along the unblemished shoreline. Beneath you, the relentless surf pounds the jagged outcroppings along the water's edge as nature continues to refine her sculpted masterpiece. Isolated beaches and secluded spots in the wilderness nearby provide momentary respite from the road for those who want to stop for private showcase views. Hard though it is to believe, each mile you pass through seems more remarkable and more titillating than the one before. Every moment you share here will be as seductive and as passionate as the first.

◆ **Romantic Suggestion:** Do not confuse **JULIA PFEIFFER BURNS STATE PARK** with Pfeiffer Big Sur State Park; Julia is 11 miles south of the other, but it offers what feels like 100 miles more privacy and landscape. Pfeiffer Big Sur State Park is exceedingly popular and disappointingly developed. Julia Pfeiffer Burns State Park, on the other hand, is 2,000 acres of prime hiking territory in nature's virgin wonderland. Enchanting waterfalls, sequestered beaches, and spellbinding views are what you can expect along the way.

In the same vicinity, **PFEIFFER BEACH** (just off Highway 1 on Sycamore Canyon Road) is an exhilarating seascape crowded with massive, eroded outcroppings and haystack rocks that are approachable during low tide. Watching the sunset from this vantage point could be a life-altering proposition, it is that beautiful.

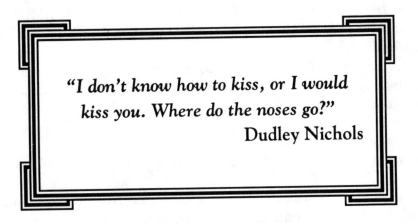

"*I don't know how to kiss, or I would kiss you. Where do the noses go?*"
Dudley Nichols

INDEX